PHILIPPIANS

A Greek Student's Intermediate Reader

JERRY L. SUMNEY

HENDRICKSON PUBLISHERS

Philippians: A Greek Student's Intermediate Reader
© 2007 by Hendrickson Publishers, Inc.
P. O. Box 3473
Peabody, Massachusetts 01961-3473

ISBN 978-1-56563-991-1

Biblical quotations designated NIV are taken from the HOLY BIBLE, NEW INTERNATIONAL VER-SION. Copyright © 1973, 1978, 1984 by International Bible Society. Used by permission of Zondervan Bible Publishers. All rights reserved. (Italics in quoted Scriptures is author's emphasis.)

Biblical quotations designated NRSV are taken from the New Revised Standard Version of the Bible, copyright © 1989 by the Division of Christian Education of the National Council of the Churches of Christ in the United States of America, and are used by permission.

Biblical quotations designated RSV are taken from the Revised Standard Version of the Bible, copyright 1952 (2nd ed., 1971) by the Division of Christian Education of the National Council of the Churches of Christ in the United States of America. Used by permission. All rights reserved.

The Greek text of Philippians is from Barbara Aland, Kurt Aland, Johannes Karavidopoulos, Carlo M. Martini, and Bruce Metzger, eds., *The Greek New Testament*, 4th rev. ed. [UBS[4]] (Stuttgart: Deutsche Bibelgesellschaft and United Bible Societies, 1993), and is used with grateful permission.

Printed in the United States of America

Second Printing – March 2008

Cover Art: "The Ship of Tarse." Bas-relief on a Phoenician sarcophagus from Sidon. 2nd c. C.E. Courtesy of the National Archaeological Museum, Beirut, Lebanon.
Photo Credit: Giraudon/Art Resource, N.Y. Used with permission.

Library of Congress Cataloging-in-Publication Data

Sumney, Jerry L.
    Philippians : a Greek student's intermediate reader / Jerry L. Sumney.
        p. cm.
    Includes bibliographical references and index.
    ISBN 978-1-56563-991-1 (alk. paper)
    1. Bible. N.T. Philippians—Translating. 2. Bible. N.T. Philippians—Criticism, interpretation, etc. I. Title.
    BS2705.55.S86 2007
    227'.6048—dc22
                    2007013976

PHILIPPIANS

For my parents,
Paul Gene and Alberta Mae Sumney,
who taught me the value and love
of reading Scripture closely and carefully

Table of Contents

⸺⦅⦆⸺

Acknowledgments

Books always bring together the work of many people, including those whom the author has read and those with whom the author has interacted in other personal ways. There are many people I am pleased to recognize as particularly important in the production of this book. I thank Dr. Harvey Floyd of David Lipscomb University for teaching me the importance of reading the New Testament in Greek. As my Greek professor through my first three years, he not only taught our classes the necessary grammar, but also showed us what difference it made. Whether it was Greek class or a New Testament class, his devotion to reading carefully and developing a clearer understanding of a passage through rigorous thought was contagious. He introduced me to the life of a scholar, and more particularly to the life of a faithful scholar. For that I am deeply grateful.

I also owe a debt of gratitude to Ms. Rachel Childress and Dr. Kathy Riley. They were brave enough to take early drafts of this book and try to use them as they sharpened their Greek-reading skills. They gave me helpful suggestions from which all subsequent readers will benefit. I am also grateful to Prof. A. K. M. Adam for his careful reading and insightful comments on early sections and drafts of the book. It has been interesting how often his comments intersected with those of Ms. Childress and Dr. Riley.

Part of the work for this book was done while I was enjoying a sabbatical leave from teaching responsibilities at Lexington Theological Seminary. I am very grateful for the opportunities and support for research and writing afforded me by the seminary's generous sabbatical policies. I also express thanks to the German Bible Society for granting permission to use the fourth revised edition of the UBS text of Philippians for this work.

A book such as this one has come from me only because of the love of Scripture that was instilled in me by my parents, Paul G. and Alberta M. Sumney. This book is dedicated to them. They taught me, by precept and example, that it is important not only to know what is in the Bible (and parts of Philippians were among my memory verses), but also to understand what is there as clearly as possible. They both modeled and explicitly taught me that detailed study of the Bible was worthwhile, noble, and of the greatest importance.

Abbreviations

General and Grammatical Abbreviations

1	first person
2	second person
2d	second
3	third person
acc.	accusative case
act.	active voice
aor.	aorist tense
B.C.E.	before the Common Era
c.	century
ca.	circa
C.E.	Common Era
cf.	confer, compare
ch(s).	chapter(s)
dat.	dative case
ed(s).	editor(s), edited by
e.g.	*exempli gratia*, for example
etc.	et cetera, and the rest
f(f).	and the verse(s) following
fem.	feminine gender
fut.	future tense
gen.	genitive case
i.e.	id est, that is
impf.	imperfect tense
impv.	imperative mood
indic.	indicative mood
inf.	infinitive
lit.	literally
masc.	masculine gender
mid.	middle voice
neut.	neuter gender
no.	number
nom.	nominative case

NT	New Testament
opt.	optative mood
p(p).	page(s)
pass.	passive voice
pf.	perfect tense
pl.	plural
ppf.	pluperfect tense
pres.	present tense
ptc.	participle
repr.	reprint
rev.	revised (b)
sg.	singular
sub.	subjunctive mood
trans.	translator
v(v).	verse(s)
voc.	vocative case
vol(s).	volume(s)
vs.	versus

Biblical Books

Lev	Leviticus
Deut	Deuteronomy
1–2 Kgs	1–2 Kings
1 Chr	1 Chronicles
Ps(s)	Psalm(s)
Isa	Isaiah
Matt	Matthew
Rom	Romans
1–2 Cor	1–2 Corinthians
Gal	Galatians
Eph	Ephesians
Phil	Philippians
Col	Colossians
1–2 Thess	1–2 Thessalonians
1–2 Tim	1–2 Timothy
Phlm	Philemon
Heb	Hebrews
Jas	James
1–2 Pet	1–2 Peter
Rev	Revelation

Bible Versions

LXX	Septuagint
NA²⁷	*Novum Testamentum Graece.* Nestle-Aland, 27th ed.
NIV	New International Version
NRSV	New Revised Standard Version
RSV	Revised Standard Version
TEV	Today's English Version (Good News Bible)
UBS⁴	*The Greek New Testament.* United Bible Societies, 4th ed.

New Testament Manuscripts

𝔓¹⁶	Papyrus Oxyrhynchus 1009 (3rd–4th c.)
𝔓⁴⁶	Papyrus Chester Beatty II (ca. 200 C.E.)
𝔓⁶¹	Papyrus Colt 5 (ca. 700 C.E.)
ℵ	London: Sinaiticus (4th c.)
Ψ (044)	Athos (8th–10th c.)
A (02)	London: Alexandrinus (5th c.)
B (03)	Rome: Vaticanus (4th c.)
C	Paris: Ephraemi Rescriptus (5th c.)
D (06)	Paris: Claromontanus (6th c.)
F (010)	Cambridge (9th c.)
G (012)	Dresden (9th c.)
K (018)	Moscow (9th c.)
L (020)	Rome (9th c.)
P (025)	St. Petersburg (9th c.)
t (56)	Paris: Latin codex (11th c.)
263	(13th c.)

Secondary Sources

ABRL	Anchor Bible Reference Library
BDAG	Bauer, W., F. W. Danker, W. F. Arndt, and F. W. Gingrich. *A Greek-English Lexicon of the New Testament and Other Early Christian Literature.* 3rd ed. Chicago, 2000.
BDF	Blass, F., A. Debrunner, and R. W. Funk. *A Greek Grammar of the New Testament and Other Early Christian Literature.* Chicago, 1961.
Dana and Mantey	Dana, H. E., and J. R. Mantey, *A Manual Grammar of the Greek New Testament.* Toronto, 1955.

Fee   Fee, G. D. *Paul's Letter to the Philippians.* NICNT. Grand Rapids, 1995.

Hawthorne   Hawthorne, G. F. *Philippians.* WBC 43. Waco, Tex., 1983.

HNTC   Harper's New Testament Commentaries

HTKNT   Herders theologischer Kommentar zum Neuen Testament

ICC   International Critical Commentary

JETS   *Journal of the Evangelical Theological Society*

JSNT   *Journal for the Study of the New Testament*

JSNTSup   Journal for the Study of the New Testament: Supplement Series

KEK   Kritisch-exegetischer Kommentar über das Neue Testament (Meyer-Kommentar)

Kennedy   Kennedy, H. A. A., "The Epistle to the Philippians," in vol. 3 of *The Expositor's Greek Testament.* Edited by W. R. Nicoll. 5 vols. London, 1897–1910.

Loh and Nida   Loh, I-Jin, and E. A. Nida, *A Translator's Handbook on Paul's Letter to the Philippians.* Helps for Translators 19. Stuttgart, 1977.

LSJ   Liddell, H. G., R. Scott, and H. S. Jones. *A Greek-English Lexicon.* 9th ed. with revised supplement. Oxford, 1996.

Metzger   Metzger, B. M. *A Textual Commentary on the Greek New Testament.* 2d ed. Stuttgart, 1994.

MM   Moulton, J. H., and G. Milligan. *The Vocabulary of the Greek Testament.* London, 1930. Reprint, Peabody, Mass., 1997.

Moule   Moule, C. F. D. *An Idiom Book of New Testament Greek.* 2d ed. Cambridge, 1959.

NIB   *New Interpreter's Bible*

N ICNT   New International Commentary on the New Testament

NIGTC   New International Greek Testament Commentary

NovT   *Novum Testamentum*

NTS   *New Testament Studies*

O'Brien   O'Brien, P. T. *The Epistle to the Philippians: A Commentary on the Greek Text.* NIGTC. Grand Rapids, 1991.

Paine   Paine, S. W. *Beginning Greek: A Functional Approach.* New York, 1961.

RNT   Regensburger Neues Testament

Smyth   Smyth, H. W. *Greek Grammar.* Revised by G. M. Messing. Cambridge, Mass., 1956.

TDNT   *Theological Dictionary of the New Testament.* Edited by G. Kittel and G. Friedrich. Translated by G. W. Bromiley. 10 vols. Grand Rapids, 1964–1976.

TLNT   *Theological Lexicon of the New Testament.* C. Spicq. Translated and edited by J. D. Ernest. 3 vols. Peabody, Mass., 1994.

Vincent   Vincent, M. R. *A Critical and Exegetical Commentary on the
                   Epistles to the Philippians and to Philemon.* ICC. Edinburgh,
                   1897.
Wallace   Wallace, D. B. *Greek Grammar Beyond the Basics: An Exegetical
                   Syntax of the New Testament.* Grand Rapids, 1996.
WBC   Word Biblical Commentary

Using This Text

This book is designed to help students who have finished their initial year of Greek grammar read a book of the New Testament, whether in conjunction with a class or as an independent study project. Its helps and aids assume that readers have a basic grasp of Greek grammar and syntax, but that they have not mastered all its finer points. It is often difficult for students to leave their readings in a grammar book and launch into texts containing much vocabulary that they do not know and constructions that they have never seen or have forgotten. This text seeks to enable that transition so that students will use the Greek that they learned in first-year classes without being frustrated to the point that they stop reading Greek.

For each section of Philippians, the book includes the Greek text, an interpretive translation, and comments on the constructions of each phrase. In most instances, a short definition is given the first time a Greek word appears. Most words are parsed, and remarks include a statement about the function of each word in its sentence. For the more difficult constructions, the discussion is more extensive than what accompanies the less complex phrases and clauses. In many places, interpretive options (perhaps the identification of the function of a participle or the meaning of a word) are discussed, with reasons given as to why one reading seems better in that particular context. It is necessary to discuss these matters in relation to context because grammatical and syntactic decisions influence interpretation, and vice versa.

Throughout the book, the first examples of important grammatical terms and constructions appear in boldface type, alerting the reader to text boxes that provide expanded definitions and simplified examples in Greek and English. The text boxes appear more frequently in the earlier parts of the book, based on the assumption that as the reader progresses through Philippians and becomes more familiar with the grammatical constructions found in the text, the need for these helps will diminish.

Included in the back of this volume are an overview of New Testament Greek syntax and a glossary of grammatical terms used in this volume. The glossary gives simple definitions that can serve as guides for reading Philippians and other Greek texts. While many of these terms appear earlier in the text boxes, the glossary provides a single place for the reader to turn when uncertain about the meaning of a term. The syntax overview offers a bit more extensive, but still brief, treatment of the items included there, often with a few examples, particularly when an example appears in Philippians. Since the syntax overview and glossary give only basic definitions, a comprehensive grammar should be consulted for more detailed study.

A short list of such sources for further study has also been included. This list identifies some of the well-known and useful tools that will help the reader do more detailed study than this book undertakes. There is a short annotation for each entry in that list. At the end of the discussions of the major sections of Philippians, there are also suggestions for further study of that section.

If this book fulfills its purpose, it will assist those who use it on their path to reading the Greek text of the New Testament with clearer and deeper understanding.

Introduction

⸺∞⸺

Philippians has been one of the best-loved letters of Paul because of its emphasis on joy that grows out of the apostle's good relations with the church in Philippi. The style and theology of the letter support the consensus view that Philippians was written by Paul. However, interpreters are divided about its provenance. Ephesus, Rome, and Caesarea[1] are the leading candidates for its place of origin. None of these hypotheses is without its problems, but recent commentators have favored Rome, the site named as early as the second century.[2] This option has in its favor that we know of a time when Paul was imprisoned there; but since the letter reflects numerous exchanges between Paul and the Philippians, some interpreters think it is unlikely that Paul is that far away. A strong case can also be made for Ephesus, since its location would have more easily allowed the travel of envoys between Paul and the Philippians.[3] We have, however, no clear evidence that Paul suffered imprisonment there.

Many readers have questioned the integrity of Philippians, with some finding three letters within the canonical text. The most problematic questions for those who maintain its integrity are the sudden discussion of "the dogs" in 3:2 after saying "finally" in 3:1 and the late appearance of what some identify as the thank you note (4:10-20) for the gift the Philippians had sent him.[4] Again, there are strong

---

[1] Those who favor Caesarea include Ernst Lohmeyer, *Die Briefe an die Philipper, an die Kolosser und an Philemon*, 13th ed., KEK (Göttingen: Vandenhoeck & Ruprecht, 1964), 3-4; Gerald F. Hawthorne, *Philippians*, WBC (Waco: Word, 1983), xxxvi-xliv.

[2] E.g., F. W. Beare, *A Commentary on the Epistle to the Philippians*, HNTC (New York: Harper & Row, 1959), 24; Gordon D. Fee, *Paul's Letter to the Philippians*, NICNT (Grand Rapids: Eerdmans, 1995), 34-37; Morna Hooker, "The Letter to the Philippians; Introduction, Commentary, and Reflections," NIB, L. E. Keck, editor (Nashville: Abingdon, 2000), 11: 474-75.

[3] A. Deissmann, "Zur ephesinischen Gefangenschaft des Apostels Paulus," *Anatolian Studies Presented to Sir William Ramsay*, W. H. Buckler and W. M. Calder, editors (Manchester: Manchester University Press, 1923), 121-27; G. S. Duncan, *St. Paul's Ephesian Ministry* (London: Hodder and Stoughton, 1929); Raymond Brown, *An Introduction to the New Testament*, ABRL (New York: Doubleday, 1997), 493-96.

[4] Those who argue against the letter's integrity include Beare, *A Commentary on the Epistle to the Philippians*, 2-5, 24-25; Jean-François Collange, *The Epistle of St. Paul to the Philippians*, trans. A. W. Heathcote (London: Epworth, 1979), 5-15; Joachim Gnilka, *Der Philipperbrief*, HTKNT (Freiburg: Herder, 1968), 5-11; Helmut Koester, "The Purpose of the Polemic of a Pauline Fragment (Philippians III)," NTS 8 (1961/1962): 317-32; John Reumann, "Philippians 3:20-21—A Hymnic Fragment?" NTS 30 (1984): 593-609;

arguments on each side that preclude complete certainty; however, several things support the integrity of the letter. First, λοιπόν (3:1), that some see as a device to signal the end of a letter, may function as a transitional word rather than signaling that the conclusion to the whole document has been reached (see the comments in the text).[5] There are also several themes (e.g., suffering, humility, and joy) that run all through Philippians, and language from the poetic material in chapter two also recurs throughout the whole text.[6] Recently, rhetorical critics have also asserted that an outburst such as that in 3:2ff. is common for speeches in the period.[7] Finally, some argue that Paul's thank you for the gift comes so late in the letter because this is where he takes the pen from the secretary and writes for himself. Writers in the ancient world did at times append paragraphs of a personal nature after their secretaries had completed the rest of the letter. Thus, the "thank you" would be made more important, not less, by waiting until this point to include it.[8] These and other considerations make it more likely that Philippians is a unity.[9]

Paul has several purposes for writing this letter. Not only does he want to thank them for their gift, he also wants to assure them about the health of Epaphroditus. He also takes this occasion to interpret his imprisonment for them, indicating that it is not inconsistent with being an apostle and that it is advancing

---

Pheme Perkins, "Philippians: Theology for the Heavenly *Politeuma*" in *Pauline Theology Vol I: Thessalonians, Philippians, Galatians, Philemon,* ed. Jouette Bassler (Minneapolis: Fortress, 1991), 89-104; Wolfgang Schenk, *Die Philipperbriefe des Paulus* (Stuttgart: W. Kohlhammer, 1984).

[5] Victor Furnish, "The Place & Purpose of Phil III," *NTS* 10 (1963/1964): 80-88; Loveday Alexander, "Hellenistic Letter-forms and the Structure of Philippians," *JSNT* 37 (1989): 90, 94-95.

[6] Robert Jewett, "The Epistolary Thanksgiving and the Integrity of Philippians," *NovT* 12 (1970): 40-53.

[7] See David Garland, "The Composition and Unity of Philippians: Some Neglected Literary Factors," *NovT* 27 (1985): 141-73; Duane F. Watson, "A Rhetorical Analysis of Philippians and Its Implications for the Unity Question," *NovT* 30 (1988): 57-88; Stanley K. Stowers, "Friends and Enemies in the Politics of Heaven: Reading Theology in Philippians," in *Pauline Theology; Vol I: Thessalonians, Philippians, Galatians, Philemon,* ed. Jouette Bassler (Minneapolis: Fortress, 1991), 89-104. See also G. B. Caird, *Paul's Letters from Prison,* New Century Bible (Oxford: Oxford University Press, 1976), 130-33; Michael White, "Morality Between Two Worlds; A Paradigm of Friendship in Philippians," in *Greeks, Romans, and Christians; Essays in Honor of Abraham J. Malherbe,* eds. D. L. Balch, E. Ferguson, W. A. Meeks (Minneapolis: Fortress, 1990), 201, 206; Ronald Russell, "Pauline Letter Structure in Philippians," *JETS* 25 (1982): 295-306.

[8] See the discussion of letter closings in Jeffrey A. D. Weima, *Neglected Endings; The Significance of the Pauline Letter Closings,* JSNTSup 101 (Sheffield: JSOT Press, 1994).

[9] Others who favor the integrity of the letter include: Josef Ernst, *Die Briefe an die Philipper, an Philemon, an die Kolosser, and die Epheser,* Regensburger Neues Testament (Regensburg: Friedrich Pustet, 1974); Berthold Mengel, *Studien zum Philipperbrief,* WUNT 8 (Tübingen: J. C. B. Mohr [Paul Siebeck], 1982); Christopher Mearns, "The Identity of Paul's Opponents at Philippi," *NTS* 33 (1987): 194-204; Peter T. O'Brien, *The Epistle to the Philippians; A Commentary on the Greek Text,* NIGTC (Eerdmans, 1991), 10-18.

the Gospel. Some interpreters have taken the many references to joy and rejoicing in Philippians to indicate that this church is not experiencing significant problems. However, both the message to Euodia and Syntyche in chapter 4 and the application of the hymn in chapter 2 show that there were tensions and arguments, perhaps over leadership. Paul faces opposition from other Christian evangelists in the city where he is imprisoned, but there is no indication that those teachers have been or are influencing the Philippians. Paul's rejection of the "dogs" in 3:2ff. seems to be an advance warning rather than a response to their success in the Philippian church.[10] So Paul calls upon this church, which has been supportive of his mission from its founding, to live in unity and humility, wanting to be certain that they remain faithful to the Gospel in their relationships within the church and that they hold fast to his understanding of the way Gentiles should live as the people of God.

The text of Philippians is fairly secure. It is well attested in multiple manuscripts, and there are fewer significant variants than we find in many New Testament texts. Fee notes that there are only ten "translationally significant" differences between the NA²⁷ and the *Textus Receptus*.[11] Our earliest witness to the text is the Chester Beatty Papyrus, 𝔓⁴⁶. It comes from about the year 200 and contains all of Philippians except for a few missing lines from the bottom of pages. 𝔓⁴⁶ belongs within the Alexandrian family of manuscripts, generally considered to be the closest to the original text. It contains less grammatical and stylistic polishing and fewer insertions of other sorts than other families of manuscripts. 𝔓⁴⁶ is our oldest extensive representative of this grouping for the Pauline Corpus. Other papyri that contain parts of Philippians include 𝔓¹⁶ and 𝔓⁶¹. 𝔓¹⁶ contains Phil 3:9-17 and 4:2-8. It comes from the third or fourth century. 𝔓⁶¹, produced around the year 700 c.e., has Phil 3:5-9, 12-16 among its sections from various Pauline letters.

The entire text of Philippians is found in eighteen uncials, according to Hawthorne.[12] Among these are the two extremely important fourth-century codices ℵ (Sinaiticus) and B (Vaticanus). Both of these also belong to the Alexandrian group, and while later than 𝔓⁴⁶, they seem to have been copied with great care. Codex B may be a bit earlier because it lacks the Eusebian canons, designations to help the reader locate passages. Codex A (Alexandrinus), a fifth-century manuscript, also contains all of Philippians. It belongs to a bit later branch of the Alexandrian group. The fifth-century Codex C (Ephraemi Rescriptus) is a palimpsest, a manuscript from which the original text was erased to make room for something new. In this case the biblical text was erased, and the sermons of Ephraem the Syrian were

---

[10] For discussion of the opponents of Philippians see Jerry L. Sumney, *"Servants of Satan," "False Brothers" and Other Opponents of Paul*, JSNTSup 188 (Sheffield: Sheffield Academic Press, 1999), 160-87.

[11] Fee, *Paul's Letter to the Philippians*, 24.

[12] Hawthorne, *Philippians*, liii.

written on the pages. The recovered biblical text is regarded as less valuable than that of Codex A because its readings more often belong to the Koine (or Byzantine) group, also referred to as the Majority text. This group, despite being widespread, is generally acknowledged to be the least valuable, being not only late but often containing additions and stylistic, grammatical, and theological corrections. The Codex Dᴾ (Claromontanus) is a sixth-century bilingual manuscript, with the text in Greek and Latin. It belongs in the Western grouping that is generally regarded as earlier than the Koine type but nonetheless has many editorial additions and some omissions. In the comments on textual problems throughout this volume, other manuscripts will be mentioned. Those not commented on here are later and of less consequence than those discussed above. The particulars of their dates and tendencies are available in the explanation of the textual apparatus of the Nestle-Aland Greek New Testament and in Bruce M. Metzger's *The Text of the New Testament; Its Translation, Corruption and Restoration* (London: Oxford University Press, 1992).

THE LETTER TO THE PHILIPPIANS

Philippians 1:1-2

Epistolary Greeting

¹Παῦλος καὶ Τιμόθεος δοῦλοι Χριστοῦ Ἰησοῦ πᾶσιν τοῖς ἁγίοις ἐν Χριστῷ Ἰησοῦ τοῖς οὖσιν ἐν Φιλίπποις σὺν ἐπισκόποις καὶ διακόνοις, ²χάρις ὑμῖν καὶ εἰρήνη ἀπὸ θεοῦ πατρὸς ἡμῶν καὶ κυρίου Ἰησοῦ Χριστοῦ.

¹Paul and Timothy, slaves of Christ Jesus, to all the saints in Christ Jesus who are in Philippi, with the bishops and deacons. ²Grace and peace to you from God our Father and the Lord Jesus Christ.

---

apposition

A construction in which a noun or substantive is used adjacent to and often in the same case as another substantive to further describe, identify, or define it.

Ἐπαφρᾶ τοῦ ἀγαπητοῦ <u>συνδούλου</u> ὑμῶν

Epaphras, our beloved <u>fellow slave</u> (Col 1:7)

ἀσπάσασθε Ἀνδρόνικον καὶ Ἰουνιᾶν τοὺς <u>συγγενεῖς</u> μου.

Greet Andronicus and Junia, my <u>kinspeople</u>. (Rom 16:7)

Παῦλος καὶ Τιμόθεος δοῦλοι Χριστοῦ Ἰησοῦ—This greeting follows the fairly standard format for Hellenistic letters in general and Paul's letters in particular. The sender(s), Παῦλος (masc. nom. sg.) καὶ Τιμόθεος (masc. nom. sg.), are identified with the nominative case. Δοῦλοι (masc. nom. pl.) stands in **apposition** to both Paul and Timothy, so formally the letter is from both. Χριστοῦ (masc. gen. sg.) Ἰησοῦ (masc. gen. sg.) is a **possessive genitive.** Commonly, greetings do not have a main verb, and a translation does not require a complete

1:1

sentence. Paul uses δοῦλος in a greeting only here and in Romans among the undisputed letters. He also refers to himself as Χριστοῦ δοῦλος in Gal 1:10. This word designates a slave, not simply a hired servant. Of the nineteen times δοῦλος appears in the undisputed letters, it clearly refers to literal slavery ten times, and in Rom 6 it is used another four times to speak of servants of sin, which Paul probably also wants to be understood as slavery. So when Paul uses it, he probably has slavery, not just

---

possessive genitive

The use of the genitive case to denote possession or ownership of objects or attributes.

οἱ ἐκ <u>τῆς Καίσαρος</u> οἰκίας

those of the <u>Caesar's</u> household (Phil 4:22)

ἕκαστος ὑμῶν λέγει, ἐγὼ μέν εἰμι <u>Παύλου</u>, ἐγὼ δὲ Ἀπολλῶ

Each of you says, "I am <u>of Paul</u>"; "I am <u>of Apollos</u>." (1 Cor 1:12)

service, in view. Given this, it is interesting to note that Paul uses it in 2 Cor 4:5 to refer to himself as a slave of the church at Corinth.

πᾶσιν τοῖς ἁγίοις ἐν Χριστῷ Ἰησοῦ–The name Χριστῷ (masc. dat. sg.) Ἰησοῦ (masc. dat. sg. [note that the dat. Ἰησοῦ has an unusual form]) serves as the object of the preposition ἐν. Just as Paul and Timothy were said to be "of Christ Jesus," so also the recipients now are said to reside in that same sphere. At this early period, the title "Messiah" (i.e., "Christ"), has already become a name by which Jesus is called. Thus the meaning that Christians assigned to the title "Messiah" has been completely taken up into their understanding of Jesus. The recipients of Hellenistic letters are usually designated with the dative, as they are here: πᾶσιν (masc. dat. pl.) τοῖς ἁγίοις (masc. dat. pl. ["saints"]). Wallace (148) calls this use the **dative of recipient.** Paul often calls Christians saints–that is, holy ones.

> **dative of recipient**
>
> The use of the dative case in a verbless construction (such as the greeting of a letter) to designate the person(s) or thing(s) receiving the implied action.
>
> Παῦλος . . . <u>πᾶσιν τοῖς οὖσιν</u> ἐν Ῥώμῃ
>
> *Paul . . . to all those living in Rome* (Rom 1:1,7)
>
> <u>τῇ ἐκκλησίᾳ</u> τοῦ θεοῦ τῇ οὔσῃ ἐν Κορίνθῳ
>
> *to the church of God which is in Corinth* (1 Cor 1:2)

τοῖς οὖσιν ἐν Φιλίπποις–The definite article τοῖς (masc. dat. pl.) with the participle οὖσιν (pres. act. ptc. masc. dat. pl. of εἰμί, "to be") stands in apposition to the first dative phrase, identifying more specifically the letter's recipients. Then the prepositional phrase ἐν Φιλίπποις (masc. dat. pl.) adds yet more specification.

σὺν ἐπισκόποις καὶ διακόνοις–Two special groups among the Philippian Christians are mentioned here: overseers/bishops and deacons. Grammatically, they are the **compound object** of the preposition σύν. Both the ἐπισκόποις (masc. dat. pl.) and the διακόνοις (masc. dat. pl.) seem to designate positions of some sort within this church. This is the only use of ἐπίσκοπος in the undisputed Pauline letters. Since mention of these positions is so singular, it is impossible to give a detailed description of their duties or even to say with certainty whether they were considered "offices" as we would use that term. The mention of overseers and deacons here does indicate, however, that these were recognized positions within this community at this

> **compound (direct) object**
>
> A construction in which two or more substantives serve as objects of a single verb or preposition.
>
> μνημονεύετε . . . <u>τὸν κόπον</u> ἡμῶν καὶ <u>τὸν μόχθον</u>.
>
> *You remember . . . our <u>work</u> and our <u>hardship</u>.* (1 Thess 2:9)
>
> ἀπὸ <u>θεοῦ</u> πατρὸς ἡμῶν καὶ <u>κυρίου</u> Ἰησοῦ Χριστοῦ
>
> *from <u>God</u> our Father and the <u>Lord</u> Jesus Christ* (Phil 1:2)

early time. The nouns δοῦλος (which Paul uses for himself and Timothy in v. 1) and διάκονος have similar meanings, but they have significantly different nuances. Δοῦλος implies servility. While δοῦλος is the more common word for a slave, διάκονος was used even to speak of those holding office as servants of the city. Still, we should perhaps not make too much of the difference, given that the designated master of the δοῦλος Paul is God (see *TDNT* 1:261–80). Also note that both terms are applied to Tychicus in Col 4:7.

χάρις ὑμῖν καὶ εἰρήνη–The greeting, found in all of the undisputed letters of Paul, begins here. The precise wording of the greeting in v. 2 is found in all the undisputed letters of Paul, with the possible exception of Galatians, which may have ἡμῶν after κυρίου. In this formula, the noun χάρις (fem. nom. sg. ["grace"]) replaces χαίρειν (pres. act. inf. of χαίρω, "to rejoice, welcome"), the usual greeting found in Hellenistic letters. Both χάρις and εἰρήνη (fem. nom. sg. ["peace"]) may be translated as constructions replicating the infinitive commonly found in the greeting formula. This construction approximates a health wish, with the infinitive having the sense of an **optative of wish** (Smyth, 2014). Compare this use of the infinitive in commands in Smyth, 2013. (German translations sometimes insert

1:2

> **optative of wish**
>
> The use of the optative mood to express a wish. This is the most common use of the optative mood in the NT.
>
> Τὸ ἀργύριόν σου σὺν σοὶ <u>εἴη</u> εἰς ἀπώλειαν.
>
> *May your money <u>be</u> with you in (or go with you into) destruction.* (Acts 8:20)
>
> <u>δῴη</u> ἔλεος ὁ κύριος τῷ Ὀνησιφόρου οἴκῳ.
>
> *May the Lord <u>give</u> mercy to the household of Onesiphorus.* (2 Tim 1:16)

the subjunctive *sei* here.) Wallace (50–51) identifies this construction as a **nominative absolute.** The pronoun ὑμῖν (dat. pl.) probably should be understood with both the preceding and following nouns.

> **nominative absolute**
>
> The use of a word in the nominative case not as the subject of a sentence but in a way grammatically unconnected to a verb. This normally occurs in greetings, salutations and titles of writings.
>
> <u>Παῦλος ἀπόστολος</u> Χριστοῦ Ἰησοῦ διὰ θελήματος θεοῦ καὶ <u>Τιμόθεος ὁ ἀδελφός</u>
>
> *<u>Paul, apostle</u> of Christ Jesus by the will of God and <u>Timothy, the brother</u>* (2 Cor 1:1)
>
> <u>Ἀποκάλυψις</u> Ἰησοῦ Χριστοῦ
>
> *<u>The revelation</u> of Jesus Christ* (Rev 1:1)

ἀπὸ θεοῦ πατρὸς ἡμῶν καὶ κυρίου Ἰησοῦ Χριστοῦ–Since ἀπὸ takes the genitive as its object, θεοῦ (masc. gen. sg.) πατρὸς (masc. gen. sg.) and κυρίου (masc. gen. sg.) Ἰησοῦ (masc. gen. sg.) Χριστοῦ (masc. gen. sg.) seem to be its compound object. Under this reading, the usual translation is "from God our Father and [from] the Lord Jesus Christ." Alternatively, and less likely, θεοῦ πατρὸς may be the sole object of ἀπὸ, with the following words modifying πατρὸς in such a way that the καὶ joins ἡμῶν (gen. pl.) and κυρίου rather than θεοῦ and κυρίου. In that case, the translation would be "from God, the Father of us and [of] the Lord Jesus Christ."

FOR FURTHER STUDY

Best, E. "Bishops and Deacons in Philippians 1,1." *Studia evangelica* 4 (1968): 190–231.

Jewett, R. "The Form and Function of the Homiletic Benediction." *Anglican Theological Review* 51 (1969): 18–34.

Malherbe, A., ed. and trans. *Ancient Epistolary Theorists.* Sources for Biblical Study 19. Atlanta: Scholars Press, 1988.

Mullins, T. Y. "Benediction as a NT Form." *Andrews University Seminary Studies* 15 (1977): 59–64.

Stowers, S. *Letter Writing in Greco-Roman Antiquity.* Library of Early Christianity 5. Philadelphia: Westminster, 1986.

White, J. L. *Light from Ancient Letters.* Philadelphia: Fortress, 1986.

Philippians 1:3-11

Thanksgiving and Prayer

1:3-8 Paul's Thankfulness for the Philippians

³Εὐχαριστῶ τῷ θεῷ μου ἐπὶ πάσῃ τῇ μνείᾳ ὑμῶν ⁴πάντοτε ἐν πάσῃ δεήσει μου ὑπὲρ πάντων ὑμῶν, μετὰ χαρᾶς τὴν δέησιν ποιούμενος, ⁵ἐπὶ τῇ κοινωνίᾳ ὑμῶν εἰς τὸ εὐαγγέλιον ἀπὸ τῆς πρώτης ἡμέρας ἄχρι τοῦ νῦν, ⁶πεποιθὼς αὐτὸ τοῦτο, ὅτι ὁ ἐναρξάμενος ἐν ὑμῖν ἔργον ἀγαθὸν ἐπιτελέσει ἄχρι ἡμέρας Χριστοῦ Ἰησοῦ ⁷καθώς ἐστιν δίκαιον ἐμοὶ τοῦτο φρονεῖν ὑπὲρ πάντων ὑμῶν διὰ τὸ ἔχειν με ἐν τῇ καρδίᾳ ὑμᾶς, ἔν τε τοῖς δεσμοῖς μου καὶ ἐν τῇ ἀπολογίᾳ καὶ βεβαιώσει τοῦ εὐαγγελίου συγκοινωνούς μου τῆς χάριτος πάντας ὑμᾶς ὄντας. ⁸μάρτυς γάρ μου ὁ θεὸς ὡς ἐπιποθῶ πάντας ὑμᾶς ἐν σπλάγχνοις Χριστοῦ Ἰησοῦ.

³I thank my God at all [my] mentionings of you, ⁴always in my every prayer for all of you, as I make petition with joy, ⁵because of your participation in the gospel from the first day until now, ⁶because I am completely confident that the one who began a good work in you will complete it at the day of Christ Jesus. ⁷So it is right for me to think this about you all because you have me in your heart, since in both my imprisonment and my defense and confirmation of the gospel, you are all my partners in grace. ⁸For God is my witness that I long for you all with the love of Christ Jesus.

Εὐχαριστῶ τῷ θεῷ μου–Εὐχαριστῶ (pres. act. indic. 1 sg. of εὐχαριστέω, "to thank") marks an interesting shift to the singular after the greeting named both Paul and Timothy as the senders of the letter. This change seems to make clear that the letter is really (or at least primarily) from Paul. This focus on Paul is continued in the indirect object τῷ θεῷ (masc. dat. sg.) and its possessive pronoun μου (gen. sg.). This same phrase begins the thanksgiving of 1 Corinthians, and is used, preceded by πρῶτον μὲν, in Romans. 1 Thessalonians, however, maintains the plural verb and has no possessive pronoun. The original hand of D, along with F and G, has τῷ κυρίῳ in place of τῷ θεῷ. But besides the weak manuscript support for the alternative reading, all the thanksgivings in the undisputed Paulines direct their thanks to "God."

ἐπὶ πάσῃ τῇ μνείᾳ ὑμῶν—The noun μνεία (fem. dat. sg.) here has the basic meaning "remembrance," but μνεία is also used to signify the mention of some-one in prayer in Romans, 1 Thessalonians, and Philemon. The adjective πάσῃ (fem. dat. sg.) in this construction would mean "all" rather than "each" or "every" and may imply something like "the whole of the mentionings of you" (BDF §275; Moule, 93–95). The preposition ἐπὶ with the dative often gives the basis for an action or result, but it may also be primarily temporal (BDF §235) (**temporal dative**). It is probably the latter here because when used in the former way, verbs of emotion are usually involved, and that is not the case here. Alternatively, Peng notes that some interpreters understand this phrase to refer to the Philippians' remembrances of Paul.

> **temporal dative**
>
> The use of the dative case to designate when something happens or how long it continues.
>
> καὶ ὅτι ἐγήγερται <u>τῇ ἡμέρᾳ τῇ τρίτῃ</u>
>
> *and that he was raised <u>on the third day</u>*
> (1 Cor 15:4)
>
> μυστηρίου <u>χρόνοις αἰωνίοις</u> σεσιγημένου
>
> *a mystery keep secret <u>for many ages</u>*
> (Rom 16:25)

1:4 **πάντοτε ἐν πάσῃ δεήσει μου ὑπὲρ πάντων ὑμῶν**—Paul seems intent on expressing the idea that they are constantly in his prayers. He uses forms of πᾶς more often in Philippians than at the beginning of any other thanksgiving. Again, πᾶς (πάσῃ [fem. dat. sg.]) with the an-arthrous noun δεήσει (fem. dat. sg. ["prayer"]) would mean "every." So it is "every prayer for all of you" (πάντων ὑμῶν [masc. gen. pl.]). This remains the individual prayer of Paul, as we see from the pronoun μου (gen. sg.).

> **circumstantial participle–attendant circumstances**
>
> The action of the participle presents an additional fact or thought closely related to or coordinated with the action of the main verb. It is often translated as a finite verb connected to the main verb with "and."
>
> <u>πορευθέντες</u> δὲ μάθετε τί ἐστιν.
>
> *But <u>go and</u> learn what it is (means).*
> (Matt 9:13)
>
> <u>πεσὼν</u> ἐξέψυξεν.
>
> *He <u>fell down and</u> died.* (Acts 5:5)

μετὰ χαρᾶς τὴν δέησιν ποιούμενος—Ποιούμενος (pres. mid. ptc. masc. nom. sg. of ποιέω, "to make, do") is dependent on the initial verb of the sentence, εὐχαριστῶ, and so retains Paul as its subject. If we identify ποιούμενος as a **circumstantial participle** of **attendant circumstances,** the resulting translation is "I give thanks . . . as I make petition." BDAG lists this passage as an example of the middle form of this verb being used with its direct object, the noun δέησιν (fem. acc. sg. ["prayer"]), as a **periphrastic construction,** ("I make for myself [the] peti-tion" = "I pray"). O'Brien (55) sees the circum-stantial participle as temporal, "when I make petition," but there is little substantial differ-

> **periphrastic construction**
>
> The use of more words than are necessary to express an idea. E.g., "I make a prayer" vs. "I pray."
>
> τὴν τούτων <u>μνήμην ποιεῖσθαι</u>
>
> *to <u>make</u> (the) <u>memory</u> of [i.e., to remember] these things* (2 Pet 1:15)
>
> Χριστοῦ Ἰησοῦ τοῦ <u>μέλλοντος κρίνειν</u> ζῶντας καὶ νεκρούς
>
> *Jesus Christ, who <u>is going to judge</u> [i.e., will judge] living and dead ones* (2 Tim 4:1)

ence in that rendering and the broader understanding of attendant circumstances given above. The rather awkward phrase (see Fee [81], who thinks that this awkwardness may be intentional) gives special emphasis to the first use of χαρᾶς (fem. gen. sg. ["joy"]) after the greeting. This noun appears often in Philippians and makes its only appearance in a Pauline thanksgiving here.

ἐπὶ τῇ κοινωνίᾳ ὑμῶν εἰς τὸ εὐαγγέλιον–The preposition ἐπὶ with the dative   1:5
gives the basis for an action, and so Paul has joy when he thinks of them "because of" τῇ κοινωνίᾳ (fem. dat. sg. ["fellowship"]) ὑμῶν (gen. pl.). This fellowship includes and probably highlights their financial support of Paul's mission because he calls it their participation εἰς τὸ εὐαγγέλιον (neut. acc. sg.). For many commentators, this prepositional phrase probably speaks of the Philippians' assistance in the furthering of the cause (or the spread) of the gospel. Thus εἰς takes on the meaning of a **dative of advantage,** or perhaps it means "with respect to, reference to" (for these uses of εἰς see BDAG).

> ### dative of advantage or disadvantage
>
> The use of the dative case to designate persons or things to whom the action or situation gives an advantage or disadvantage.
>
> εἴτε σωφρονοῦμεν, ὑμῖν.
> If we are in our right mind, [it is] for your benefit. (2 Cor 5:13)
>
> μαρτυρεῖτε ἑαυτοῖς.
> You are testifying against yourselves. (Matt 23:31)

ἀπὸ τῆς πρώτης ἡμέρας ἄχρι τοῦ νῦν–The adverb νῦν ("now") combined with the preceding definite article τοῦ (masc. gen. sg.) forms a genitive construction that serves as the object of the improper preposition ἄχρι ("until"), which is also a **temporal conjunction.** The preposition ἀπὸ with the genitive often designates the starting point for something. This starting point is τῆς πρώτης ἡμέρας (fem. gen. sg. ["day"]). This πρώτης (fem. gen. sg. ["first"]) day may mean the day of their conversion or the day Paul left Philippi and so the point at which they are more likely to have become financial supporters of the Pauline mission. Perhaps Paul was not trying to be so specific with this expression.

> ### temporal conjunction
>
> A conjunction that expresses something about the time when an action occurs in the clause or phrase it introduces.
>
> μετὰ ἔτη τρία ἀνῆλθον εἰς Ἱεροσόλυμα.
> After three years I went up to Jerusalem. (Gal 1:18)
>
> ἄχρι γὰρ τῆς σήμερον ἡμέρας τὸ αὐτὸ κάλυμμα . . . μένει.
> For until this very day, the same veil . . . remains. (2 Cor 3:14)

πεποιθὼς αὐτὸ τοῦτο–Αὐτὸ (neut. acc. sg.)   1:6
τοῦτο (neut. acc. sg.) forms an emphatic construction ("of this very thing," "of precisely this") that could refer to what comes before it or what comes after it; the ensuing ὅτι indicates that it points to what follows. The participle πεποιθὼς (2d pf. act. ptc. masc. nom. sg. of πείθω, "to convince") is causal (Wallace 631–32; O'Brien, 63). Grammatically, this participle could be dependent on εὐχαριστῶ and so supply another reason why Paul gives thanks or has joy when he prays for them. But Fee (85) seems

more correct in seeing it as depending on the preceding participle (ποιούμενος) so that these words are further reflection on the phrase "from the first day until now." The temporal elements of v. 6 commend this reading. BDF (§154) sees αὐτὸ τοῦτο as an example of an **accusative of content,** a construction that ties the accusative adjective or pronoun very closely to the verb. The result is that the phrase should be rendered "in just this confidence" or "I am sure." This gives the expression an adverbial function (see BDF §290).

> **accusative of content**
>
> The use of the object of the verb in the accusative case to indicate something implied within the verb itself; e.g., *to fight a war*. Such accusatives are often cognates of the governing verb.
>
> ἐφοβήσαν <u>φόβος μέγαν</u>.
> *They feared <u>with great fear</u>.*
> (Mark 4:41).

ὅτι ὁ ἐναρξάμενος ἐν ὑμῖν ἔργον ἀγαθὸν ἐπιτελέσει–Wallace (459, 665) gives this ὅτι as an example of the appositional use of this conjunction so that it can be translated "namely, that." There is no clear antecedent for ὁ ἐναρξάμενος (aor. mid. [deponent] ptc. masc. nom. sg. of ἐνάρχομαι, "to begin"), the subject of this clause, but it seems to be God rather than Christ because Christ has not been mentioned in the sentence to this point, and Christ is mentioned in the immediately following prepositional phrase but only used in connection with the Parousia. The direct object of ἐναρξάμενος is ἔργον (neut. acc. sg. ["work"]). Here the adjective ἀγαθὸν (neut. acc. sg. ["good"]) is in the **attributive position** since both the noun and the adjective are anarthrous (without the article). The "good work" ἐν ὑμῖν (dat. pl.) is given no content by Paul here, but given that its completion is an eschatological matter, it must be broader than participation in Paul's mission. Ἐπιτελέσει (fut. act. indic. 3 sg. of ἐπιτελέω, "to end, accomplish") may be described as a **predictive future.** The progressive nature of this completing is grounded in the placement of this verb between the past (ὁ ἐναρξάμενος) and future fulfillment (ἄχρι) rather than in the nature of the tense (see Wallace, 568). Paul gives no object for ἐπιτελέσει, but clearly it is the "good work" that God had begun in the Philippians. We may insert the object "it" into our translation to make a smoother English sentence.

> **attributive position**
>
> The placement of an adjective or other modifier between the article and the noun it modifies, or following the noun with its own article.
>
> ἀπὸ τῆς <u>πρώτης</u> ἡμέρας ἄχρι τοῦ νῦν
> *from the <u>first</u> day until the present* (Phil 1:5)
>
> Σὺ εἶ ὁ υἱός μου <u>ὁ ἀγαπητός</u>.
> *You are my <u>beloved</u> son.* (Mark 1:11)

> **predictive future**
>
> The use of the future tense to signify that something is expected with certainty to take place in the future.
>
> Πρὶν ἀλέκτορα φωνῆσαι σήμερον <u>ἀπαρνήσῃ</u> με τρίς.
> *Before the rooster crows today, <u>you will deny</u> me three times.* (Luke 22:61)
>
> οἱ νεκροὶ ἐν Χριστῷ <u>ἀναστήσονται</u> πρῶτον.
> *The dead in Christ <u>will rise</u> first.* (1 Thess 4:16)

ἄχρι ἡμέρας Χριστοῦ Ἰησοῦ–This is an unusual use of the improper preposition ἄχρι, which usually means "until." The context indicates that it is best rendered "at" in this use because it specifies when God will complete the work begun in the Philippians (Fee, 86). The noun ἡμέρας (fem. gen. sg. ["day"]) is a common way for Paul to refer to the Parousia. Paul seldom uses Χριστοῦ (masc. gen. sg.) with ἡμέρας; instead, he more commonly uses κυρίου. This is the first major break in the sentence structure of this thanksgiving. The semicolon in the Greek text may be best used here to signal a place to end the English sentence. Still, the translation needs to reflect the very close connection that Paul makes between vv. 3-6 and vv. 7-8.

καθώς ἐστιν δίκαιον ἐμοὶ τοῦτο φρονεῖν ὑπὲρ πάντων ὑμῶν–Although the   1:7 conjunction καθώς does not begin a sentence here, it may still signal that the grounds for what went before are being given. Even if it is playing its usual role as a comparative, it introduces a justification for Paul's thanksgiving for the Philippians. The **predicate accusative** δίκαιον (neut. acc. sg.) has no specific religious connotations here, but rather means "right" or "just." BDAG gives this passage as an example of the neuter of this adjective pointing to "that which is obligatory in view of the certain requirements of justice." Perhaps that is reading more into this fairly casual usage than is necessary, but it does capture the sense. Ἐμοὶ (dat. sg.) serves as an indirect object and as the subject of φρονεῖν (pres. act. inf. of φρονέω, "to think"). Although the subject of an infinitive is usually in the accusative case, occasionally another case is used, as it is here (Wallace, 192). The object of φρονεῖν is the ambiguous τοῦτο (neut. acc. sg.). The antecedent of this pronominal adjective is probably the whole of vv. 3-6. This is the first appearance of the verb φρονέω in this letter. This word appears twenty-six times in the NT. Twenty-three of those are in Paul's writings; of those twenty-three, ten are in Philippians, and another nine are in Romans. Although it is rendered "feel" in the NIV, its focus is better seen in the cognitive with the recognition that it is sometimes meant to encompass more of life than just thought. Πάντων (masc. gen. pl.) ὑμῶν (gen. pl.) continues Paul's emphasis on all of the Philippians.

> **predicate accusative**
>
> A type of double accusative used with verbs of having, designating, regarding, etc. The first accusative designates the object, while the second indicates what is said about the object.
>
> ἀλλήλους ἡγούμενοι ὑπερέχοντας ἑαυτῶν.
>
> *Consider others [as] better than yourselves.* (Phil 2:3)
>
> ἐάν τις αὐτὸν ὁμολογήσῃ Χριστόν
>
> *if anyone confessed him [to be] the Christ* (John 9:22)

διὰ τὸ ἔχειν με ἐν τῇ καρδίᾳ ὑμᾶς–The neuter accusative singular τὸ with the infinitive ἔχειν functions as the object of διὰ. The construction that begins here is difficult because there are two accusative nouns, με (acc. sg.) and ὑμᾶς (acc. pl.), attached to the **articular infinitive** τὸ ἔχειν (pres. act. inf. of ἔχω,

> **articular infinitive**
>
> An infinitive preceded by an article that gives it the force of a substantive.
>
> Πρὸ τοῦ δὲ ἐλθεῖν τὴν πίστιν
>
> Now before the coming of faith (Gal 3:23)
>
> ὥστε ἐξαπορηθῆναι ἡμᾶς καὶ τοῦ ζῆν
>
> so that we despaired, even of life (2 Cor 1:8)

"to have"). The difficulty is in determining which is the subject and which is the object of the infinitive. The guidelines that Wallace (193-94) gives are not determinative in this case, as he acknowledges (196). Although word order often is determinative (see those who argue that it is determinative here in Fee, 90), that is not always the case, so we are left to discern subject and object from the context. But even that is not as clear. The matter is made yet more ambiguous by the absence of a pronoun accompanying τῇ καρδίᾳ (fem. dat. sg. ["heart"]), the object of the preposition ἐν. Nor does the use of the singular help us determine how to read the verse, since Paul uses the singular of καρδία with plural pronouns (e.g., 2 Cor 3:15). The RSV and NIV treat με as the subject and thus render the phrase so that Paul has the Philippians in his heart (so also O'Brien, 68; Fee, 90). The oath formula that begins v. 8, with its connective γάρ, may support this view. The NRSV and Hawthorne (22-23), however, treat ὑμᾶς as the subject so that the Philippians hold Paul in their heart. This reading makes a good connection with the following clause, which speaks of their sharing in his imprisonment. That would mean that the γάρ of v. 8 introduces an oath that reaffirms that their love for him is matched by his love for them. Although there can be no certainty here, this latter option seems to fit the flow of the sentence a bit better.

ἐν τε τοῖς δεσμοῖς μου καὶ ἐν τῇ ἀπολογίᾳ καὶ βεβαιώσει τοῦ εὐαγγελίου—
These two prepositional phrases are dependent on the following participle συγκοινωνούς. The enclitic particle τε draws together the prepositional phrase that it appears in and the following one, introduced by καί, so that one translates "both . . . and . . ." Paul uses τοῖς δεσμοῖς (masc. dat. pl. ["bond, fetter"]) figuratively to refer to his imprisonment here. This is a common use of this term in early Christian writings. The compound object of the second ἐν is τῇ ἀπολογίᾳ (fem. dat. sg. ["defense"]) καὶ βεβαιώσει (fem. dat. sg. ["confirmation, establishment"]). Both of these nouns probably have specific reference to Paul's coming trial, but they may also have a broader reference to Paul's witness τοῦ εὐαγγελίου through his faithfulness despite persecution. Τοῦ εὐαγγελίου (masc. gen. sg. ["gospel"]) should be understood with ἀπολογίᾳ and βεβαιώσει, both of which are governed by a single article.

> ### circumstantial participle
> The use of the participle in the predicate position to define the circumstances in which the main action takes place, or the state of affairs that exists in the context of that action. Circumstances may include such things as cause, manner, means, purpose, result, time, etc.
>
> Οὐκ ἐντρέπων ὑμᾶς γράφω ταῦτα.
> *I do not write these things (for the purpose of) shaming you.*
> (1 Cor 4:14)–showing purpose
>
> ἑαυτὸν ἐκένωσεν μορφὴν δούλου λαβών.
> *He emptied himself (by) taking the form of a servant.* (Phil 2:7)–showing means

συγκοινωνούς μου τῆς χάριτος πάντας ὑμᾶς ὄντας—The **circumstantial participle** ὄντας (pres. act. ptc. masc. acc. pl. of εἰμί, "to be"), governing the whole clause that begins with ἐν τε τοῖς δεσμοῖς, expresses the reason why they have Paul in their hearts. Once again, he says that this is true for πάντας (masc. acc. pl.) ὑμᾶς (acc. pl.). They feel this way about him because they are συγκοινωνούς (masc. acc.

predicate nominative

The use of the nominative case to form the predicate of a verb of being, knowing, or thinking.

πνεῦμα ὁ θεός.
God is a spirit. (John 4:24)

οὗτος <u>ἄρχων</u> τῆς συναγωγῆς ὑπῆρχεν.
He was <u>a ruler</u> of the synagogue. (Luke 8:41)

---

pl. of συγκοινωνός, "partner"). This term was commonly used to refer to business partners, and a following genitive often designates what they share, as τῆς χάριτος (fem. gen. sg.) does here. The pronoun μου (gen. sg.) should be understood to modify συγκοινωνούς rather than τῆς χάριτος. This is seen from the article, which may designate this "grace" as the grace of God, and from the context, which is emphasizing the relationship between Paul and the Philippians. So here they are designated as Paul's partners. This partnership probably has a broad reference to their relationship, but it may also be related to their repeated, and now renewed, financial support of his mission.

μάρτυς γάρ μου ὁ θεός–Finally a new sentence begins here. Θεός (masc. nom. sg.) is the subject of the understood ἐστί in this oath formula, as the presence of its article suggests (Wallace, 242–43). So μάρτυς (masc. nom. sg. ["witness"]) is the **predicate nominative** with the possessive genitive μου attached to it.   1:8

ὡς ἐπιποθῶ πάντας ὑμᾶς–Here the conjunction ὡς is used in a fairly unusual way. It is better rendered "that" rather than "how [much]." This is in accord with the way it is used with verbs of knowing (here ἐπιποθῶ [pres. act. indic. 1 sg. of ἐπιποθέω, "to desire, long for"] functions as such a verb). Fee (94) suggests that it is somewhat awkward and thus is similar to the English "how that." Paul continues to emphasize his

---

causal/instrumental

A word or phrase that indicates the means or instrument by which an action is accomplished; often translated with: *through, by means of, because of.*

Τῇ γὰρ <u>πίστει</u> ἑστήκατε.
For you stand <u>by means of</u> (the) faith. (2 Cor 1:24)

ἐγὼ ἐβάπτισα ὑμᾶς <u>ὕδατι</u>.
I baptize you <u>with water</u>. (Mark 1:8)

---

thanksgiving for πάντας (masc. acc. pl.) ὑμᾶς (acc. pl.), "all of you" or "you all." This is one of the means that Paul uses to prepare for his discussion of the strife present in the Philippian church.

---

subjective genitive

The use of the genitive case to designate the subject of the action implied in the word it modifies. Thus "the love of Christ" would indicate the love Christ has for others.

τὸ κρίμα <u>τοῦ θεοῦ</u>
judgment <u>rendered by God</u> (Rom 2:3)

ἵνα δικαιωθῶμεν ἐκ πίστεως <u>Χριστοῦ</u>
so that we might be justified by the faithfulness <u>of Christ</u> (Gal 2:16)

ἐν σπλάγχνοις Χριστοῦ Ἰησοῦ–Ἐν may be either locative, pointing to the sphere in which Paul's love exists, or **causal/instrumental,** indicating that Paul longs for them through, by means of, the love of Christ. Σπλάγχνοις (masc. dat. pl.) literally refers to the organs of the body that were seen as those in which the emotions are rooted. The word often is used to mean "love," just as "heart" is in English. Χριστοῦ (masc. gen. sg.) Ἰησοῦ (masc. gen. sg.) may be a **subjective genitive** and so designate this love as the love that Christ has for them.

1:9-11   Paul's Prayer for Love and Discernment

⁹καὶ τοῦτο προσεύχομαι, ἵνα ἡ ἀγάπη ὑμῶν ἔτι μᾶλλον καὶ μᾶλλον περισσεύῃ ἐν ἐπιγνώσει καὶ πάσῃ αἰσθήσει ¹⁰εἰς τὸ δοκιμάζειν ὑμᾶς τὰ διαφέροντα, ἵνα ἦτε εἰλικρινεῖς καὶ ἀπρόσκοποι εἰς ἡμέραν Χριστοῦ, ¹¹πεπληρωμένοι καρπὸν δικαιοσύνης τὸν διὰ Ἰησοῦ Χριστοῦ εἰς δόξαν καὶ ἔπαινον θεοῦ.

⁹And I pray this, that your love might abound yet more and more through knowledge and all insight, ¹⁰so that you may discern what is important in order that you might be blameless and spotless on the day of Christ, ¹¹having been filled with the fruit of righteousness that comes through Jesus Christ for the glory and praise of God.

1:9   **καὶ τοῦτο προσεύχομαι**–Paul continues his prayer, προσεύχομαι (pres. mid./pass. [deponent] indic. 1 sg. ["to pray"]), still using the singular. Thus it is clear that he alone is the actual author of the letter. Τοῦτο (neut. acc. sg.) refers to what comes after it in this sentence. This is made clear by the ἵνα clause that follows.

ἵνα ἡ ἀγάπη ὑμῶν ἔτι μᾶλλον καὶ μᾶλλον περισσεύῃ–This ἵνα clause is a **purpose clause.** As usual, ἵνα is followed by a subjunctive verb, here περισσεύῃ (pres. act. sub. 3 sg. of περισσεύω, "to abound, overflow"). This is the first of only four appearances of ἀγάπη (fem. nom. sg. ["love"]) in Philippians. In this letter that expresses much affection and trust in the recipients, it is interesting that this word appears so few times and that the last of these is in 2:2. The **comparative adverb** μᾶλλον is repeated for emphasis, and the emphasis is heightened by the ἔτι–"yet more and more." The possessive pronoun ὑμῶν (gen. pl.) shows clearly that this love is the love that the Philippians possess, but it is not clear whom they are loving. It may be Paul, one another, or God, or perhaps it is unspecified to include all of these.

ἐν ἐπιγνώσει καὶ πάσῃ αἰσθήσει–The entire prepositional phrase may be understood to indicate the sphere in which their love is to abound (O'Brien, 74). In that case, ἐν denotes place (locative sense) (BDAG). Alternatively, ἐν may be instrumental, indicating the means

> **purpose clause**
>
> A clause that expresses the purpose for which the action or state of the governing verb is accomplished.
>
> ἦλθεν γὰρ ὁ υἱὸς τοῦ ἀνθρώπου ζητῆσαι καὶ σῶσαι τὸ ἀπολωλός.
>
> *For the son of man came to seek and to save the lost.* (Luke 19:10)
>
> τοῖς πᾶσιν γέγονα πάντα, ἵνα πάντως τινὰς σώσω.
>
> *I have become all things to all people, in order that by all means I might save some.* (1 Cor 9:22)

> **comparative adverb**
>
> An adverb that expresses comparison or contrast with another element in the sentence.
>
> ἀδελφὸν ἀγαπητόν, μάλιστα ἐμοί, πόσῳ δὲ μᾶλλον σοί
>
> *a beloved brother, especially to me, but much more to you* (Phlm 16)
>
> πολλῷ οὖν μᾶλλον δικαιωθέντες νῦν ἐν τῷ αἵματι αὐτοῦ σωθησόμεθα.
>
> *Therefore, having now been justified through his blood, much more will we be saved.* (Rom 5:9)

by which love is to grow. The latter reading seems to fit better with beginning of v. 10; that is, the knowledge and insight that increase love will also help them discern what matters. This use of αἰσθήσει (fem. dat. sg. ["perception, discernment"]) here marks the only use of that word in the NT. Its broad meaning refers to perception, but in the proper contexts it signifies intellectual, especially moral, perception or insight (BDAG; *TDNT* 1:187-88).

εἰς τὸ δοκιμάζειν ὑμᾶς τὰ διαφέροντα–Dana and Mantey (285-86) identify this phrase as one of the rare instances in which the articular infinitive with εἰς signifies result. However, since this meaning is rare, and since the purpose rendering fits the context well, it seems best to take it as an articular **infinitive expressing purpose.** Thus the phrase expresses the goal or purpose of the Philippians abounding in love through knowledge and (intellectual and moral) insight. The accusative articular infinitive τὸ δοκιμάζειν (pres. act. inf. of δοκιμάζω, "to examine, prove") serves as the object of εἰς, with ὑμᾶς (acc. pl.) as its subject and τὰ διαφέροντα (pres. act. ptc. neut. acc. pl. of διαφέρω, "to be worth more than, be superior to") as its object. Use of διαφέρω may have reminded the recipients of the ethical discussions among Stoics and Cynics. In these discussions the negative form of the adjective, ἀδιάφορον, played an important role. It designated those things that were not of moral significance. Stoics and Cynics differed over whether such things were of no consequence at all or whether some indifferent things led to immorality.

1:10

> ### infinitive expressing purpose
>
> The common use of the infinitive to express the goal or purpose of the governing verb. The infinitive may be anarthrous, have the genitive article τοῦ, and/or have the preposition εἰς or πρός. On rare occasions it may follow ὥστε or ὥς.
>
> ἀποκατήλλαξεν ... <u>παραστῆσαι</u> ὑμᾶς ἁγίος.
>
> *He has reconciled [you] ... <u>to present</u> you [as] holy.* (Col 1:22)
>
> μὴ νομίσητε ὅτι ἦλθον <u>καταλῦσαι</u> τὸν νόμον.
>
> *Do not think that I have come <u>to abolish</u> the law.* (Matt 5:17)

ἵνα ἦτε εἰλικρινεῖς καὶ ἀπρόσκοποι–The two adjectives εἰλικρινεῖς (masc. nom. pl. ["pure"]) and ἀπρόσκοποι (masc. nom. pl. ["blameless"]) serve as predicate nominatives with the verb ἦτε (pres. act. sub. 2 pl. of εἰμί, "to be"), whose subject is an understood "you." The ἵνα clause expresses the purpose of their being able to properly discern, "that you might be blameless and spotless." To avoid repetition in translation, the ἵνα has been translated "in order that."

εἰς ἡμέραν Χριστοῦ–Εἰς has its temporal meaning with the object ἡμέραν (fem. acc. sg. ["day"]), and so it may be translated "at" or "on." The preposition εἰς appears with ἡμέρα only here and in 2:16 in all the Pauline corpus. The expression ἡμέραν Χριστοῦ (masc. gen. sg.) appears in the NT only in Philippians (though there is a variant for 2 Thess 2:2 that has it). It has the same basic meaning as the "Day of the Lord" (the Parousia), and this carries with it the idea of judgment.

1:11　πεπληρωμένοι καρπὸν δικαιοσύνης τὸν διὰ Ἰησοῦ Χριστοῦ–The use of the perfect tense, πεπληρωμένοι (pf. pass. ptc. masc. nom. pl. of πληρόω, "to fill"), signals that the Philippians have already been filled and remain filled with καρπὸν (masc. acc. sg. ["fruit"]) δικαιοσύνης (fem. gen. sg. ["righteousness"]). The latter word could be a **genitive of apposition** (see BDF §167), meaning the fruit that is righteousness, a **genitive of content** (see Smyth, 1323), designating what one receives because one is righteous, or a genitive of origin, showing that this fruit comes from righteousness. The masc. acc. sg. article τὸν governs the prepositional phrase διὰ Ἰησοῦ (masc. gen. sg.) Χριστοῦ (masc. gen. sg.), showing that the phrase modifies καρπὸν. Thus it indicates that this fruit comes through, by means of, Christ.

> **genitive of apposition**
>
> The use of a substantive in the genitive case to refer to the same person or thing as the substantive it modifies. Often the genitive word provides more specific information about a general or ambiguous word.
>
> ἀρραβῶνα τοῦ πνεύματος
> *the guarantee, that is the Spirit*
> (2 Cor 5:5)

εἰς δόξαν καὶ ἔπαινον θεοῦ–This prepositional phrase specifies the purpose (as εἰς often does with accusative objects) of the Philippians being filled. It is interesting to note that the goal of their being filled and, if the reference goes back to the prior clause, of their being blameless in judgment is δόξαν (fem. acc. sg. ["glory"]) καὶ ἔπαινον (masc. acc. sg. ["praise"]) of θεοῦ (masc. gen. sg. ["God"]), with Christ as the one through whom the Philippians possess these things. Thus the goal of their being filled and being blameless is not ultimately that they receive salvation, but rather that God is recognized and praised for who God is. (For discussion of δόξα see 4:20.)

> **genitive of content**
>
> The use of the genitive case to specify the contents of the word modified.
>
> τὸ δίκτυον τῶν ἰχθύων
> *the net of [i.e., containing] fish*
> (John 21:8)
>
> οἱ θησαυροὶ τῆς σοφίας καὶ γνώσεως
> *the treasures [consisting] of wisdom and knowledge* (Col 2:3)

FOR FURTHER STUDY

Artz, P. "The 'Epistolary Introductory Thanksgiving' in the Papyri and Paul." *Novum Testamentum* 36 (1994): 28-46.

Jewett, R. "The Epistolary Thanksgiving and the Integrity of Philippians." *Novum Testamentum* 12 (1970): 40-53.

O'Brien, P. T. *Introductory Thanksgivings in the Letters of Paul.* Supplements to Novum Testamentum 49. Leiden: Brill, 1977.

Peng, K. "Do We Need an Alternative Rendering for Philippians 1.3?" *Bible Translator* 54 (2003): 415-19.

Schubert, P. *Form and Function of the Pauline Thanksgivings.* Beihefte zur Zeitschrift für die neutestamentliche Wissenschaft 20. Berlin: Töpelmann, 1939.

Stowers, S. *Letter Writing in Greco-Roman Antiquity.* Library of Early Christianity 5. Philadelphia: Westminster, 1986.

White, J. L. *The Form and Function of the Body of the Greek Letter: A Study of the Letter-body in the Non-literary Papyri and in Paul the Apostle.* Society of Biblical Literature Dissertation Series 2. Missoula, Mont.: Scholars Press, 1972.

———. *Light from Ancient Letters.* Foundations and Facets: New Testament. Philadelphia: Fortress, 1986.

Wiles, G. P. *Paul's Intercessory Prayers: The Significance of the Intercessory Prayer Passages in the Letters of St. Paul.* Society for New Testament Studies Monograph Series 24. Cambridge: Cambridge University Press, 1974.

Philippians 1:12-26

⸺ ∾∾∾ ⸺

Report of Paul's Circumstances with Related Examples to Imitate and to Avoid

1:12-14 Paul's Imprisonment and Its Effects

¹²Γινώσκειν δὲ ὑμᾶς βούλομαι, ἀδελφοί, ὅτι τὰ κατ' ἐμὲ μᾶλλον εἰς προκοπὴν τοῦ εὐαγγελίου ἐλήλυθεν, ¹³ὥστε τοὺς δεσμούς μου φανεροὺς ἐν Χριστῷ γενέσθαι ἐν ὅλῳ τῷ πραιτωρίῳ καὶ τοῖς λοιποῖς πᾶσιν, ¹⁴καὶ τοὺς πλείονας τῶν ἀδελφῶν ἐν κυρίῳ πεποιθότας τοῖς δεσμοῖς μου περισσοτέρως τολμᾶν ἀφόβως τὸν λόγον λαλεῖν.

¹²I want you to know, brothers and sisters, that my circumstances have turned out rather for the advance of the gospel, ¹³so that my imprisonment is clearly seen to be for Christ among the whole praetorian guard and all the rest, ¹⁴and most of the brothers and sisters have been made confident in the Lord by my imprisonment; they are more bold so that they speak the Word fearlessly.

1:12 **Γινώσκειν δὲ ὑμᾶς βούλομαι, ἀδελφοί**—The vocative ἀδελφοί (masc. voc. pl.) is intended to include all members of the Christian community, not only the men, so we translate it as "brothers and sisters." Βούλομαι (pres. mid./pass. [deponent] indic. 1 sg. ["to want, wish, desire"]) has γινώσκειν (pres. act. inf. of γινώσκω, "to know") as its complement, with ὑμᾶς (acc. pl.) as the subject of the infinitive.

ὅτι τὰ κατ' ἐμὲ—The conjunction ὅτι often comes after verbs that denote mental perception, here γινώσκω, and introduces the content of what is known (BDAG). The verb of the ὅτι clause, which appears at the end of the clause, is ἐλήλυθεν. The subject of that verb and the whole clause is the phrase τὰ κατ' ἐμὲ. This and similar constructions are used often in Philippians. The phrase κατ' ἐμὲ consists of the elided form of κατά with its accusative singular object, the personal pronoun ἐμέ. The definite article τὰ (neut. nom. pl.) functions as a **substantive,** with κατ' ἐμὲ modifying it. Somewhat woodenly, it may be

> **substantive**
>
> An adjective or other word (e.g. pronoun, participle) that functions as a noun.
>
> μακάριοι <u>οἱ πραεῖς</u>.
> Blessed are <u>the meek</u>. (Matt 5:5)
> <u>ὁ ἐγείρας</u> τὸν κύριον Ἰησοῦν
> <u>the one who raised</u> the Lord Jesus
> (2 Cor 4:14)

translated "the things about me"; more idiomatically, we may render it "my circumstances" or "my affairs."

μᾶλλον εἰς προκοπὴν τοῦ εὐαγγελίου ἐλήλυθεν–Ἐλήλυθεν (pf. act. indic. 3 sg. of ἔρχομαι, "I come, go") is singular because a neuter plural subject (τὰ κατ᾽ ἐμὲ) can take a singular verb, perhaps because the neuter plural was considered a **collective noun** (Smyth, 958). Εἰς designates a result of Paul's circumstances. With this εἰς we may translate ἐλήλυθεν as "have turned out" (see BDAG). Since they know that Paul is in prison, they probably were surprised, as the adverb μᾶλλον ("more, rather") indicates, to hear that his circumstances had led to προκοπὴν (fem. acc. sg.) τοῦ εὐαγγελίου (masc. gen. sg.). Μᾶλλον in some contexts marks an **alternative** (meaning "rather") instead of a simple **comparative** (meaning "more"). In the next clause he explains how this alternative effect is possible.

ὥστε τοὺς δεσμούς μου φανεροὺς ἐν   1:13
Χριστῷ γενέσθαι–The particle ὥστε here introduces a **dependent clause** that designates a result from the previous clause (BDAG), with the accusative τοὺς δεσμούς (masc. acc. pl.) as the subject of the infinitive γενέσθαι (aor. mid. [deponent] inf. of γίνομαι, "I am produced, happen, turn out," see BDF §§391, 406). Δεσμός literally refers to anything that hinders or binds a person; it is even used of diseases (e.g., Mark 7:35). Paul, of course, uses it for his imprisonment. Φανεροὺς (masc. acc. pl. ["visible, plainly seen"]), then, is the predicate adjective of the infinitive and so describes what has come about. So we translate "my imprisonment is clearly seen to be . . ." In this clause the prepositional phrase ἐν Χριστῷ (masc. dat. sg.) expresses the cause or the reason for Paul's imprisonment. Thus the cause of Paul's circumstances is his participation in the sphere of existence, his identity as one who is "in Christ."

ἐν ὅλῳ τῷ πραιτωρίῳ καὶ τοῖς λοιποῖς πᾶσιν–This second ἐν designates the place or sphere in which this understanding of Paul's

---

collective noun

A singular noun that stands for a group; e.g., when "Israel" refers to all those who are Jews.

Ἄκουε, Ἰσραήλ, κύριος ὁ θεὸς ἡμῶν κύριος εἷς ἐστιν.

Listen, Israel, the Lord our God, the Lord is one. (Mark 12:29)

Ἰουδαίῳ τε πρῶτον καὶ Ἕλληνι

To Jews first and also to Greeks (Rom 1:16)

---

alternative comparative

A comparison that expresses contrast, often using the expression μᾶλλον (ἢ) to introduce the second element of the contrast.

Πειθαρχεῖν δεῖ θεῷ μᾶλλον ἢ ἀνθρώποις.

We must obey God rather than humans. (Acts 5:29)

ἠγάπησαν οἱ ἄνθρωποι μᾶλλον τὸ σκότος ἢ τὸ φῶς.

People loved darkness rather than light. (John 3:19)

---

dependent clause

A clause in a complex sentence that cannot stand on its own as a complete sentence. Such clauses can function as nouns, adjectives, or adverbs for the main clause

Εἰδότες . . . τὸν φόβον τοῦ κυρίου ἀνθρώπους πείθομεν.

Knowing . . . the fear of the Lord, we persuade people. (2 Cor 5:11)

οὐκ εἰδότες θεὸν ἐδουλεύσατε τοῖς φύσει μὴ οὖσιν θεοῖς.

When you did not know God, you served those who by nature are not divine. (Gal 4:8)

imprisonment is known. Both τῷ πραιτωρίῳ (masc. dat. sg.) and τοῖς λοιποῖς (masc. dat. pl.) are objects of ἐν. The adjective ὅλῳ (masc. dat. sg.) is in the predicate position, and, according to BDAG, the word never appears in the attributive position in the NT. Πραιτώριον is a loanword from Latin (*praetorium*). In Greek it may signify the emperor's palace or the barracks attached to it, the body of soldiers broadly comprising the emperor's bodyguard, or an encampment of these soldiers (see O'Brien, 93). If Philippians was written from Rome, it probably signifies the corps of the emperor's bodyguard. That Paul is influencing the Praetorian Guard indicates that he must be imprisoned in a place that has an imperial residence or a provincial governor. It is not clear who τοῖς λοιποῖς πᾶσιν (masc. dat. pl.) includes, but it must extend at least as far as others connected with running the prison.

> **partitive genitive**
>
> The use of the genitive case to designate the whole (thing or group) of which the substantive is a part.
>
> τοὺς πλείονας <u>τῶν ἀδελφῶν</u>
> *the majority <u>of the brothers</u>* (Phil 1:14).
> τινες <u>τῶν κλάδων</u>
> *some <u>of the branches</u>* (Rom 11:17)

1:14 καὶ τοὺς πλείονας τῶν ἀδελφῶν ἐν κυρίῳ πεποιθότας τοῖς δεσμοῖς μου—
The comparative τοὺς πλείονας (masc. acc. pl.) serves as the subject of πεποιθότας (pf. act. ptc. masc. acc. pl. of πείθω, "to convince, persuade"), so we may translate the phrase as "most . . . have been made confident." Τῶν ἀδελφῶν, a **partitive genitive,** modifies "the majority" and, as is nearly always the case, "brothers" refers to Christians generally, not just males. Since this expression is qualified by "most," it is clear that not all Christians are convinced that Paul is imprisoned for the sake of the gospel. The prepositional phrase ἐν κυρίῳ (masc. dat. sg.) may modify τῶν ἀδελφῶν. If so, it is somewhat redundant because "brothers" means "Christians," who by definition are "in the Lord." However, it seems more likely that ἐν κυρίῳ is attached to the following participle, even though this would be a unique construction in the undisputed Paulines. Thus it emphasizes that the confidence of these Christians is in the Lord. Τοῖς δεσμοῖς (masc. dat. pl.) μου (gen. sg.) is an instrumental dative or **dative of cause** attached to the preceding participle, conveying that they have been made confident *by means of* or *because of* Paul's imprisonment.

> **dative of cause**
>
> The use of the dative case to designate the cause of something.
>
> τῇ ἀπιστίᾳ ἐξεκλάσθησαν.
> *They were cut off <u>because of unbelief</u>.*
> (Rom 11:20)
> ἐγὼ δὲ λιμῷ ὧδε ἀπόλλυμαι.
> *And I am perishing here <u>due to famine</u>.*
> (Luke 15:17)

περισσοτέρως τολμᾶν ἀφόβως τὸν λόγον λαλεῖν—The comparative adverb περισσοτέρως attaches to the main verb in the clause, τολμᾶν (pres. act. inf. of τολμάω, "to dare, be courageous"). The tense of τολμᾶν may be significant in its contrast with the perfect tense πεποιθότας: having been given confidence, they are now emboldened. Τοὺς πλείονας also serves as the subject of τολμᾶν. The infinitive λαλεῖν (pres. act. inf. of λαλέω, "to speak") is dependent on τολμᾶν, expressing a result of their boldness, and has λόγον (masc. acc. sg. ["word"]) for its object. The adverb ἀφόβως ("without fear") seems to modify λαλεῖν rather than τολμᾶν. Remembering that the subject of λαλεῖν is "the majority," we translate "so that they speak the word fearlessly." This may be the earliest extant use of "the Word" to mean the gospel (see O'Brien, 96).

1:15-20　Responses to Paul's Imprisonment

1:15-17　Antagonists and Colleagues

¹⁵Τινὲς μὲν καὶ διὰ φθόνον καὶ ἔριν, τινὲς δὲ καὶ δι' εὐδοκίαν τὸν Χριστὸν κηρύσσουσιν· ¹⁶οἱ μὲν ἐξ ἀγάπης, εἰδότες ὅτι εἰς ἀπολογίαν τοῦ εὐαγγελίου κεῖμαι, ¹⁷οἱ δὲ ἐξ ἐριθείας τὸν Χριστὸν καταγγέλλουσιν, οὐχ ἁγνῶς, οἰόμενοι θλῖψιν ἐγείρειν τοῖς δεσμοῖς μου.

¹⁵On the one hand, some preach Christ through envy and strife; on the other hand, some preach Christ through good will; ¹⁶some proclaim Christ out of love, knowing that I have been appointed for a defense of the gospel; ¹⁷but others proclaim Christ out of selfish ambition, not sincerely, because they think they are increasing the affliction of my imprisonment.

Τινὲς μὲν καὶ διὰ φθόνον καὶ ἔριν, τινὲς δὲ καὶ δι' εὐδοκίαν τὸν Χριστὸν ‖1:15‖ **κηρύσσουσιν**—The μὲν ... δὲ particles may simply mark off words in a series, but more often they carry an adversative force: "on the one hand, some ..., on the other hand, others ..." The **adversative** force is the sense of the **particles** here, where they mark the first of several antithetical parallels in the next few verses. The **compound subject** of κηρύσσουσιν (pres. act. indic. 3 pl. of κηρύσσω, "to proclaim, preach") includes both uses of τινὲς (masc. nom. pl.), the one before μὲν and the other before δὲ. The first καὶ of the verse may be superfluous, or it may make the contrast more emphatic, thus rendered "Indeed, ..." or "Certainly, ..." Διὰ in both halves of the adversative bears an instrumental sense ("through the agency of," "by means of") with the accusatives. The first group, who are given as bad examples, preach from motives of φθόνον (masc. acc. sg. ["envy, jealousy"]) and ἔριν (fem. acc. sg. ["strife, discord"]). These words are seldom used in the NT. Φθόνος appears five times in the Pauline corpus and only four other times in the NT; ἔρις appears only in the Pauline corpus, and only eight times there. In the three places that φθόνος is used in the undisputed letters (Rom 1:29; Gal 5:20-21; Phil 1:15), it is used

adversative particle

A word that expresses opposition or contrast between sentences or elements within a sentence (e.g., ἀλλά or δέ).

μηδὲ κατὰ κενοδοξίαν *ἀλλὰ* τῇ ταπεινοφροσύνῃ

not according to vanity, but with humility (Phil 2:3)

ἐφρονεῖτε, ἠκαιρεῖσθε *δέ*.

You were concerned, but you were without opportunity. (Phil 4:10)

with ἔρις. In Romans and Galatians these words appear in vice lists. In their only other appearances in the Pauline corpus they are again connected; in 1 Tim 6:4 they are together, and in Titus they are found only six verses apart (φθόνος in 3:3; ἔρις in 3:9). In Philippians these terms seem to foreshadow the coming discussions of discord within the community. The second διὰ is elided and has a single object, εὐδοκίαν (fem. acc. sg. ["goodwill, favor"]). (See the discussion of εὐδοκία at 2:13.) It is clear that the word here refers to the disposition toward Paul of those who are preaching. Whatever their motives, Paul evidently considers their message to be the authentic gospel, because he says that they preach τὸν Χριστὸν (masc. acc. sg.). The following verses make this more clear.

> **compound subject**
>
> A construction in which two or more substantives function as the subjects of a single verb.
>
> Ἀσπάζεται ὑμᾶς Τιμόθεος ὁ συνεργός μου καὶ Λούκιος καὶ Ἰάσων καὶ Σωσίπατρος οἱ συγγενεῖς μου.
>
> *Timothy* my co-worker *and Luke and Jason and Sosipater* my kinspeople greet you. (Rom 16:21)
>
> σὰρξ καὶ αἷμα βασιλείαν θεοῦ κληρονομῆσαι οὐ δύναται.
>
> *Flesh and blood* cannot inherit the kingdom of God. (1 Cor 15:50)

1:16   οἱ μὲν ἐξ ἀγάπης–Verses 16-17 build upon the adversative μὲν ... δὲ construction and through v. 17a are completely parallel with v. 15, although reversed so that the good example comes first. So vv. 15-17a are a clear example of **chiasmus.** The parallel is carried on with the main verb of the sentence and its object, τὸν Χριστὸν καταγγέλλουσιν, which have the same meaning here as τὸν Χριστὸν κηρύσσουσιν in v. 15. The definite article οἱ (masc. nom. pl.) functions as a substantive, governing its immediately following prepositional phrase, which

> **chiasmus**
>
> An arrangement of parallel words or ideas in an A-B-B-A pattern such that the order of the elements in the first half are reversed in the second half.
>
> ὅπου οὐκ ἔνι Ἕλλην καὶ Ἰουδαῖος,
>   περιτομὴ καὶ ἀκροβυστία
>
> *where there is neither Greek nor Jew,*
>   *circumcision nor uncircumcision* (Col 3:11)
>
> ἡμεῖς ἀσθενεῖς, ὑμεῖς δὲ ἰσχυροί· ὑμεῖς ἔνδοξοι, ἡμεῖς δὲ ἄτιμοι.
>
> *We are weak, but you are strong; you are held in honor, but we in disrepute.* (1 Cor 4:10)

characterizes the motivation of those who are a good example–they act out of love, ἀγάπης (fem. gen. sg.)–and serving as the first part of the compound subject of καταγγέλλουσιν (pres. act. indic. 3 sg. of καταγγέλλω, "to proclaim").

εἰδότες ὅτι εἰς ἀπολογίαν τοῦ εὐαγγελίου κεῖμαι–Εἰδότες (pf. act. ptc. masc. nom. pl. of οἶδα, "to know") is either a circumstantial participle of attendant circumstances ("while knowing") or a participle expressing cause ("because they know"). The former reading implies that Paul's situation is one of several motives they may have for preaching. On the other hand, understanding it to be a causal participle limits the scope of vision to Paul's circumstances and makes a better parallel to the following contrast with those who preach in order to increase Paul's suffering. That rather polemical statement also does not exhaust the motives of those Paul mentions. Ὅτι often follows verbs of perception, indicating what is known (BDAG). Κεῖμαι (pres. pass. [deponent] indic. 1 sg. of κεῖμαι, "to lie, set, be appointed, be destined") could indicate that something is appointed by God for Paul or that he is set to do it. If it is correct that this word is to be read as a passive of this deponent verb, the former meaning is clearly preferable, as most commentators agree. Paul has been appointed εἰς ἀπολογίαν (fem. acc. sg. ["defense"]) τοῦ εὐαγγελίου (masc. gen. sg. ["gospel"]). The εἰς with the accusative here indicates the purpose (Smyth, 1686d) of Paul's imprisonment, with τοῦ εὐαγγελίου being an **objective genitive.**

> ### objective genitive
>
> The use of the genitive case to designate the object of the action implied in the word it modifies. Thus "the love of Christ" would indicate love *for* or *toward* Christ, the love of which Christ is the object.
>
> ἔχετε πίστιν <u>θεοῦ</u>.
> *Have faith <u>in God</u>.* (Mark 11:22)
> τῆς ἐπιγνώσεως <u>τοῦ υἱοῦ</u> τοῦ θεοῦ
> *the knowledge <u>of the son</u> of God* (Eph 4:13)

οἱ δὲ ἐξ ἐριθείας τὸν Χριστὸν καταγγέλλουσιν, οὐχ ἁγνῶς–The adverbial   1:17
expression οὐχ ἁγνῶς ("not sincerely, not from pure motives"), modifying καταγγέλλουσιν (pres. act. indic. 3 pl. of καταγγέλλω, "to proclaim"), ascribes another derogatory motivation to those who preach out of strife. Again, οἱ (masc. nom. pl.) serves as a substantive with its prepositional phrase, ἐξ ἐριθείας (fem. gen. sg. ["strife, contentiousness"]). Despite their bad motives, Paul continues to recognize that they do preach an acceptable message, because he again says that they proclaim τὸν Χριστὸν (masc. acc. sg.).

> ### circumstantial participle of cause
>
> The participle provides a reason for the state or action of the main verb. It if often translated *because*.
>
> Τοῦτο <u>πεποιθὼς</u> οἶδα.
> *<u>Because I am confident</u> of this, I know.* (Phil 1:25)
> Ἰωσὴφ . . . δίκαιος <u>ὢν</u>
> *Joseph, . . . <u>because he was</u> a righteous person* (Matt 1:19)

οἰόμενοι θλῖψιν ἐγείρειν τοῖς δεσμοῖς μου–This participial phrase carries the negative description of their motives further. Οἰόμενοι (pres. mid./pass. [deponent] ptc. masc. nom. pl. of οἴομαι, "to think, suppose") is a **circumstantial participle denoting cause** ("because they think . . ."). The infinitive ἐγείρειν (pres. act. inf. of ἐγείρω, "to raise") completes the thought begun with the participle. Given that Paul is in prison, the combination of this verb with θλῖψιν (fem. acc. sg.) as its object seems to mean "to increase affliction." Τοῖς δεσμοῖς (masc. dat. pl. ["bonds"]) is a **dative of respect.** To translate this clause into smooth English, it is perhaps better to translate the infinitive as an indicative: "because they think *they are increasing* the affliction of my imprisonment."

> ### dative of respect (reference, relation)
>
> The use of the dative case to limit the persons or things for which a statement or perspective holds true, often when the statement might not otherwise be true.
>
> οἵτινες ἀπεθάνομεν <u>τῇ ἁμαρτία</u>
> *we who have died [<u>with respect</u>] <u>to sin</u>* (Rom 6:2)
> αἱ ἐκκλησίαι ἐστερεοῦντο <u>τῇ πίστει</u>.
> *the churches were strengthened <u>in [relation to] faith</u>.* (Acts 16:5)

1:18-20 Paul's Response to Both

[18]τί γάρ; πλὴν ὅτι παντὶ τρόπῳ, εἴτε προφάσει εἴτε ἀληθείᾳ, Χριστὸς καταγγέλλεται, καὶ ἐν τούτῳ χαίρω. ἀλλὰ καὶ χαρήσομαι, [19]οἶδα γὰρ ὅτι τοῦτό μοι ἀποβήσεται εἰς σωτηρίαν διὰ τῆς ὑμῶν δεήσεως καὶ ἐπιχορηγίας τοῦ πνεύματος Ἰησοῦ Χριστοῦ [20]κατὰ τὴν ἀποκαρα-δοκίαν καὶ ἐλπίδα μου, ὅτι ἐν οὐδενὶ αἰσχυνθήσομαι ἀλλ' ἐν πάσῃ παρρησίᾳ ὡς πάντοτε καὶ νῦν μεγαλυνθήσεται Χριστὸς ἐν τῷ σώματί μου, εἴτε διὰ ζωῆς εἴτε διὰ θανάτου.

[18]What do I say about this? Nothing, except that Christ is preached in [any and] every way, whether from false motives or true, and I rejoice about that. And I will continue to rejoice [19]because I know that this will turn out for my salvation through your prayers and the supply of the Spirit of Jesus Christ, [20]in accord with my eager expectation and hope, so that I will not be put to shame by anything, but with all boldness Christ, now as always, will be magnified through my body, whether I live or die.

1:18   **τί γάρ**–The question formed by the conjunction γάρ and the **interrogative adjective** τί might be rendered "And what do I have to say about this state of affairs?" This translation, however, takes the emotional impact out of the terse question. So perhaps we might translate it as "What do I say about that?" or even "So what?" The γάρ indicates that the question relates back to the preceding statement about some preaching Christ from pure motives and others from impure motives.

πλὴν ὅτι παντὶ τρόπῳ, εἴτε προφάσει εἴτε ἀληθείᾳ–The adversative conjunction πλὴν with ὅτι begins the answer to Paul's rhetorical question. BDAG gives two possibilities for translation. First, it may be breaking off a discussion to focus on an important aspect, and thus it would be rendered "in any case" or "only." The second option (preferred by BDAG) is that it there is less disjunction with the previous phrase, and so it is translated "except that." If τί γάρ is given the impact suggested above, this latter meaning seems more likely, though there is little difference. BDF (§198) identifies παντὶ τρόπῳ (masc. dat. sg. ["manner, way"]) as a **dative of manner** in a formulaic expression (similarly O'Brien, 106). The coordinating conjunction εἴτε usually appears in pairs, as it does here.

> **interrogative (adjective, pronoun, particle)**
>
> An adjective or other word that indicates that a question is being asked. Interrogatives may be particles or pronouns that sometimes have an adjectival function.
>
> τίς με ῥύσεται ἐκ τοῦ σώματος τοῦ θανάτου τούτου;
> _Who_ will rescue me from this body of death? (Rom 7:24)
>
> ποῦ σοφός; ποῦ γραμματεύς;
> _Where_ is the wise person? _Where_ is the scholar? (1 Cor 1:20)

> **dative of manner**
>
> The use of the dative case to indicate the manner or method in which something is accomplished.
>
> χάριτι μετέχω.
> I partake _with joy_. (1 Cor 10:30)
>
> παρρησίᾳ λαλεῖ.
> He speaks _boldly_. (John 7:26)

Both προφάσει (fem. dat. sg. ["motive, pretext"]) and ἀληθείᾳ (fem. dat. sg. ["truth"]) are datives of manner. Given the preceding contrasting motivations, the context indicates that προφάσει has the sense of pretext, even though it can mean that one gives a valid reason. These two nouns specify the meaning of παντὶ τρόπῳ, which we may then render "in any and every way."

Χριστὸς καταγγέλλεται, καὶ ἐν τούτῳ χαίρω–We finally come to the main clause of this sentence, Χριστὸς (masc. nom. sg.) καταγγέλλεται (pres. pass. indic. 3 sg. of καταγγέλλω, "to proclaim, preach"). It is interesting that Paul switches to the passive voice here. It is clear that he is pleased that Christ is preached, not that some preach from impure motives. As is often the case in the NT, ἐν (with the dative) designates the object of χαίρω (pres. act. indic. 1 sg. of χαίρω, "to rejoice"). Τούτῳ (dat. sg.) is neuter, apparently signifying that what Paul rejoices in is this preaching of Christ.

Ἀλλὰ καὶ χαρήσομαι–Ἀλλὰ καὶ is used here to introduce a point in an emphatic way (BDF §448). The new point is that Paul will continue to rejoice; thus he uses the future tense χαρήσομαι (fut. pass. [deponent] indic. 1 sg. of χαίρω). The γάρ of v. 19 introduces his explanation of this rejoicing.

οἶδα γὰρ ὅτι τοῦτό μοι ἀποβήσεται εἰς σωτηρίαν–The perfect οἶδα (pf. act. indic. 1 sg. of οἶδα, "to know") functions as a present and is the main verb of the sentence. Within the dependent ὅτι clause, τοῦτο (neut. nom. sg.) is the subject of ἀποβήσεται (fut. mid. [deponent] indic. 3 sg. of ἀποβαίνω, "to go away, turn out"), which has an active sense. The antecedent for τοῦτο is unclear, but it seems to refer to Paul's circumstances, especially how his trial goes, rather than just to the preaching from various motives. The prepositional phrase εἰς σωτηρίαν expresses the goal of ἀποβήσεται. Σωτηρίαν (fem. acc. sg.) may point to final judgment, or, since it can mean simply "deliverance," to an acquittal in Paul's trial, or to a vindication of Paul's faith at the trial, whatever the verdict, because of his faithfulness. The first option seems least likely, given what follows in the context. Perhaps a combination of the last two options encompasses the range of meaning that Paul had in mind. Several commentators note that what follows the ὅτι in this verse is a quotation of Job 13:16 (LXX); so Paul is drawing on Job to understand his situation and to express his faith in God.

διὰ τῆς ὑμῶν δεήσεως καὶ ἐπιχορηγίας τοῦ πνεύματος Ἰησοῦ Χριστοῦ–This prepositional phrase modifies εἰς σωτηρίαν. Δεήσεως (fem. gen. sg. ["prayer"]) and ἐπιχορηγίας (fem. gen. sg. ["assistance, support"]) form the compound object of διὰ and are closely related, as is seen in their sharing of a single article, τῆς (fem. gen. sg.). This sharing makes the meaning difficult, but perhaps it indicates that there is a close relationship between the prayer of the Philippians (ὑμῶν [gen. pl.]) and a special measure of the Spirit granted to Paul in his defense that is the answer to their prayer (so O'Brien, 110; Fee, 132). Ἐπιχορηγία

1:19

appears only one other time in the NT (Eph 4:16). Although it is often translated "help" (e.g., RSV, NIV, NRSV), Fee (132–33) argues that "help" is inaccurate because the word always points to the provision or material itself that was given or supplied. Thus the thing provided is identified by the ensuing phrase, τοῦ πνεύματος (neut. gen. sg.). Another difficulty presented by this phrase is the meaning of Ἰησοῦ (masc. gen. sg.) Χριστοῦ (masc. gen. sg.) in conjunction with the Spirit. Paul nearly always speaks of the Spirit as from God, not from Christ. So it seems unlikely that it is a genitive of origin or a subjective genitive. Some have even suggested that it is appositional, so that the Spirit is Christ. One might also see it as a possessive genitive. Usual Pauline usage contributes little in this case because this is the only place where Paul uses this exact expression, although he speaks of the Spirit of Christ in Rom 8:9 and Gal 4:6. Commentators often do not specify what sort of genitive this is, but rather prefer to speak of what it signifies in the context. Perhaps there is no single type of genitive that sufficiently describes the intent of this construction. It seems correct that it refers both to the Holy Spirit who was in the earthly Jesus and in the risen Christ (so Hawthorne, 41) and to the Spirit as that which mediates the presence and life (including endurance of persecution) of Christ to Paul (Fee, 134–35). Since Paul's σωτηρία is accomplished through a special supply of the Spirit, the primary emphasis in his use of σωτηρία seems to be on his trial (though not necessarily pointing to his acquittal, but rather to his faithfulness in the proceedings) and less on eschatological salvation. Still, what follows shows that these are not to be viewed as mutually exclusive concerns.

> **hendiadys**
>
> The use of two words to express a single idea.
>
> ἐξίσταντο . . . ἐπὶ τῇ συνέσει καὶ ταῖς ἀποκρίσεσιν αὐτοῦ.
>
> *They were amazed . . . at his <u>understanding answers</u>.* (lit. "understanding and answers") (Luke 2:47)
>
> ζωὴν καὶ ἀφθαρσίαν
>
> *immortal life* (lit. *life and immortality*) (2 Tim 1:10)

1:20   **κατὰ τὴν ἀποκαραδοκίαν καὶ ἐλπίδα μου**—This κατὰ phrase goes back to either εἰς σωτηρίαν or ἀποβήσεται in v. 19. O'Brien (112) connects it to the whole phrase τοῦτό μοι ἀποβήσεται εἰς σωτηρίαν. Again the close relationship between the two accusative objects of κατὰ–ἀποκαραδοκίαν (fem. acc. sg. ["eager expectation"]) and ἐλπίδα (fem. acc. sg. ["hope"])–is seen by their sharing of a single article. Perhaps this is a case of **hendiadys,** expressing a single idea using two substantives. Alternatively, ἐλπίδα may be epexegetical, so that "hope" defines Paul's expectation. In either case, the close relationship between the two nouns also suggests that the μου (gen. sg.) following ἐλπίδα modifies both objects.

ὅτι ἐν οὐδενὶ αἰσχυνθήσομαι ἀλλ᾽ ἐν πάσῃ παρρησίᾳ—The ὅτι may express purpose here, especially given the second verb that it governs. Αἰσχυνθήσομαι (fut. pass. indic. 1 sg. of αἰσχύνω, "to be ashamed, be put to shame"), with Paul as the implied subject, and μεγαλυνθήσεται (fut. pass. indic. 3 sg. of μεγαλύνω, "to make large, exalt, glorify"), with Christ as its subject, are the main verbs of the ὅτι clause. Ἐν οὐδενὶ (neut. dat. sg. ["no, nothing"]) functions adverbially, modifying αἰσχυνθήσομαι so that it reads "I will be put to shame by nothing" or, more idiomatically, "I will not be put to shame by anything." The conjunction ἀλλ' either marks the point at which members of the sentence begin to modify the following verb or forms its contrast between ἐν οὐδενὶ and ἐν πάσῃ (fem. dat. sg.) παρρησίᾳ (fem. dat. sg. ["boldness"]). O'Brien (113-14) chooses the former, seeing the two clauses in antithetic parallel. The length of the second member gives the proper emphasis to the glorification of Christ, the main point of the clause, and may count against O'Brien's understanding.

ὡς πάντοτε καὶ νῦν—Loh and Nida (30) translate this adverbial construction "at all times and especially now." More idiomatically, if less emphatic, we may translate it "now as always." The phrase modifies the following verb and explains what Paul understands to be the basic purpose of his life, whether speaking of his current circumstances or any other.

μεγαλυνθήσεται Χριστὸς ἐν τῷ σώματί μου—The prepositional phrase ἐν τῷ σώματί (neut. dat. sg.) μου (gen. sg.) functions adverbially, being governed by μεγαλυνθήσεται (fut. pass. indic. 3 sg. of μεγαλύνω, "to exalt, glorify"). The subject of this passive verb is Χριστὸς (masc. nom. sg.). This part of the ὅτι clause indicates that Paul's whole being is dedicated to glorifying Christ.

εἴτε διὰ ζωῆς εἴτε διὰ θανάτου—Loh and Nida (31) see the grammatical connection between this phrase and the preceding material as rather loose. However, it indicates the extent of the dedication of Paul to Christ and serves as a transition to the topic of the next paragraph. Since Paul seems unsure whether his trial will conclude with life (διὰ ζωῆς [fem. gen. sg.]) or death (διὰ θανάτου [masc. gen. sg.]), the σωτηρία in v. 19 should not be understood primarily as acquittal in Paul's trial. This is the second time the particle εἴτε (a combination of εἴ and τε) has been used in this chapter without a verb following it (cf. v. 18). This type of **ellipsis** is found elsewhere in Paul's writings (e.g., Rom 12:6-8 [where we find εἴτε three times in succession with no verb]; 2 Cor 5:10). In 1 Cor 8:5 it is

> **ellipsis**
>
> The literary device of omitting one or more words to the sense of the statement, often to add force and vigor.
>
> μόνον μὴ τὴν ἐλευθερίαν εἰς ἀφορμὴν τῇ σαρκί.
>
> *Only, do not [use] the freedom for an opportunity for the flesh.* (Gal 5:13)
>
> Εἰ καὶ πάντες σκανδαλισθήσονται, ἀλλ' οὐκ ἐγώ.
>
> *Even if all are offended, I will not [be offended].* (Mark 14:29)

used much as it is here, with a two-word prepositional phrase following each particle, although different prepositions are used there. Perhaps a smooth translation of these prepositional phrases here in Philippians is "whether by living or by dying," or one might even render them "whether I live or die."

1:21-26 Paul's Care for the Philippians Seen in His Choice to Continue His Life and Mission

²¹ἐμοὶ γὰρ τὸ ζῆν Χριστὸς καὶ τὸ ἀποθανεῖν κέρδος. ²²εἰ δὲ τὸ ζῆν ἐν σαρκί, τοῦτό μοι καρπὸς ἔργου, καὶ τί αἱρήσομαι οὐ γνωρίζω. ²³συνέχομαι δὲ ἐκ τῶν δύο, τὴν ἐπιθυμίαν ἔχων εἰς τὸ ἀναλῦσαι καὶ σὺν Χριστῷ εἶναι, πολλῷ (γὰρ) μᾶλλον κρεῖσσον· ²⁴τὸ δὲ ἐπιμένειν (ἐν) τῇ σαρκὶ ἀναγκαιότερον δι᾽ ὑμᾶς. ²⁵καὶ τοῦτο πεποιθὼς οἶδα ὅτι μενῶ καὶ παραμενῶ πᾶσιν ὑμῖν εἰς τὴν ὑμῶν προκοπὴν καὶ χαρὰν τῆς πίστεως, ²⁶ἵνα τὸ καύχημα ὑμῶν περισσεύῃ ἐν Χριστῷ Ἰησοῦ ἐν ἐμοὶ διὰ τῆς ἐμῆς παρουσίας πάλιν πρὸς ὑμᾶς.

²¹For, from my perspective, to live is Christ and to die is gain. ²²And if I live in the flesh, this is fruit of labor for me, but which I prefer I do not know. ²³And I am torn between the two: I want to depart and be with Christ, for that is better by far, ²⁴but remaining in the flesh is more necessary for you. ²⁵I am very confident of this: I know that I will remain with all of you for the progress and joy of your faith, ²⁶so that your boasting might abound in Christ Jesus through me because of my coming to you again.

1:21 **ἐμοὶ γὰρ τὸ ζῆν Χριστὸς καὶ τὸ ἀποθανεῖν κέρδος**–The postpositive particle γὰρ shows that vv. 21–26 are closely related to the preceding paragraph. The γὰρ is causal; that is, it gives an explanation for what went before. The articular infinitive τὸ (neut. nom. sg.) ζῆν (pres. act. inf. of ζάω, "to live") serves as the subject of the sentence, with the understood verb ἐστί, which has Χριστὸς (masc. nom. sg.) as its predicate nominative. So we translate "to live is Christ." The personal pronoun ἐμοὶ (dat. sg.) stands in an emphatic position and seems to be a dative of relation or reference. Wallace (146) sees it as an **ethical dative,** a type of dative close to, perhaps even a subset of, the dative of reference. The second clause of the sentence is joined to the first by a coordinating conjunction and so does not so much imply a contrast to the first half as correlate an idea. The structure of the second clause is parallel to that of the first, with the articular infinitive τὸ (neut. nom. sg.) ἀποθανεῖν (aor. act. inf. of ἀποθνήσκω, "to die") serving as the subject of the understood ἐστὶ, along with the predicate nominative κέρδος (neut. nom. sg. ["gain"]).

> **ethical dative**
>
> The use of the dative case to indicate whose point of view is being expressed. Some consider it a subcategory under dative of reference.
>
> ἦν ἀστεῖος τῷ θεῷ.
>
> he was beautiful to God (i.e., from God's perspective). (Acts 7:20)
>
> ἐμοὶ γὰρ τὸ ζῆν Χριστὸς.
>
> For me (i.e., from my perspective) to live is Christ. (Phil 1:21)

1:22 **εἰ δὲ τὸ ζῆν ἐν σαρκί**–It is possible that the first two clauses of this verse as found in the UBS⁴ text constitute a sentence by themselves (BDF §442[8] gives v. 22b as an example of an interrogative apodosis beginning with καί; that is, the καί is rendered "then," and the sentence ends with "which will I prefer?"). However, the parallel in structure between the first two clauses and v. 21 (see below)

anaphora

The literary device of repeating the same word or phrase in successive clauses.

Πίστει νοοῦμεν . . . <u>Πίστει</u> . . .
Ἄβελ . . . προσήνεγκεν . . . <u>Πίστει</u>
Ἐνὼχ μετετέθη . . .

By faith . . . we understand . . . *By faith*
Abel offered . . . *By faith* Enoch was
taken . . . (Heb 11:3-5)

<u>διαιρέσεις</u> δὲ χαρισμάτων . . . καὶ
<u>διαιρέσεις</u> διακωνιῶν . . . καὶ
<u>διαιρέσεις</u> ἐνεργημάτων

a *diversity* of gifts . . . and a *diversity* of
ministries . . . and a *diversity* of workings
(1 Cor 12:4-6)

and the balance in reasoning that Paul gives following v. 21 (i.e., v. 22b gives a reason for remaining in the flesh and so makes the dilemma of v. 22c more understandable) make it more likely that the protasis is v. 22a, and the apodosis includes all of the rest of v. 22. The protasis of this conditional sentence has, as did the preceding sentences, the articular infinitive τὸ (neut. nom. sg.) ζῆν (pres. act. inf. of ζάω, "to live") as its subject. Wallace identifies this repetition of infinitives as an example of **anaphora.** Ἐστί is the understood verb of this clause. BDAG gives denoting "a state of being" as one of the uses of ἐν, especially with εἶναι. LSJ lists a less specific but compatible use of ἐν, noting that it sometimes indicates a state or condition (of life). In this verse, such ranges of meaning for ἐν seem to capture Paul's idea best. Σαρκί (fem. dat. sg. ["flesh"]), the object of ἐν, probably has no distinctively theological implications in this context. Rather, it refers to bodily or earthly existence as opposed to postearthly existence, as v. 23 shows.

τοῦτό μοι καρπὸς ἔργου–The antecedent of τοῦτο (neut. nom. sg.) is the entire protasis, Paul's continuing his earthly existence. Τοῦτο is the subject of the understood verb of this apodosis, ἐστί, though perhaps this verb could be construed as a future. Καρπὸς (masc. nom. sg.) functions as a predicate nominative, a function found with intransitive verbs. Μοι seems to be either a dative of reference, designating "the person in whose opinion a statement holds good" (Smyth, 1496), or an ethical dative, referring to the person whose interest is being spoken of (Smyth, 1486). Ἔργου (neut. gen. sg.) clearly modifies καρπὸς, but the meaning of the phrase remains obscure. Perhaps ἔργου is a **genitive of source.** Then the meaning would be "fruit that comes from labor."

genitive of source

The use of the genitive case to identify the source from which an object derives.

καρπὸν <u>δικαιοσύνης</u>
fruit *that comes from righteousness*
(Phil 1:11)

ἐστὲ ἐπιστολὴ <u>Χριστοῦ</u>.
You are a letter *from Christ*. (2 Cor 3:3)

καὶ τί αἱρήσομαι οὐ γνωρίζω.–The καὶ that begins this clause is mildly adversative. BDF (§368), among others, suggests that the proper punctuation is to insert a question mark after αἱρήσομαι (fut. mid. indic. 1 sg. of αἱρέω, "to prefer, choose"). This reading seems to give the more proper sense to the interrogative pronoun τί (neut. acc. sg.), but the meaning is substantively the same regardless of which punctuation is accepted. Still, see the comments above on εἰ δὲ . . . σαρκί for reasons to accept the punctuation given here. BDAG gives "prefer" as a secondary meaning of αἱρέω in the middle voice. If that meaning were accepted, Paul would be saying that he did not know whether he preferred to live or to die. Some have suggested that the meaning "choose" for this verb indicates that Paul is considering whether he should reveal his Roman citizenship at his trial, but since it is not certain that Paul was a citizen (that asserted only in Acts), this is probably not the best understanding of this verse. Seeking a clear understanding of this verse from another angle, O'Brien (127–28) argues that in the NT γνωρίζω (pres. act. indic. 1 sg. of γνωρίζω) means "to make known" rather than "to know." Thus the use of this verb indicates that God had not revealed to Paul what would happen during his trial. Perhaps what finally weighs against this understanding of γνωρίζω is that αἱρήσομαι is in the first person, so it seems Paul is expressing his own view. However, that the matter is completely in Paul's hands seems unlikely. In the end, the meaning remains unclear.

1:23 **συνέχομαι δὲ ἐκ τῶν δύο**—The postpositive δὲ is more copulative than adversative here. The main verb of the sentence, συνέχομαι (pres. pass. indic. 1 sg. of συνέχω, "to hold together, press hard, be absorbed in"), is followed by the unusual use of ἐκ to mean "between," which BDAG mentions only under συνέχω. This verb is used only one other time in the Pauline corpus (only ten other times in the NT, nine of which are in Luke and Acts), 2 Cor 5:14, where Paul says that "the love of Christ constrains us." It is sometimes used in extrabiblical literature to describe being torn between two things, as it is here. Although its form is unusual, δύο (neut. gen. pl.) serves as the object of ἐκ.

τὴν ἐπιθυμίαν ἔχων εἰς τὸ ἀναλῦσαι καὶ σὺν Χριστῷ εἶναι—The circumstantial participle ἔχων (pres. act. ptc. masc. nom. sg. of ἔχω, "to have, hold") serves as the main verb of the following subordinate clause and has τὴν ἐπιθυμίαν (fem. acc. sg. ["desire, longing"]) for its object and Paul as its subject. Rather than translating the words as "having the desire," we may render them as a finite verb and translate "I desire" or "I want." An articular **infinitive** with εἰς usually denotes purpose or **result;** however, BDF (§402[2]) asserts that it has a looser sense here, more akin to a genitive articular infinitive. The strangeness of the phrase is reflected in the textual tradition. The εἰς is absent (forming a construction that BDF says is impossible) in 𝔓⁴⁶, D, F, and G. Perhaps the εἰς helps Paul signal the close connection between ἀναλῦσαι (aor. act. inf. of ἀναλύω, "to untie, depart") and the second infinitive of the prepo-

> ### infinitive in result clause
>
> The use of the infinitive to express the result that is produced by the governing verb. Such infinitives commonly follow ὥστε, although sometimes the infinitive has no particle or preposition and may be articular or anarthrous.
>
> ἐπισυναχθεισῶν τῶν μυριάδων τοῦ ὄχλου, <u>ὥστε καταπατεῖν</u> ἀλλήλους
>
> *a very large crowd was gathered, <u>so that they were crushing</u> one another*
> (Luke 12:1)
>
> ἵνα ὁ Θεὸς ἀνοίξῃ ἡμῖν θύραν τοῦ λόγου <u>λαλῆσαι</u> τὸ μυστήριον
>
> *that God might open for us a door of speech <u>to tell</u> the mystery* (Col 4:3)

sitional phrase, εἶναι (pres. act. inf. of εἰμί, "to be"), as does their sharing the single article τὸ (neut. acc. sg.). Paul uses ἀναλύω, which in the passive voice means to depart or return, metaphorically for death. This usage of the passive is also known from other literature. So he understands death to bring Christians into a state that he describes as σὺν Χριστῷ (masc. dat. sg.). Paul does not give any explanation (here or elsewhere) of the difference in the way he understands this existence and what he expects from the transformation at the Parousia.

πολλῷ (γὰρ) μᾶλλον κρεῖσσον—We identify κρεῖσσον (neut. nom. sg.) as a nominative rather than an accusative because of the understood verb attached to it. If it is correct that ἐστί is to be supplied, with its understood subject being "it" or "that," then κρεῖσσον is a predicate adjective. Perhaps the verb was omitted to emphasize the comparatives. This phrase has several textual variants. D and a few other manuscripts omit γὰρ, and 𝔓⁴⁶ omits κρεῖσσον. ℵ, A, B, and C have the text given here, which is the most difficult reading by virtue of its seeming repetitiveness because of the buildup of comparatives. The adverb μᾶλλον ("more") is, of course, not inflected. The preceding adjective, πολλῷ (neut. dat. sg.), intensifies the comparison and is a **dative of degree of difference.** BDF (§246) notes that such an accumulation of comparatives heightens a comparison.

> **dative of degree of difference**
>
> The use of the dative case with a comparative to designate the degree of difference between (or among) things.
>
> ἀλλὰ νῦν <u>πολλῷ μᾶλλον</u> ἐν τῇ ἀπουσίᾳ μου
>
> but now <u>much more</u> in my absence (Phil 2:12)
>
> ὁ δὲ <u>πολλῷ μᾶλλον</u> ἔκραζεν.
>
> But he cried out <u>all the more</u>. (Mark 10:48)

τὸ δὲ ἐπιμένειν (ἐν) τῇ σαρκὶ ἀναγκαιότερον δι᾽ ὑμᾶς.—Δὲ has its full adversative force here. The comparison is with the double infinitive clause of v. 23 ("I want to depart and be with Christ"). The ἐν is missing from ℵ, A, and C (among others), but is found in 𝔓⁴⁶, B, and D. O'Brien (116) suggests that the ἐν may have been added by scribes to make the sentence grammatically correct. Its insertion also makes it more parallel to 1:22 and other passages in which Paul uses σάρξ. Furthermore, Paul on occasion does use forms of ἐπιμένω with a dative without a preposition (e.g., Rom 6:1; 11:22, 23; cf. Col 1:23). So the better reading omits ἐν, making τῇ σαρκὶ (fem. dat. sg. ["flesh"]) the direct object of the substantivized articular infinitive τὸ (neut. nom. sg.) ἐπιμένειν (pres. act. inf. of ἐπιμένω, "to remain"), even though the accusative case would be grammatically more common. We may translate the phrase as "but remaining in the flesh." This articular infinitive serves as the subject of the understood ἐστίν, and the comparative ἀναγκαιότερον (neut. nom. sg. ["more necessary"]) is the understood verb's predicate adjective. The pronoun ὑμᾶς (acc. pl.) is the object of the elided (contracted) form of διά.   1:24

καὶ τοῦτο πεποιθὼς οἶδα—Οἶδα (pf. act. indic. 1 sg. of οἶδα, "to know"), although formed from the perfect tense of εἶδον, is used as a present and treated as   1:25

a distinct word with its own principle parts. This is the main clause of the sentence that comprises vv. 25-26. The conjunction καὶ puts stress on τοῦτο (see the adverbial use of καί in Smyth, 2881). Τοῦτο (neut. acc. sg.) is the object of οἶδα, the main verb of the sentence, which is also modified by the participle πεποιθὼς. used as an adverb ("confidently"). So we translate the clause as "I know this confidently" or "I am very confident of this." Kennedy (429) suggests the translation "With this conviction I know." This translation makes it clear that the phrase intends to indicate that Paul is so sure of their need for him that even though he does not yet know the outcome of his trial, he is certain that it will be God's will that he return to them.

ὅτι μενῶ καὶ παραμενῶ πᾶσιν ὑμῖν–῞Οτι introduces the first dependent clause of the sentence. ῞Οτι often appears with verbs of mental perception (here οἶδα), designating the content of what is known. The phrase gives the preceding "this" (τοῦτο) content: Paul knows that μενῶ (fut. act. indic. 1 sg. of μένω, "to remain, stay") and παραμενῶ (fut. act. indic. 1 sg. of παραμένω, "to remain, continue in an office"). As is the case here, the dative is often used in conjunction with παραμενῶ to designate the person(s) with whom one remains (both the adjective πᾶσιν and the pronoun ὑμῖν are dat. pl.).

εἰς τὴν ὑμῶν προκοπὴν καὶ χαρὰν τῆς πίστεως–Εἰς with accusative objects designates the purpose or goal of the governing verb. Both προκοπὴν (fem. acc. sg. ["progress, advancement"]) and χαρὰν (fem. acc. sg. ["joy']) are governed by the definite article τὴν (fem. acc. sg.), which indicates their close connection. It seems likely, then, that ὑμῶν (gen. pl.) modifies both objects. Although the position of τῆς πίστεως, at the end of the clause and fairly distant from προκοπὴν, may count against it being seen to modify both, the context, including the single article for the two nouns, seems to indicate that it does. Τῆς πίστεως (fem. gen. sg. ["faith, faithfulness"]) and ὑμῶν do not need to be repeated in the translation. Putting the two together and reading "for the progress and joy of your faith" conveys the attachment to both.

1:26   ἵνα τὸ καύχημα ὑμῶν περισσεύῃ–As it often does, ἵνα, used with a subjunctive verb, expresses purpose. So v. 26 gives another reason why Paul will "remain." Paul uses the word καύχημα (neut. nom. sg.), here the subject of περισσεύῃ (pres. act. sub. 3 sg. of περισσεύω, "to abound"), in various ways. Here it has a positive connotation, but that is not always the case, especially as it is used in 2 Corinthians. BDAG suggests "what you can be proud of" as the translation here. Just as it was in the preceding clause, the benefit of Paul remaining accrues to the Philippians, so it is "your [ὑμῶν (gen. pl.)] boasting" that abounds.

ἐν Χριστῷ Ἰησοῦ ἐν ἐμοὶ–Ἐν with the dative Χριστῷ (masc. dat. sg.) Ἰησοῦ (masc. dat. sg.) has its locative meaning here, but the immediately following ἐν phrase has an instrumental meaning, as the preceding and following statements suggest. So their boast is "in Christ Jesus because of me [ἐμοὶ (dat. sg.)]" or "through me."

διὰ τῆς ἐμῆς παρουσίας πάλιν πρὸς ὑμᾶς—These phrases further specify how their pride may increase because of Paul (so Vincent, 31). Paul uses the same word for his own return to Philippi (πρὸς ὑμᾶς [acc. pl.]) that he often uses for the second coming of Christ. However, here παρουσίας (fem. gen. sg.) reverts to its more common meaning and so simply refers to his return with no hint of the sort of honored reception that it often implied when used for a visit of a dignitary. The genitive possessive adjective/pronoun ἐμῆς is feminine singular because it conforms to the noun that it modifies rather than to its referent.

FOR FURTHER STUDY

Green, J. B. "Resurrection of the Body: New Testament Voices Concerning Personal Continuity and the Afterlife." Pp. 85-100 in *What about the Soul? Neuroscience and Christian Anthropology*. Edited by J. B. Green. Nashville: Abingdon, 2004.

Gundry, R. *Soma in Biblical Theology: With Emphasis on Pauline Anthropology*. Society for New Testament Studies Monograph Series 29. Cambridge: Cambridge University Press, 1976.

Jewett, R. *Paul's Anthropological Terms: A Study of Their Use in Conflict Settings*. Arbeiten zur Geschichte des antiken Judentums und der Urchristentums 10. Leiden: Brill, 1971.

Mullins, T. Y. "Disclosure: A Literary Form in the New Testament." *Novum Testamentum* 7 (1964): 44-50.

Peng, K. "Do We Need an Alternative Rendering for Philippians 1.3?" *Bible Translator* 54 (2003): 415-19.

Sanders, J. T. "The Transition from Opening Epistolary Thanksgiving to Body in the Letters of the Pauline Corpus." *Journal of Biblical Literature* 81 (1962): 348-62.

Stowers, S. *Letter Writing in Greco-Roman Antiquity*. Library of Early Christianity 5. Philadelphia: Westminster, 1986.

Thrall, M. E. *Greek Particles in the New Testament: Linguistic and Exegetical Studies*. New Testament Tools and Studies 3. Leiden: Brill, 1962.

White, J. L. *The Form and Function of the Body of the Greek Letter: A Study of the Letter-body in the Non-literary Papyri and in Paul the Apostle*. Society of Biblical Literature Dissertation Series 2. Missoula, Mont.: Scholars Press, 1972.

Philippians 1:27-2:18

※

Exhortations to Conform Community Life to the Example of Christ

1:27-30 Exhortation to Live in Harmony as the Gospel Demands

²⁷Μόνον ἀξίως τοῦ εὐαγγελίου τοῦ Χριστοῦ πολιτεύεσθε, ἵνα εἴτε ἐλθὼν καὶ ἰδὼν ὑμᾶς εἴτε ἀπὼν ἀκούω τὰ περὶ ὑμῶν, ὅτι στήκετε ἐν ἑνὶ πνεύματι, μιᾷ ψυχῇ συναθλοῦντες τῇ πίστει τοῦ εὐαγγελίου ²⁸καὶ μὴ πτυρόμενοι ἐν μηδενὶ ὑπὸ τῶν ἀντικειμένων, ἥτις ἐστὶν αὐτοῖς ἔνδειξις ἀπωλείας, ὑμῶν δὲ σωτηρίας, καὶ τοῦτο ἀπὸ θεοῦ ²⁹ὅτι ὑμῖν ἐχαρίσθη τὸ ὑπὲρ Χριστοῦ, οὐ μόνον τὸ εἰς αὐτὸν πιστεύειν ἀλλὰ καὶ τὸ ὑπὲρ αὐτοῦ πάσχειν, 30 τὸν αὐτὸν ἀγῶνα ἔχοντες, οἷον εἴδετε ἐν ἐμοὶ καὶ νῦν ἀκούετε ἐν ἐμοί.

²⁷Only, live worthily of the gospel of Christ, so that whether coming I see you or being absent I hear about your affairs, I find that you stand firm in one spirit, striving together with one life for faithfulness to the gospel, ²⁸and do not be at all frightened by anything that comes from opponents; this is a sign of destruction for them and of your salvation, and this is from God, ²⁹because it has been granted to you to suffer on behalf of Christ; I mean you have been granted not only to believe in him, but also to suffer for him ³⁰as you have the same struggle that you saw with me and now hear about me.

1:27 **Μόνον ἀξίως τοῦ εὐαγγελίου τοῦ Χριστοῦ πολιτεύεσθε**—Μόνον, the neuter accusative of the adjective μόνος, here functions as an adverb. Brewer suggests that we translate πολιτεύεσθε (pres. mid./pass. [deponent] impv. 2 pl. of πολιτεύομαι, "to live, conduct one's life"), the main verb of this sentence, as "discharge your obligations as citizens." However, understanding this as an exhortation to live as good citizens of Philippi seems unlikely. Rather, Paul's statement seems to be a broader exhortation that uses language especially appropriate for the city addressed. (See the discussion of options offered for rendering πολιτεύεσθε in O'Brien 146-47; see also 3:20 below.) Perhaps the simple "live" remains the best rendering. Τοῦ εὐαγγελίου (masc. gen. sg. ["gospel"]) seems to modify the adverb ἀξίως ("worthily") (see examples of genitive nouns with ἀξίως in Kennedy, 430; BDAG). O'Brien (148 n. 25) finds τοῦ Χριστοῦ (masc. gen. sg.) to be both an objective genitive (about Christ, has Christ as its content) and a subjective genitive (Christ is the one speaking). It may even be that this is a genitive of origin, suggesting that the gospel comes from Jesus, or maybe even that it is the gospel that Christ proclaimed. The objective genitive seems to fit the context of this exhortation best: they are urged live in accord with the content of the gospel, which is about Christ himself. BDF (§163) notes that Paul often uses the objective genitive with εὐαγγέλιον.

ἵνα εἴτε ἐλθὼν καὶ ἰδὼν ὑμᾶς εἴτε ἀπὼν ἀκούω τὰ περὶ ὑμῶν—The first reason Paul gives for the Philippians to "live worthily of the gospel" concerns his relationship with them. The NT commonly expresses purpose with ἵνα plus a subjunctive, here ἀκούω (pres. act. sub. 1 sg. of ἀκούω, "to hear"). Each occurrence of the disjunctive particle εἴτε has its own circumstantial participle(s). Ἐλθὼν (aor. act. ptc. masc. nom. sg. of ἔρχομαι, "to come") after the first εἴτε is parallel with ἀπὼν (pres. act. ptc. masc. nom. sg. of ἄπειμι, "to be absent, be away") after the second. Ἰδὼν (aor. act. ptc. masc. nom. sg. of εἶδον, "to see") is parallel with the main verb of the clause, ἀκούω. Ὑμᾶς (acc. pl.) is the object of ἰδὼν, so the phrase reads "whether coming and seeing you . . ." The definite article τὰ (neut. acc. pl.) here exercises its substantivizing function (see BDF §266) and so designates the prepositional phrase περὶ ὑμῶν (gen. pl.) as the object of ἀκούω. This clause is difficult to translate smoothly because of the relationship between ἀκούω and the preceding participle that creates an imbalance with the prior phrase and its two participles. The basic statement of the clause is "so that I might hear about your affairs." Of course, if Paul does come and see them, as the first phrase allows, then the verb ἀκούω is not really fitting. To restore a balance, ἰδὼν would need to be a subjunctive to match ἀκούω with both verbs attached to the ἵνα. To prepare for the following clause, we may translate this clause "so that whether coming I see you or being absent I hear about your affairs."

ὅτι στήκετε ἐν ἑνὶ πνεύματι—This second purpose clause, having στήκετε (pres. act. indic. 2 pl. στήκω, "to stand, stand firm") as its main verb, modifies the preceding purpose clause. Στήκω is a new word in Greek that appears for the first time in the NT (BDAG). It seems to be derived from the perfect tense form of ἵστημι. When Paul uses στήκω to specify the content of the position that one is to maintain, he always designates that position with ἐν followed by a dative, as he does here: ἐν ἑνὶ (neut. dat. sg. ["one"]) πνεύματι (neut. dat. sg. ["spirit"]). To connect this clause with the preceding one, our translation inserts "I find," which restates the seeing and/or hearing of the prior clause.

μιᾷ ψυχῇ συναθλοῦντες τῇ πίστει τοῦ εὐαγγελίου—The meaning of "standing firm in one spirit" is further defined by this phrase. Μιᾷ (fem. dat. sg. ["one"]) ψυχῇ (fem. dat. sg. ["life, soul"]) is an instrumental dative (or dative of means) and probably is parallel to ἐνὶ πνεύματι in the previous clause and so shows that πνεύματι refers not to the Holy Spirit, but to the Philippians' unity of thought and life. Συναθλοῦντες (pres. act. ptc. masc. nom. pl. of συναθλέω, "to contend along with") and other forms of συναθλέω occur only in Philippians in the NT. As is often the case with verbs compounded with σύν, συναθλοῦντες takes a dative as its object. Thus the Philippians are to struggle together τῇ πίστει (fem. dat. sg. ["faith"]). As the object of συναθλοῦντες, τῇ πίστει may be understood as a dative of advantage (so BDAG). The faith τοῦ εὐαγγελίου (neut. gen. sg. ["gospel"]) may mean a number of things, depending on how one understands the genitive and πίστις. Τοῦ εὐαγγελίου may be an objective genitive (faith that has the gospel as its object),

> **genitive of origin or relationship**
>
> The use of the genitive case to specify one's family or place of origin.
>
> Μαρία <u>ἡ Ἰωσῆτος</u>
> *Mary, <u>the [mother]</u> of Joses*
> (Mark 15:47)
>
> πάντες γὰρ ὑμεῖς υἱοὶ <u>φωτός</u> ἐστε.
> *For you are all children <u>of light</u>.*
> (1 Thess 5:5)

genitive of origin or relationship (faith that *comes from* or *is related to* the gospel), or genitive of apposition (faith that *is* the gospel). All of these understandings of this phrase depend on πίστις meaning "belief" or standing for the content of what is believed. However, πίστις may also mean "faithfulness." Thus Paul may be calling them to struggle together "for faithfulness to the gospel." This would make τοῦ εὐαγγελίου an objective genitive. Such an understanding fits well with Paul's comments about his joy that his bonds have emboldened others to preach, his desire for boldness in his trial, and his prayer for the Philippians in vv. 9–11. Even though it would be an unusual construction for πίστις to mean "faithfulness" and to have something other than a person in the gen. following it, in the context such a reading seems preferable. This is confirmed by what follows: an admonition to faithfulness in the face of opposition.

1:28   **καὶ μὴ πτυρόμενοι ἐν μηδενὶ ὑπὸ τῶν ἀντικειμένων**–This second participial phrase modifies στήκετε, not the immediately preceding participial phrase. Μὴ πτυρόμενοι (pres. pass. ptc. masc. nom. pl. of πτύρω, "to be frightened, terrified"

> **imperatival participle**
>
> The use of the participle to issue a command.
>
> <u>ἀποστυγοῦντες</u> τὸ πονηρόν, <u>κολλώμενοι</u> τῷ ἀγαθῷ.
> <u>*Hate*</u> *(the) evil;* <u>*cling to*</u> *(the) good.*
> (Rom 12:9)

[a NT *hapax legomenon*]), is an example of Paul's practice of using a **participle** to serve the function of an **imperative** (BDF §468). It is possible that συναθλοῦντες in v. 27 should be understood as an imperative as well, although this is less likely because of its more direct connection to the finite verb στήκετε. Paul's use of μηδενὶ (neut. dat. sg. ["no, nothing"]) as a substantive fits with a common use of the word in the NT. The double negative (not permissible in English) gives emphasis to the injunction but may be expressed with something such as "do not be at all frightened by anything." The preposition ὑπὸ here designates the person through whom the action of the verb takes place (see BDAG). If the emphatic negative is expressed as I have suggested, then this prepositional phrase may need to be translated by using a paraphrase like "that comes from opponents." Τῶν ἀντικειμένων (pres. mid./pass. [deponent] ptc. masc. gen. pl. of ἀντίκειμαι, "to be in opposition to"), the participle used as a substantive, probably refers to non-Christian opposition rather than to the teachers mentioned in vv. 15–18. Of the eight times ἀντίκειμαι appears in the NT (six of which are in the Pauline corpus), it nearly always refers to non-Christian opposition. The only exceptions are Gal 5:17 (the Spirit and the flesh oppose each other) and 1 Tim 1:10 (whatever opposes healthy teaching), and these do not point to groups of Christians with which the addressed group is in conflict.

ἥτις ἐστὶν αὐτοῖς ἔνδειξις ἀπωλείας, ὑμῶν δὲ σωτηρίας—The case, number, and gender of the indefinite relative pronoun ἥτις (fem. nom. sg.) have been determined by its attraction to the predicate nominative ἔνδειξις (fem. nom. sg. ["sign, proof"]) and by its function as the subject of ἐστὶν (pres. act. indic. 3 sg. of εἰμί, "to be"]). Thus its gender and number are of little help in finding its antecedent. The most likely options are that it refers to the sense of the preceding phrase (their not being afraid of their opposition) or to τῇ πίστει in v. 27 (see further options in O'Brien, 154). If it is correct to understand πίστις as "faithfulness," then this latter option makes good sense of the passage because Paul is then saying that their faithfulness is evidence of their salvation and their persecutors' condemnation. Even though πίστις is rather distant from the pronoun, this seems the better option. The sign given is a sign for the opposition (αὐτοῖς [masc. dat. pl.]) that they will receive destruction (ἀπωλείας [fem. gen. sg.]), although, of course, they do not understand this. Simultaneously, it is an evidence of the σωτηρίας (fem. gen. sg. ["salvation"]) of the faithful Philippians (ὑμῶν [gen. pl.]) (but see the alternative understanding in Hawthorne, 58–60).

> **divine passive**
>
> The use of the passive voice to refer to God indirectly as the cause of an action.
>
> μακάριοι οἱ πενθοῦντες, ὅτι αὐτοὶ <u>παρακληθήσονται</u>.
>
> *Blessed [are] those who are mourning, for <u>they will be comforted</u> [i.e., by God].* (Matt 5:4)
>
> τιμῆς <u>ἠγοράσθητε</u>.
>
> <u>*You were bought*</u> *[i.e., God bought you] with a price.* (1 Cor 7:23)

καὶ τοῦτο ἀπὸ θεοῦ—The antecedent of τοῦτο (neut. nom. sg.) is grammatically unclear, but it seems to refer to the idea of whole preceding phrase: the twofold nature of the sign. The verb in this clause is an understood ἔστιν with τοῦτο as its subject. As always, ἀπό has a genitive object, here θεοῦ (masc. gen. sg.).

ὅτι ὑμῖν ἐχαρίσθη τὸ ὑπὲρ Χριστοῦ—The conjunction ὅτι makes a causal or an explanatory connection between this difficult clause and the preceding clause. Ἐχαρίσθη (aor. pass. indic. 3 sg. of χαρίζομαι, "to give graciously, forgive") is a **divine passive.** It is not unusual for the activity of God to be indicated with a

1:29

passive verb. At this point the focus remains on the situation that the Philippians are facing, ὑμῖν (dat. pl.), rather than expanding to include Paul. Τὸ (neut. nom. sg.) substantivizes the prepositional phrase ὑπὲρ Χριστοῦ (masc. gen. sg.) so that the phrase appears to function as the subject of ἐχαρίσθη. The syntax of the sentence breaks down here. Paul's original intent seems to have been to place πάσχειν here. That would make the construction the same sort as is found with the immediately following infinitives and elsewhere in Paul's writings. But Paul breaks off before completing this thought in order to expand it with the following construction. Some (e.g., Fee, 171) see this as a result of Paul's spontaneously expanding this thought as he is dictating. Given the break in the syntax, it seems better to complete the thought in translation and then to expand it; so we translate "it has been granted to you to suffer on behalf of Christ."

οὐ μόνον τὸ εἰς αὐτὸν πιστεύειν ἀλλὰ καὶ τὸ ὑπὲρ αὐτοῦ πάσχειν—The comparative construction οὐ μόνον . . . ἀλλὰ καὶ . . . (not only . . . but also . . .) is used fairly often by Paul to emphasize a point. Given the difficult nature of this sentence, one might bring out the emphasis by inserting a phrase that repeats the main verb, such as "I mean you have not only been granted to believe . . ." The articular infinitives τὸ (neut. nom. sg.) πιστεύειν (pres. act. inf. of πιστεύω, "to believe") and τὸ (neut. nom. sg.) πάσχειν (pres. act. inf. of πάσχω, "to suffer") function as additional subjects of the preceding ἐχαρίσθη and thus explicate what the Philippians have been granted: to believe εἰς αὐτὸν (masc. acc. sg.) and to suffer ὑπὲρ αὐτοῦ (masc. gen. sg.). The antecedent of these pronouns is Christ. BDAG cites Acts 5:41, 9:16, 21:13, and 2 Thess 1:5, along with Phil 1:29, as examples of ὑπὲρ being used with verbs of suffering to denote the reason for the suffering. Among Acts 9:16, 21:13, 2 Thess 1:5, and Phil 1:29, only the verse from Philippians is certainly Pauline, but Paul does use this preposition with a noun that denotes suffering in 2 Cor 12:10.

1:30   **τὸν αὐτὸν ἀγῶνα ἔχοντες**—This clause begins with a broken construction. Ἔχοντες (pres. act. ptc. masc. nom. pl. of ἔχω, "to have") should formally be dative to agree with ὑμῖν at the beginning of v. 29, but the long clause based on the passive and the following finite verbs (εἴδετε and ἀκούετε) with understood second-person plural subjects seem to have drawn Paul to employ the nominative case. Paul here begins to identify their struggles with his own. He and the Philippians are enduring τὸν αὐτὸν (masc. acc. sg.) ἀγῶνα (masc. acc. sg. ["struggle"]), "the same struggle." Some interpreters have suggested that this means that both Paul and the Philippians are facing persecution at the hands of the Romans, but that probably is reading too much into this statement.

οἷον εἴδετε ἐν ἐμοὶ καὶ νῦν ἀκούετε ἐν ἐμοί—The antecedent of the relative pronoun οἷον (masc. acc. sg. ["of what sort"]) is ἀγῶνα. BDAG asserts that use of this pronoun suggests that the struggles that the Philippians faced were of the same intensity as those faced by Paul. Perhaps this reads too much into the selection of this term, and rather we should understand it simply to say that they were suffering the same sort of troubles that Paul suffered. The different tenses of the two verbs in this clause, εἴδετε (aor. act. indic. 2 pl. of εἶδον, "to see") and ἀκούετε (pres. act. indic. 2 pl. of ἀκούω, "to hear"), indicate that this suffering is characteristic of Paul's experience because not only did they see it when Paul was present, but also they now hear about it as a part of his life. The preposition ἐν often designates the object or person to which something occurs (BDAG). That seems to be its function here with the dative ἐμοί. Translating ἐν with English prepositions that convey this thought produces "that you saw with me and now hear about me."

2:1-4   Exhortation to Unity and Humility

¹Εἴ τις οὖν παράκλησις ἐν Χριστῷ, εἴ τι παραμύθιον ἀγάπης, εἴ τις κοινωνία πνεύματος, εἴ τις σπλάγχνα καὶ οἰκτιρμοί, ²πληρώσατέ μου τὴν χαρὰν ἵνα τὸ αὐτὸ φρονῆτε, τὴν αὐτὴν ἀγάπην ἔχοντες, σύμ-ψυχοι, τὸ ἓν φρονοῦντες, ³μηδὲν κατ' ἐριθείαν μηδὲ κατὰ κενοδοξίαν ἀλλὰ τῇ ταπεινοφροσύνῃ ἀλλήλους ἡγούμενοι ὑπερέχοντας ἑαυτῶν, ⁴μὴ τὰ ἑαυτῶν ἕκαστος σκοποῦντες ἀλλὰ (καὶ) τὰ ἑτέρων ἕκαστοι.

¹Therefore, if there is any encouragement in Christ, if any consolation of love, if any fellowship of the Spirit, if any loving compassion, ²fulfill my joy by living harmoniously through having the same love, being united in spirit, and being of one mind, ³doing nothing that comes from contentiousness, nor from vanity, but with humility consider others better than yourselves. ⁴Do not look after your own affairs only, but also the affairs of others.

---

simple (real) conditional sentence

A conditional sentence in which it is assumed, at least for the sake of argument, that what is stated in the protasis is true. The protasis is formed with εἰ plus an indicative of any tense and the apodosis with any mood and tense.

εἰ δὲ ἀνάστασις νεκρῶν οὐκ ἔστιν, οὐδὲ Χριστὸς ἐγήγερται.

But if [indeed] there is no resurrection of the dead, then neither has Christ been raised. (1 Cor 15:13)

εἰ δέ τις ἀγαπᾷ τὸν θεόν, οὗτος ἔγνωσται ὑπ' αὐτοῦ.

If anyone loves God, this person is known by him. (1 Cor 8:3)

Verses 1–4 form a single complex sentence in Greek that serves as an introduction to the hymnic material of vv. 6–11. It is a present conditional sentence with a fourfold protasis. Each part of the protasis begins with εἰ followed by a nominative form of the indefinite pronoun τὶς and a noun (in the fourth phrase two nouns) in the nominative. This compounding of characteristics gives emphasis to the point Paul is about to make.

Εἴ τις οὖν παράκλησις ἐν Χριστῷ—The conjunctive particle οὖν indicates that the following exhortations build on the asserted common citizenship and suffering of the Philippian Christians. Since this is a **simple conditional sentence,** the "if" (εἰ τι[ς]) does not express

2:1

doubt; rather, it assumes that there is "encouragement in Christ" (παράκλησις [fem. nom. sg.] ἐν Χριστῷ [masc. dat. sg.]) and so on. The relative pronoun τις (fem. nom. sg.) functions adjectivally and so is translated "any" (see Wallace, 347). The same construction is present in all four segments of the protasis. There is no expressed verb in the protasis, but the understood verb is the pres. act. indic. ἐστί, which must be supplied in each of the four phrases.

εἴ τι παραμύθιον ἀγάπης—Given that Paul is about to talk about love within the community, it seems possible that it is their love (ἀγάπης [fem. gen. sg.]) for one another that he cites here. Παραμύθιον (neut. nom. sg.) is nearly a synonym of παράκλησις. Rather than seeking differences in nuance between these two words, we do better to see them as complementary, pointing to the Philippians' experience of God's presence. The difference in the form of the relative pronoun occurs, of course, because it must match the gender of the following noun. Thus τι is neut. nom. sg.

εἴ τις κοινωνία πνεύματος—The absence of the article before πνεύματος (neut. gen. sg. ["spirit"]) allows that this may be a reference to the spirit of the Philippians. A few early interpreters opted for this understanding, but it is now nearly universally held to refer to the Holy Spirit. Even though Paul is interested in focusing their attention on their common life, the reference to Christ in the first element of the protasis points to understanding this as a reference to the Spirit. So their fellowship (κοινωνία [fem. nom. sg.]) is with the Spirit.

εἴ τις σπλάγχνα καὶ οἰκτιρμοί—The adjective οἰκτιρμοί (masc. nom. pl. ["pity, compassion"]) appears to function substantivally so that it parallels the preceding three phrases, which all have a second noun following the initial noun. Since the parallel with the preceding two phrases could have been maintained by using this adjective in the genitive, we probably are not to understand the καὶ epexegetically. Σπλάγχνα (neut. nom. pl.) literally refers to inner parts of the body, especially the heart, but it also stands for the affection or love that was thought to have its seat in the heart. This phrase contains a solecism, an incongruity between the adjective (τις [masc./fem. nom. sg.]) and its noun. This may have occurred because εἴ τις was viewed as a single word (note that οὖν is after both of these words rather than after just the first one at the beginning of this verse) and because τινά would have broken the pattern of the previous three phrases. The indefinite pronoun τις still functions adjectivally.

2:2   **πληρώσατέ μου τὴν χαρὰν**—This is the main clause of the sentence and comprises the apodosis. Paul's use of πληρώσατε (aor. act. impv. 2 pl. of πληρόω, "to fill, complete") affirms a close relationship between Paul's own joy (μου [gen. sg.] τὴν χαρὰν [fem. acc. sg.]) and the Philippians' experience of the working of God in the context of their community and their relations with one another. Their inner-community relations are the focus of all the dependent constructions through v. 4.

ἵνα τὸ αὐτὸ φρονῆτε—The ἵνα of v. 2 functions in an unusual manner. Ἵνα usually has a final sense denoting purpose, but here that is not the case. O'Brien (177) lists three possible understandings: it functions (1) as the direct object of a supplied verb of request (for use of ἵνα with such verbs see BDF §392), (2) as an imperative, or (3) epexegetically. This last option seems preferable because ἵνα is used this way in John, and it does not require us to supply more verbs than necessary (so Wallace, 476). Thus what follows it designates the ways in which the Philippians may complete Paul's joy (see Moule, 145–46). Φρονῆτε is the pres. act. sub. 2 pl. of φρονέω ("to think"). With this verb the phrase could call them to hold the same opinions. In this context, however, it probably means something like "by living harmoniously" or "by being on the same side, of the same party," or "by being like-minded." BDAG and LSJ find such meanings of this phrase as early as Herodotus. (For use of αὐτός with φρονέω in Philippians see 4:2.)

τὴν αὐτὴν ἀγάπην ἔχοντες—This participial phrase continues to explain how the Philippians may complete Paul's joy. The next two phrases serve the same purpose. The participle ἔχοντες (pres. act. ptc. masc. nom. pl. of ἔχω, "to have") may tie the phrase to the preceding ἵνα or may give content to being like-minded. Τὴν αὐτὴν ἀγάπην (fem. acc. sg. ["love"]) with αὐτὴν (fem. acc. sg.) in the attributive position means here the same type of love. The context implies that this love is directed toward others in the Christian community.

σύμψυχοι—This masc. nom. pl. adjective, meaning "harmonious," may be attached to the following phrase or may stand independently. Either construal disrupts the pattern of the three consecutive phrases among which it appears. It is more commonly taken to be independent. In that case, it has been substantivized and functions as the subject of an implied verbal form (probably a participle to parallel the surrounding phrases). This is the only place in the NT σύμψυχος appears; however, this chapter does contain two other compounds formed with ψυχή: εὐψυχέω in 2:19, and ἰσόψυχος in 2:20. By using these various compounds of ψυχή, formed with prefixes that relate to togetherness, good will, and equality, Paul is seeking ways to emphasize the unity to which he is calling the Philippians.

τὸ ἓν φρονοῦντες,—The pattern of having αὐτός in the attributive position in these phrases is broken by the use of ἓν (neut. acc. sg.) with φρονοῦντες (pres. act. ptc. masc. nom. pl. of φρονέω, "to think, hold an opinion") following. Some copyists thought that this difference was a mistake. Thus a corrector of ℵ and the copyist of A inserted αὐτό. Most other major manuscripts have the reading given here, and it is the more difficult reading. The change to ἓν allows reiteration for emphasis without repetition of the first dependent phrase and perhaps with a different shade of meaning, now perhaps more in the sense of agreement in thought. But as was the case with the four parts of the protasis, the four phrases in the apodosis express the same basic sentiment in somewhat different ways.

2:3　**μηδὲν κατ' ἐριθείαν**–The elided κατά, which commonly takes an accusative, takes ἐριθείαν (fem. acc. sg. ["strife, selfish ambition"]) as its object. There is no expressed verb in this clause to which μηδὲν (neut. acc.) may be attached. Fee (186) comments that this sentence starts to get away from Paul at this point. Some suggest that φρονοῦντες should be repeated from v. 2. That may be the best grammatical sense that one can make of what follows. Thus Paul is specifying what is excluded when they have their minds set as they should (Fee, 186), but supplying πράσσετε (as in 4:9) seems to bring out the sense of the passage better (similarly O'Brien, 179; Loh and Nida, 51). The precise meaning of ἐριθεία in the NT is difficult to determine. Prior to the NT and in the first century it was used particularly of those who seek political office for self-serving purposes. The implication of this term seems to go beyond contentiousness to include a baseness of character evidenced by unscrupulous manipulation for one's own gain (for discussion of the insulting nature of this characterization see *TDNT* 2.660-61).

μηδὲ κατὰ κενοδοξίαν–Μηδὲ, the negative coordinating conjunction, includes the second negative particle in this clause, which signals that the rejection of this mode of behavior is emphatic. Κενοδοξίαν (fem. acc. sg. ["vanity, conceit, excessive ambition]" [BDAG]) here marks the only occurrence of this word in the NT, although it is not especially rare in other literature. Its cognate adjective, κενόδοξος, is also a NT *hapax legomenon,* with its one occurrence coming from the hand of Paul (Gal 5:26).

ἀλλὰ τῇ ταπεινοφροσύνῃ–The instrumental dative τῇ ταπεινοφροσύνῃ (fem. dat. sg.) is connected to the construction following it rather than the one preceding it. Thus "with humility" introduces the thought following it. Note that this compound word contains yet another cognate of φρονέω.

ἀλλήλους ἡγούμενοι ὑπερέχοντας ἑαυτῶν–Ἀλλήλους (masc. acc. pl.) is the object of ἡγούμενοι (pres. mid./pass. [deponent] ptc. masc. nom. pl. of ἡγέομαι, "to consider, regard"). Ἡγέομαι often takes a double accusative when the subject of the verb is thinking of something or someone in a particular way. The second accusative in this clause, ὑπερέχοντας (pres. act. ptc. masc. acc. pl. of ὑπερέχω, "to be better than"), implies a **comparison** when used in conjunction with a **genitive,** as it is here with ἑαυτῶν (masc. gen. pl.). So they are to "consider others better than" themselves. Used in this way, ὑπερέχοντας is an example of an acc. participle serving within **indirect discourse.** That is, it speaks of (in a way paraphrases) what the readers should be thinking. The reflexive pronoun ἑαυτῶν may be rendered with a sec-

> **genitive of comparison**
>
> The use of the genitive case with a comparative verb, adjective, or adverb to form a comparison. It is normally translated using *than.*
>
> ὁ πατὴρ μείζων μού ἐστιν.
> *The Father is greater than I.*
> (John 14:28)
>
> κρείττων γενόμενος τῶν ἀγγέλων
> *being better than the angels* (Heb 1:4)

ond person here, "yourselves," because grammatically the clause is still connected to πληρώσατε at the beginning of v. 2. Ὑπερέχω is found only five times in the NT, three of which are in Philippians. The other two occurrences (Rom 13:1; 1 Pet 2:13) refer to governing authorities and so do not have the comparative force, found only in the Philippian passages within the NT. This meaning is well attested outside the NT.

> ### indirect discourse
>
> The use of the direct object clause, often introduced by ὅτι, following a verb of perception, to express reported thought or speech. Unlike direct discourse, which involves a direct quotation of what was said, indirect discourse recasts the thought or statement into an indirect form.
>
> ἠκούσθη ὅτι ἐν οἴκῳ ἐστίν.
>
> *It was reported that he was in the house.* (Mark 2:1)
>
> ἀνήγγειλεν . . . ὅτι Ἰησοῦς ἐστιν ὁ ποιήσας αὐτὸν ὑγιῆ.
>
> *He reported . . . that Jesus was the one who made him whole.* (John 5:15)

μὴ τὰ ἑαυτῶν ἕκαστος σκοποῦντες–This 2:4 participial clause has an imperative force. To indicate this, it is probably best to begin a new English sentence here with "Do not look after . . ." Ἕκαστος (masc. nom. sg.) is the first element of the compound subject of the plural participle. Use of the singular conforms to early Christian usage, but the plural form, found only a few words away, is rare in early Christian literature. The strangeness of the lack of agreement in number was sensed by the copyists of some manuscripts, and so the plural is found in A, B, F, and G. But the singular may serve to individualize the admonition. The definite article τὰ (acc. pl.) serves as a substantive and is the direct object of σκοποῦντες (pres. act. ptc. masc. nom. pl. of σκοπέω, "to look out for"), with ἑαυτῶν (masc. gen. pl.) as a possessive genitive. So τὰ ἑαυτῶν can be rendered "your own affairs." As with the previous pronoun, it is appropriate to render this one in the second person because of the grammatical connection with πληρώσατε at the beginning of v. 2.

ἀλλὰ (καὶ) –The presence of both of these conjunctions may signal an emphatic contrast (see BDF §448; Smyth, 2764). On the other hand, O'Brien (185) (apparently also Loh and Nida, 52–53) sees it as a softening of the contrast so that one is allowed to be concerned with one's own affairs as well as those of others. This seems probable, but it is also possible that this is simply an unusual use of an idiomatic expression that signals neither of these alternatives (see the various uses of ἀλλὰ καί in Smyth, 2763).

τὰ ἑτέρων ἕκαστοι–As in the preceding part of this compound direct object, the definite article τὰ (neut. pl.) serves as a substantive, here with ἑτέρων (masc. gen. pl.)–the opposite of ἑαυτῶν–as a possessive genitive. The unusual plural ἕκαστοι (masc. nom. pl.) is the second part of the compound subject of σκοποῦντες. The Majority Text has ἕκαστος in conformity with its occurrence earlier in this verse; however, ℵ, A, B, C, and 𝔓⁴⁶, among other manuscripts, have the plural.

2:5-11 A Hymnic Account of the Gospel

⁵τοῦτο φρονεῖτε ἐν ὑμῖν ὃ καὶ ἐν Χριστῷ Ἰησοῦ, ⁶ὃς ἐν μορφῇ θεοῦ ὑπάρχων οὐχ ἁρπαγμὸν ἡγήσατο τὸ εἶναι ἴσα θεῷ, ⁷ἀλλὰ ἑαυτὸν ἐκένωσεν μορφὴν δούλου λαβών, ἐν ὁμοιώματι ἀνθρώπων γενόμενος· καὶ σχήματι εὑρεθεὶς ὡς ἄνθρωπος ⁸ἐταπείνωσεν ἑαυτὸν γενόμενος ὑπήκοος μέχρι θανάτου, θανάτου δὲ σταυροῦ. ⁹διὸ καὶ ὁ θεὸς αὐτὸν ὑπερύψωσεν καὶ ἐχαρίσατο αὐτῷ τὸ ὄνομα τὸ ὑπὲρ πᾶν ὄνομα, ¹⁰ἵνα ἐν τῷ ὀνόματι Ἰησοῦ πᾶν γόνυ κάμψῃ ἐπουρανίων· καὶ ἐπιγείων καὶ καταχθονίων ¹¹καὶ πᾶσα γλῶσσα ἐξομολογήσηται ὅτι κύριος Ἰησοῦς Χριστὸς εἰς δόξαν θεοῦ πατρός.

⁵Have this way of thinking in you, which was also in Christ Jesus, ⁶who existing in the form of God did not consider equality with God something to be seized ⁷but emptied himself by taking the form of a slave, by taking on the likeness of humanity, and by being found in appearance as a human. ⁸He humbled himself by being obedient unto death, even a death on a cross. ⁹For this reason, God highly exalted him and gave him a name that is above every name, ¹⁰so that at the name of Jesus every knee might bow, the knee of those in the heavens and on earth and below the earth, ¹¹and so that every tongue might confess that the Lord is Jesus Christ, to the glory of God the Father.

Separating these verses from the preceding four verses is rather artificial. The hymn in vv. 6–11 gives direct support to the admonitions of vv. 1–4 and should be understood as the primary sanction given these instructions. While vv. 5–11 are a subsection that gives the basis for the exhortations, the hymn and its introduction have been separated here from the preceding (and following) verses only for the sake of keeping the translation of the verses closer to the discussion, not because there is a break in the thought.

> **relative clause**
>
> A clause introduced by a relative pronoun, relative adjective, or relative adverb that connects the clause to an antecedent in the main clause of the sentence.
>
> εἴπερ εἷς ὁ θεός <u>ὃς δικαιώσει περιτομὴν ἐκ πίστεως</u>
>
> *since it is the one God <u>who justifies the circumcised through faith</u>* (fulness) (Rom 3:30)
>
> ἐν τῇ νυκτὶ <u>ἧ παρεδίδετο</u>
>
> *on the night <u>in which he was betrayed</u>* (1 Cor 11:23)

2:5 **τοῦτο φρονεῖτε ἐν ὑμῖν**–Τοῦτο (neut. acc. sg.) is the direct object of φρονεῖτε (pres. act. impv. 2 pl. of φρονέω, "to think, consider"), on which the **relative clause** following it builds. The antecedent of τοῦτο is not clear. It may refer back to what is described in the preceding verses, or it may point forward, in which case it is a more direct call to imitate Christ. 𝔓⁴⁶, a corrector of ℵ, and D, F, and G have a γάρ following τοῦτο. Since the phrase is an **asyndeton** (lacking a conjunction at its

> **asyndeton**
>
> The omission of conjunctions or other connecting words (e.g. "and," "but") that typically coordinate words and clauses, often resulting in a staccato effect that adds passion or vividness to an expression (cf. 2 Tim 4:2).

beginning) without the γάρ, it seems more likely that the transition was eased by the addition of the γάρ than that it was omitted, even though this is the beginning of a reading in some lectionaries. Although its use in that context can explain the absence of the γάρ in the lectionaries themselves, it is unlikely that such usage would have influenced the text early enough to account for its absence in ℵ, A, B, and C. Ἐν ὑμῖν (dat. pl.) may be translated "in you" or "among you." The first translation indicates that it is a manner of life that each person is to have; the second, that this attitude is to be among them as a characteristic of the group. Perhaps Paul would not have distinguished these meanings.

ὃ καὶ ἐν Χριστῷ Ἰησοῦ–The relative pronoun ὃ (neut. nom. sg.) directly introduces the hymn of vv. 6–11 and has τοῦτο as its antecedent. The understood verb of this relative clause is ἦν (impf. act. indic. 3 sg. of εἰμί, "to be"). Ἐν Χριστῷ (masc. dat. sg.) Ἰησοῦ (masc. dat. sg.) clearly means that this way of thinking was in Christ. If the parallel with the preceding clause is precise, this favors understanding ἐν ὑμῖν as "in each of you" rather than "among you." But the parallel may not be intended to be that precise.

ὃς ἐν μορφῇ θεοῦ ὑπάρχων–The relative pronoun ὃς (masc. nom. sg.) begins a hymn that goes through v. 11. This is a common way for NT writings to introduce hymnic and other types of confessional material (see, e.g., Col 1:15). The circumstantial participle ὑπάρχων (pres. act. ptc. masc. nom. sg. of ὑπάρχω, "to be, exist") has been understood as causal by some and as **concessive** by others. Perhaps the absence of significant textual variants in this first clause is explained in part by how open it is to a wide range of interpretations. It is perhaps best to leave it less narrowly circumscribed and so translate it simply as "being." Μορφῇ (fem. dat. sg.) is the object of ἐν and is modified by θεοῦ (masc. gen. sg.). There has been extensive discussion of this use of μορφή. In the NT this word appears only once outside Philippians, in Mark 16:12 (thus in a part of Mark that probably was composed later than the bulk of that Gospel); in Philippians, only here and in v. 7. Although the basic meaning of the word is clear, its significance for christological issues has made determining the term's precise nuance in this context important. Μορφή had different nuances depending on whether it was being used in Aristotelian thought, in Gnosticism and Hellenistic religions, in connection with Adam typologies, and so on. Various modern interpreters have argued that one or the other of these contexts is the key to understanding its use here. With O'Brien (210), it seems best to see it "against the background of the glory of God"

2:6

> ### concessive clause
>
> A clause presenting a state of affairs that exists despite what the main clause asserts. The translation is often introduced with "though" or "although."
>
> καὶ μηδεμίαν αἰτίαν θανάτου εὑρόντες ᾐτήσαντο Πιλᾶτον ἀναιρεθῆναι αὐτόν.
>
> *Even though they found no cause for death,* they asked Pilate to condemn him to death. (Acts 13:28)
>
> ὅτι εἰ καὶ ἐλύπησα ὑμᾶς ἐν τῇ ἐπιστολῇ οὐ μεταμέλομαι.
>
> *Even if I grieved you with the letter,* I do not regret it. (2 Cor 7:8)

as it is discussed in the Hebrew Bible (see the discussion of this question in O'Brien, 206-11). However, one should not put too much weight on a single word used in early liturgical material that Paul quotes to make quite another point.

οὐχ ἁρπαγμὸν ἡγήσατο τὸ εἶναι ἴσα θεῷ–ʽΗγήσατο (aor. mid. [deponent] indic. 3 sg. of ἡγέομαι, "to consider, think") again appears with a double accusative: ἁρπαγμὸν (masc. acc. sg.) and the substantivized articular infinitive τὸ (neut. acc. sg.) εἶναι (pres. act. inf.) (see BDF §399; Wallace, 602). Together, τὸ εἶναι and ἴσα (neut. acc. pl.) may be translated simply as "equality" because the adjective ἴσα functions here as an adverb, as it often does when appearing in the neuter plural. Θεῷ (masc. dat. sg.) could be construed as a dative of manner (perhaps Loh and Nida, 56), a dative of respect, or a dative used with adjectives or adverbs connected with εἶναι. Ἁρπαγμός is a fairly rare term outside the NT and is found only here in the NT. Its cognate ἁρπαγή is found only three times in the NT, none of these in Paul's writings (Matt 23:25; Luke 11:39; Heb 10:34). The normal meaning of ἁρπαγμός is "robbery," "a seizing," or "booty"; however, some have found this meaning unacceptable for this passage (e.g., BDAG), opting instead for "grasping." There has been extensive controversy about this matter and its significance for understanding the nature of the preexistent Christ.

2:7 **ἀλλὰ ἑαυτὸν ἐκένωσεν**–Paul's use of ἀλλὰ signals a stronger opposition than would the use of δέ, although this distinction should not be pressed. The reflexive pronoun ἑαυτὸν (masc. acc. sg.) indicates that this emptying, ἐκένωσεν (aor. act. indic. 3 sg. of κενόω, "to empty"), was done by Christ himself.

μορφὴν δούλου λαβών–This participial phrase is parallel to the first line of the hymn. Μορφὴν (fem. acc. sg.) δούλου (masc. gen. sg.) clearly parallels the ἐν μορφῇ θεοῦ ὑπάρχων of v. 6. This phrase is also the first of three parallel phrases that add specificity to the contrast signaled by ἀλλὰ and so define the ways in which Christ "emptied himself." Since this is the phrase's relationship with the preceding clause, we may identify λαβών (aor. act. ptc. masc. nom. sg. of λαμβάνω, "to take") as **a circumstantial participle of means.** The meaning then is that Christ humbled himself "by taking the form of a slave."

> **circumstantial participle of means**
>
> The use of the participle to tell how or to describe the means by which the action of the main verb takes place. It is often translated *by* or *by means of.*
>
> ἀλλὰ ἑαυτὸν ἐκένωσεν μορφὴν δούλου <u>λαβών</u>.
>
> *But he emptied himself <u>by taking</u> the form of a slave.* (Phil 2:7)
>
> κοπιῶμεν <u>ἐργαζόμενοι</u> ταῖς ἰδίαις χερσίν.
>
> *We labor, <u>working</u> with our own hands.* (1 Cor 4:12)

ἐν ὁμοιώματι ἀνθρώπων γενόμενος–The participle γενόμενος (aor. mid. [deponent] ptc. masc. nom. sg. of γίνομαι, "to be born") is also to be understood as circumstantial, expressing means or manner. If we understand γενόμενος in this way, we may render it "by taking on." Within this second of the three parallel participial phrases, the meaning of ὁμοιώματι (neut. dat. sg.)

ἀνθρώπων (masc. gen. pl.) is discussed widely because of the christological implications of its translation. The question is whether ὁμοίωμα, meaning "likeness, image, copy, form, appearance" (all meanings given in BDAG), can also mean "full identity." Clearly, the word does not imply identity in Rom 8:3, but many commentators hold that it carries the meaning of full identity here in Philippians. The further statement in the third participial phrase presents a similar difficulty. Perhaps this is an ambiguity that the hymn does not want to resolve. 𝔓⁴⁶, along with some Coptic and Syriac manuscripts, has the singular ἀνθρώπου rather than the plural that stands in the text here. The singular appears probably because it conforms to the preceding δούλου and the following participle, both of which are singular. Perhaps these readings also worked from the logic that Jesus was one person.

καὶ σχήματι εὑρεθεὶς ὡς ἄνθρωπος—It may be significant that ἄνθρωπος (masc. nom. sg. ["human"]) is singular. The **relative adverb** ὡς functions here to introduce the perspective from which a person is viewed, particularly as to the person's character, function, or role (see BDAG, ὡς, 3.a.γ.). The grammatical point cannot be pressed to determine whether it denotes an actual quality or one that is wrongly claimed and thus whether it affirms a clear incarnational Christology. Again, the christological point must be made with more than syntactical and philological considerations. As with the previous two participles, εὑρεθεὶς (aor. pass. ptc. masc. nom. sg. of εὑρίσκω, "to find") expresses means, and its understood subject is Christ. Σχήματι (masc. dat. sg.) is a dative of respect (BDF §197). Σχῆμα refers to the form or appearance of something. In classical use this appearance may reflect reality or be opposed to reality (LSJ). In the NT it appears only here and in 1 Cor 7:31, where it refers to the "form of this world." BDAG gives σχῆμα the meaning "way of life" for this 1 Corinthians use, and this might be an interesting nuance to consider here in Philippians. However, these two uses are insufficient to establish a common meaning for Paul, especially since the 1 Corinthians passage refers to the κόσμος rather than to a person. Thus any more precise meaning for the word will be derived from context rather than from lexicography. The precision of understanding that we would like to attain for σχήματι eludes us here in part because it appears in a preformed piece being cited by Paul. Thus, we cannot even be certain that its meaning would conform precisely to his understanding as expressed elsewhere in his own words.

> **relative adverb**
>
> An adverb that introduces a relative clause. Common NT relative adverbs include ὅπου, ὅπως, and ὅτε.
>
> Ὅτε δὲ ἦλθεν Κηφᾶς εἰς Ἀντιόχειαν, κατὰ πρόσωπον αὐτῷ ἀντέστην.
>
> And _when_ Cephas came to Antioch, I opposed him publicly. (Gal 2:11)
>
> τὸ πνεῦμα ὅπου θέλει πνεῖ.
>
> The wind blows _wherever_ it wants. (John 3:8)

ἐταπείνωσεν ἑαυτὸν—The understood subject of ἐταπείνωσεν (aor. act. indic. 3 sg. of ταπεινόω, "to lower, humble") is Christ. The voluntary nature of Christ's   **2:8** descension is emphasized with the reflexive pronoun ἑαυτὸν (masc. acc. sg.). This phrase seems parallel, both formally (though it lacks the conjunction) and stylistically, with the first phrase of v. 7. In v. 7 Christ "emptied himself"; in v. 8 he "humbled himself."

γενόμενος ὑπήκοος μέχρι θανάτου–Just as in v. 7, γενόμενος (aor. mid. [deponent] ptc. masc. nom. sg. of γίνομαι, "to become") is dependent on the preceding finite verb and is a circumstantial participle of means or manner. Thus it indicates the way Christ humbled himself. As usual, the predicate of γίνομαι, here ὑπήκοος (masc. nom. sg. ["obedient"]), is in the nominative; so Christ humbled himself "by being obedient." Although one might expect that a word such as ὑπήκοος would appear often in the NT, particularly in hortatory contexts, it occurs only two other times (Acts 7:39; 2 Cor 2:9). The prepositional phrase μέχρι θανάτου (masc. gen. sg.) specifies the extent of Christ's obedience.

θανάτου δὲ σταυροῦ–The postpositive conjunction δέ sometimes introduces an intensification or an explanation (BDF §447[8]). Here it seems to be an intensification. When Paul uses δέ in this way, the nouns that it introduces usually are of the same case and number (see, e.g., 1 Cor 2:6), as they are here. It may be worth noting that Smyth (2836) does not mention such a use of δέ but notes that it marks a continuation, especially when a subordinate thought or idea is given. Specifying the means of Christ's death, θανάτου (masc. gen. sg. ["death"]) is in some senses subordinate to the fact of the death itself, but it also signals an intensification here. Wallace (105) identifies σταυροῦ (masc. gen. sg. ["cross"]) as a **genitive of production** because in his view this brings out the force of the statement more than seeing it as a genitive of means. One might also see it as a qualitative genitive.

> **genitive of production**
>
> The use of the genitive case to designate the thing that produced the modified noun.
>
> θανάτου δὲ <u>σταυροῦ</u>
> *death <u>produced by the cross</u>* (Phil 2:8).
> Ὁ δὲ καρπὸς <u>τοῦ πνεύματος</u>
> *the fruit <u>the Spirit produces</u>* (Gal 5:22)

2:9 **διὸ καὶ ὁ θεὸς αὐτὸν ὑπερύψωσεν**–When the two conjunctions διὸ καί appear together, they often introduce a result (BDF §442[12]). Thus we may render them "for this reason" or "therefore." Here the result follows from the obedience of Christ. Now, for the first time in the hymn, the actor is ὁ θεὸς (masc. nom. sg. ["God"]). This seems to mark a major point of transition in the hymn. Ὑπερύψωσεν is the aor. act. indic. 3 sg. of ὑπερυψόω ("to raise to the highest position"), a NT *hapax legomenon*, although ὑψόω ("to exalt") is fairly common. Bertram asserts that the compounding of this common verb with the preposition is a genuine strengthening of its sense (*TDNT* 8.608–9). Thus it may be translated "highly exalted."

καὶ ἐχαρίσατο αὐτῷ τὸ ὄνομα τὸ ὑπὲρ πᾶν ὄνομα–Ἐχαρίσατο (aor. mid. [deponent] indic. 3 sg. of χαρίζομαι, "to grant, bestow upon") is the second verb in the compound predicate of this sentence. The verb χαρίζομαι usually indi-

cates that the giver is pleased to be bestowing the gift (LSJ; BDAG). The antecedent of αὐτῷ (masc. dat. sg.) is, of course, Christ. To speak of "bestowing a name"
meant more than just the giving of a title, because a name often was thought to indicate something about the character of its possessor. Giving Jesus a name therefore most likely implies that certain characteristics were bestowed or perhaps
recognized. Many commentators assert that the name given is the divine name,
especially since the article τὸ precedes ὄνομα (neut. acc. sg. ["name"]). These
commentators often see the passage as an echo of what is said about the name of
God in Isa 41-55 (see O'Brien, 237-38; Fee, 220-23; TDNT 5:270-74). The
definite article before ὄνομα is not found in D, G, F, and the Majority Text. However, it does appear in ℵ, A, B, and C, and it appears to be the better reading. The
second τὸ (neut. acc. sg.) in this phrase serves to make the following prepositional
phrase modify the preceding ὄνομα. When used with the accusative, ὑπέρ has
the meaning of "excelling" or "being above." Those who assert that the name
"Christ" is the divine name may find support for that view with this prepositional
phrase because we hear that this name is above πᾶν (neut. acc. sg.) ὄνομα.

ἵνα ἐν τῷ ὀνόματι Ἰησοῦ πᾶν γόνυ κάμψη–The ἵνα clause with the subjunc-   2:10
tive verb comprises a purpose clause. Wallace identifies this clause as an example
of what he calls a purpose-result clause. This is a ἵνα clause that indicates "both
the intention and its sure accomplishment" (Wallace, 473). What is sure to be accomplished is that πᾶν (neut. nom. sg.) γόνυ κάμψη (aor. act. sub. 3 sg. of
κάμπτω, "to bend, bow"). In classical usage κάμπτω with γόνυ (neut. nom. sg.
["knee"]) usually meant "to sit in order to rest." It was sometimes used metaphorically to mean that one was humble. In the passive κάμπτω also meant "to submit."
The expression "to bend one's knee" seems to have implied worship only when
used in the LXX. When LSJ gives the meaning "to worship," all the examples of this
meaning come from the LXX. Κάμπτω appears in the NT only four times. In Rom
11:4 and 14:11 it appears in biblical citations, and so these uses probably draw on
LXX usage. The citation of 1 Kgs 19:18 in Rom 11:4 gives the meaning of worship
to "bending one's knee," but the LXX uses the verb ὀκλάζω ("to bend or crouch")
here rather than κάμπτω. The citation of Isa 45:23 in Rom 14:11 seems to imply
submission at judgment more than worship, although the second phrase of the
quotation certainly designates worship. The only other place that κάμπτω appears outside Philippians in the NT is in Eph 3:14, where it is associated with
prayer, as it is often in the LXX (e.g., 1 Chr 29:20). In the Philippians hymn "bending the knee" almost certainly derives its meaning from the LXX and may have
been suggested to the author of the hymn by Isa 45:23. In Isa 45 the context suggests that "bending the knee" includes worship; however, κάμπτω sometimes indicates submission rather than worship in the LXX (e.g., 2 Kgs 1:13 [see TDNT
3:594-95]). When "every knee" (πᾶν γόνυ) is said to bend in the Philippians
hymn, it certainly includes submission (as one must submit to a higher or more
powerful authority such as a king or a master) and may include worship. Whether

it includes the idea of worship may depend on how familiar or comfortable the author was with this unusual meaning given to the expression in the LXX. The prepositional phrase ἐν τῷ ὀνόματι (neut. dat. sg.) Ἰησοῦ (masc. gen. sg.) complicates the claim that the name "Christ" given in the previous clause is the divine name, because it may be taken as a reference to the name that Christ is given.

ἐπουρανίων καὶ ἐπιγείων καὶ καταχθονίων–All three of the these adjectives (masc. gen. pl.) are being used as substantives and may be seen as **genitives of place.** It may be helpful to repeat "the knee" for clarity and to retain in English the parallel with the following clause. Together, these three genitives signify the universal recognition of place given to Christ by God. This is the only use of καταχθόνιος in the NT. It is a reference to the underworld–the abode of the dead and the deities who rule that sphere. Its cognate verb καταχθονίζω means "to devote something to the infernal gods" (LSJ). The adjective often is used to refer to the divine beings of the underworld in sepulchral inscriptions. Sasse asserts that this adjective is always used in connection with either gods or δαίμονες (TDNT 3:634). It is not unusual to find ἐπουράνιος in the plural because many conceived of multiple realms in the part of the cosmos above the earthly realm,

> **genitive of place**
>
> The use of the genitive case to designate the place in which the word modified is located or situated.
>
> ἐκείνης ἤμελλεν διέρχεσθαι.
> *He was about to go through that place.*
> (Luke 19:4)
>
> ὁ κρυπτὸς τῆς καρδίας
> *the hidden thing in the heart*
> (1 Pet 3:4)

in that area called the heavens. Perhaps all three adjectives are plural because they have been substantivized and so stand for all those who live in these realms. Thus the point of these three substantivized adjectives is to include all beings, divine and human, in every realm among those who submit to Christ.

2:11   **καὶ πᾶσα γλῶσσα ἐξομολογήσηται**–Ἐξομολογήσηται (aor. mid. sub. 3 sg. of ἐξομολογέω, "to confess") is the second subjunctive governed by the ἵνα at the beginning of v. 10. Thus it gives a second purpose for God's exaltation of Jesus. Some manuscripts (including A and C) have the future indicative here rather than the aorist subjunctive. That makes an improper construction by classical standards, although it had begun to appear a few places (e.g., Revelation) in the first century (see BDF §369[2]). Given that the subjunctive appears in 𝔓46, ℵ, and B, it is the more probable reading. Πᾶσα (fem. nom. sg.) γλῶσσα (fem. nom. sg.) literally means "every tongue." If we give γλῶσσα one of its common meanings, "languages," the expression means that all languages of all realms will confess Jesus. Using γλῶσσα in this phrase presses beyond the previous claim that every knee will bow because they not only submit by bowing, but also they must actively confess that "Jesus is Lord."

ὅτι κύριος Ἰησοῦς Χριστὸς–As is the case here, ὅτι is often used with verbs that denote thinking, judging, and expressing an emotion to designate the content of what is thought or felt. Ἐξομολογέω uses ὅτι in this way when it means "to acknowledge" (BDAG) as opposed to "confess" in the sense that one confesses sins. The understood verb of this clause is ἐστί (pres. act. indic. 3 sg. of εἰμί, "to be") with Ἰησοῦς (masc. nom. sg.) Χριστός (masc. nom. sg.) as the predicate nominative. So what all these beings confess is the status of Christ: he is κύριος (masc. nom. sg. ["Lord"]). Some Western witnesses omit Χριστός. Metzger (546) conjectures that the omission was intended to bring this verse into conformity with v. 10.

εἰς δόξαν θεοῦ πατρός–The concluding phrase of the hymn seems to express the ultimate goal of all the action spoken of in the hymn, but more specifically that in vv. 9–11 (for εἰς used to indicate a goal, see BDAG, meaning 4). Thus the point of these acts of Christ and the response of God is to bring δόξαν (fem. acc. sg. ["glory"]) to θεοῦ (masc. gen. sg. ["God"]) πατρός (masc. gen. sg. ["Father"]). Πατρός stands in apposition to θεοῦ. (For a discussion of δόξα, see 4:20.) Here it seems to refer to recognition of the divine nature.

2:12-18 Application of the Hymn

¹²Ὥστε, ἀγαπητοί μου, καθὼς πάντοτε ὑπηκούσατε, μὴ ὡς ἐν τῇ παρουσίᾳ μου μόνον ἀλλὰ νῦν πολλῷ μᾶλλον ἐν τῇ ἀπουσίᾳ μου, μετὰ φόβου καὶ τρόμου τὴν ἑαυτῶν σωτηρίαν κατεργάζεσθε· ¹³θεὸς γάρ ἐστιν ὁ ἐνεργῶν ἐν ὑμῖν καὶ τὸ θέλειν καὶ τὸ ἐνεργεῖν ὑπὲρ τῆς εὐδοκίας. ¹⁴πάντα ποιεῖτε χωρὶς γογγυσμῶν καὶ διαλογισμῶν, ¹⁵ἵνα γένησθε ἄμεμπτοι καὶ ἀκέραιοι, τέκνα θεοῦ ἄμωμα μέσον γενεᾶς σκολιᾶς καὶ διεστραμμένης, ἐν οἷς φαίνεσθε ὡς φωστῆρες ἐν κόσμῳ, ¹⁶λόγον ζωῆς ἐπέχοντες, εἰς καύχημα ἐμοὶ εἰς ἡμέραν Χριστοῦ, ὅτι οὐκ εἰς κενὸν ἔδραμον οὐδὲ εἰς κενὸν ἐκοπίασα. ¹⁷ἀλλὰ εἰ καὶ σπένδομαι ἐπὶ τῇ θυσίᾳ καὶ λειτουργίᾳ τῆς πίστεως ὑμῶν, χαίρω καὶ συγχαίρω πᾶσιν ὑμῖν· ¹⁸τὸ δὲ αὐτὸ καὶ ὑμεῖς χαίρετε καὶ συγχαίρετέ μοι.

¹²Therefore, my loved ones, just as you are always obedient, not only while in my presence but much more in my absence, with fear and trembling work out your own salvation, ¹³for God is the one who works in you both the willing and the working of good will. ¹⁴Do everything without murmurings and disputes ¹⁵so that you may be blameless and pure children of God who are spotless in the midst of an unscrupulous and perverse generation, in which you shine as stars in the world ¹⁶by holding on to the word of life, that I might have something to boast of in the day of Christ, so that I did not run for nothing nor did I work for nothing. ¹⁷And even if I am poured as a libation on the altar of service for your faith, I rejoice, and I rejoice with all of you. ¹⁸In the same way you also rejoice, and rejoice with me.

These verses are the direct application of the hymn to the Philippian readers. Just as v. 5 indicated, these verses confirm that the hymn is given as a sanction for the exhortations that precede and follow it.

2:12   **Ὥστε ἀγαπητοί μου**—The vocative plural ἀγαπητοί renews the warm tone of ch. 1, especially since they are the beloved not only of God, but also of Paul (μου [gen. sg.]). This tone helps prepare for the instructions that follow. The conjunction ὥστε indicates that the following sentence or paragraph is based on what preceded. This grammatical connection confirms that the following paragraph is the application of the hymn to the Philippians' situation.

καθὼς πάντοτε ὑπηκούσατε—Interestingly, Paul does not specify the one to whom they are always obedient, ὑπηκούσατε (aor. act. indic. 2 pl. of ὑπακούω, "to obey"). Perhaps this ambiguity is intended so that they may think of obedience to God or to him, or even to local leaders. Although the rest of the sentence points to Paul as the one whom they obey, he may intentionally want to conflate obedience to him with obedience to God.

μὴ ὡς ἐν τῇ παρουσίᾳ μου μόνον—The neut. acc. sg. form of the adjective μόνος sometimes functions adverbially, especially used in conjunction with a negative particle (BDAG). The term τῇ παρουσίᾳ (fem. dat. sg.) is used here in its common sense of "being present." Codex B omits the ὡς in this phrase, perhaps by accident or perhaps because it was thought to be redundant. The word is found in 𝔓⁴⁶, ℵ, A, C, and many other witnesses.

ἀλλὰ νῦν πολλῷ μᾶλλον ἐν τῇ ἀπουσίᾳ μου—The dative adjective πολλῷ (neut. dat. sg.) that precedes the comparative adverb μᾶλλον intensifies the comparison and is sometimes called a dative of degree of difference. (Smyth [1513-15] classifies this usage under dative of manner and refers to it specifically as a dative of measure of difference.) This construction continues Paul's development of a positive pathos in preparation for the commands to come. As this letter indicates, Paul's absence (τῇ ἀπουσίᾳ [fem. dat. sg.]) is now necessitated by his imprisonment. This absence provides the Philippians an opportunity to live out their faith without dependence on Paul's immediate presence.

μετὰ φόβου καὶ τρόμου—These two nouns are found together in the LXX and the Pauline corpus. Besides Phil 2:12, the combination appears three times in the NT (1 Cor 2:3; 2 Cor 7:15; Eph 6:5). In this hortatory context φόβου (masc. gen. sg. ["fear"]) καὶ τρόμου (masc. gen. sg. ["trembling"]) probably includes a fear of judgment. (On the fear of God in Paul's thought, see *TDNT* 9.213-17.)

τὴν ἑαυτῶν σωτηρίαν κατεργάζεσθε—This final word of v. 12 is the main verb of the sentence to which the beginning ὥστε looked and so is the first exhortation based on the hymn of vv. 6-11. The primary sense of κατεργάζεσθε (pres. mid./pass. [deponent] impv. 2 pl. of κατεργάζομαι, "to work out") is to achieve or accomplish something by work (see LSJ). Here they are to accomplish ἑαυτῶν (masc. gen. pl.) σωτηρίαν (fem. acc. sg.). This does not mean that they are to earn their salvation; rather, the sense is similar to that expressed in 1:27, where they are exhorted to "live worthy of the gospel." It is significant that the verb and the reflexive pronoun that modify σωτηρίαν are plural. This shows that the call to live out their salvation is a call to the Philippians as a community and anticipates that the matters to be raised in the following verses involve relations within the community.

θεὸς γάρ ἐστιν ὁ ἐνεργῶν ἐν ὑμῖν—The postpositive γάρ indicates that this sentence provides the reason they can be commanded to embody their salvation (v. 12). The emphatic placement of θεὸς (masc. nom. sg.) indicates that Paul does not want the Philippians to think that they "work out" their salvation on their own; rather, with the **predicate** nominative **participle** ὁ ἐνεργῶν (pres. act. ptc. masc. nom. sg. of ἐνεργέω, "to work, be effective"), he asserts that God empowers them to accomplish this task. The preposition ἐν is commonly used with ἐνεργέω. Θεὸς is missing from D and the Majority Text (excluding K and P) but is found in the earlier manuscripts ℵ and B as well as in A, C, F, and others. The prepositional phrase ἐν ὑμῖν (dat. pl.) may indicate again that this salvation is to be "worked out" in the context of the community because God is working "among you."

2:13

---

predicate participle

The use of the participle to function as a predicate adjective or predicate nominative.

Θεὸς γάρ ἐστιν <u>ὁ ἐνεργῶν</u> ἐν ὑμῖν.
For God is <u>the one who works</u> in you.
(Phil 2:13)

<u>ζῶν</u> γάρ ὁ λόγος τοῦ θεοῦ.
For the word of God is <u>living</u>.
(Heb 4:12)

καὶ τὸ θέλειν καὶ τὸ ἐνεργεῖν ὑπὲρ τῆς εὐδοκίας—The double καὶ, one preceding the substantivized τὸ (neut. acc. sg.) θέλειν (pres. act. inf. of θέλω, "to will") and the other preceding the substantivized τὸ (neut. acc. sg.) ἐνεργεῖν (pres. act. inf. of ἐνεργέω, "to work"), signifies that both articular infinitives are given separate emphasis (Smyth, 2877). Thus the conjunctions are to be translated "both . . . and . . ." or "not only . . . but also . . ." Both infinitives serve as the direct object of ὁ ἐνεργῶν. Wallace (602) brings these elements together to translate the first part of the phrase as "both the willing and the working." When ὑπὲρ is followed by a genitive, it sometimes designates something that one wants to attain (BDF §231[2]). Εὐδοκία (of which τῆς εὐδοκίας is the fem. gen. sg.) is very rare outside Jewish and Christian writers. Spicq (TLNT 2:103) can cite only three occurrences of it outside such writers. In these three it means "kindness" and "happiness." Until the second century B.C.E., it was used almost universally in connection with God so that it referred to God's favor or benevolence. After that time it sometimes refers to human contentment or to a favorable disposition (see TLNT 2:104; BDAG). It is unclear whether εὐδοκία points to divine favor or to human good will here in Phil 2:13. The ambiguity was significant enough that C clarified it by adding αὐτοῦ so that it clearly refers to God's good purpose. However, Paul sometimes uses it to refer to human good will (see especially Rom 10:1: Paul's own εὐδοκία, "heartfelt desire"). Furthermore, Paul has already used it in Phil 1:15 to speak of human disposition. The arguments for εὐδοκία referring to God's good purpose (O'Brien, 288-89; Loh and Nida, 68-69) are plausible but not decisive. The context tends to favor seeing it as a reference to human disposition, since it stands at the beginning of a section on community relations. Paul's previous use of the term in this letter also favors this rendering. Finally, it seems unlikely that this last prepositional phrase of v. 13 should be attached to the sentence that begins in v. 14 (as BDF §213 suggests). Grammatically it could go with either sentence, but it seems to fit the flow of the preceding sentence better than it does the following sentence.

2:14   **πάντα ποιεῖτε**—With the imperative ποιεῖτε (pres. act. impv. 2 pl. of ποιέω, "to do, make"), attention turns more directly to relations among the Christians at Philippi. Still, the πάντα (neut. acc. pl.) remains rather broad, encompassing everything about their community life.

χωρὶς γογγυσμῶν καὶ διαλογισμῶν—Γογγυσμῶν (masc. gen. pl.) marks another word that is fairly uncommon outside the LXX, where γογγυσμός appears eleven times (with two additional occurrences in apocryphal texts), and in the NT, where it appears only four times. Nearly all of its eleven uses in the LXX refer to the grumbling of the Israelites in the desert. It is possible that Paul is intentionally making this connection when he uses the term here. In addition to excluding murmuring from their community life, he also tells them to reject διαλογισμῶν (masc. gen. pl.), "disputes, arguments." Although the word can mean simply a "thought" or "opinion," in this context it clearly refers to arguing.

2:15   **ἵνα γένησθε ἄμεμπτοι καὶ ἀκέραιοι τέκνα θεοῦ**—Both ἄμεμπτοι (masc. nom. pl. of ἄμεμπτος, "blameless") and ἀκέραιοι (masc. nom. pl. of ἀκέραιος, "pure, innocent") are predicate adjectives dependent on γένησθε. Ἵνα γένησθε (aor. mid. [deponent] sub. 2 pl. of γίνομαι, "to be, become") governs the rest of this sentence (i.e., through v. 16), making all that follows a purpose clause that explains why they should avoid murmuring and arguing. Although γένητε is found in 𝔓⁴⁶, A, and D in place of γένησθε, the deponent form is always used in the NT. Τέκνα (neut. nom. pl.) is a predicate nominative that goes back to γένησθε. The word τέκνον does not specify the gender of a child, but it is no less personal or affectionate than θυγάτηρ ("daughter") or υἱός ("son").

ἄμωμα—This adjective (neut. nom. pl.) may go back to γένησθε and function as another predicate adjective, or it may simply modify τέκνα. The latter seems more likely because its gender and number conform to that of τέκνα and because of its proximity to that noun. To make this connection clear, one might render τέκνα ἄμωμα as "children who are spotless." In this passage there is no clear difference in meaning between ἄμωμον and ἄμεμπτος, although the latter is used elsewhere almost exclusively for humans, while the former is used more broadly.

μέσον γενεᾶς σκολιᾶς καὶ διεστραμμένης–The neut. nom. sg. adjective μέσον functions here as a preposition, as it does on occasion (BDAG; Moule, 85). When it functions in this way, its object is in the genitive, as we find γενεᾶς (fem. gen. sg. ["generation"]) to be here. Σκολιᾶς (fem. gen. sg. ["crooked, dishonest"]) and διεστραμμένης (pf. pass. ptc. fem. gen. sg. of διαστρέφω, "to deform, pervert") are meant to be the direct opposites of the pure and unblemished of the previous phrase.

ἐν οἷς φαίνεσθε–The verb φαίνεσθε is the pres. mid./pass. indic. 2 pl. of φαίνω. In the passive φαίνω has a somewhat broader semantic field than in the active voice. In the passive it may connote "becoming," "being visible," or "being revealed." Since the play on words in the following phrase shows that "shine" is a primary sense of the verb, it may well also carry the intimation of being visible/revealed. Grammatically there is no proper antecedent for οἷς (masc. dat. pl.); however, contextually it clearly refers to the collective noun γενεᾶς (see BDF §296).

ὡς φωστῆρες ἐν κόσμῳ–Ὡς introduces a characteristic of those under discussion. The Philippians' rejection of arguing and murmuring will make them so distinctive that they will shine like φωστῆρες (masc. nom. pl. ["stars"]). It is interesting to note that Paul speaks of the stars being in the κόσμος (masc. dat. sg.) rather than in the heavens. Perhaps this should be understood as a reference to any place in the cosmos from which they might be seen. Thus they may be observed by beings in realms other than the earth. Alternatively, it might emphasize the contrast between the Philippian Christians (who are spotless) and those around them (who are crooked and perverse).

λόγον ζωῆς ἐπέχοντες–Ἐπέχοντες is the pres. act. ptc. masc. nom. pl. of ἐπέχω.   **2:16** This verb may mean either "to hold onto" or "to offer to another." Which construal translators choose depends on whether they think that the verb emphasizes the influence of the church on the world or the contrast between the two. One's choice will depend on how one construes the whole clause. It may relate to the rest of the sentence in at least three different ways: (1) it may attach to the immediately preceding clause and so explain the manner in which or means by which the Philippians shine as stars; (2) it may be a new sentence with the participle being construed as imperative; or (3) it may be dependent on the **ἵνα clause** (ἵνα γένησθε ἄμεμπτοι καὶ ἀκέραιοι) of v. 15. Which option Paul intended determines what the immediately following boast is about: (1) their distinctiveness from the world, or (2) their holding to the

---

ἵνα clause

A clause that begins with ἵνα and is usually followed by a subjunctive verb. Such clauses often express a purpose or result of the main verb.

τὰ μωρὰ τοῦ κόσμου ἐξελέξατο ὁ θεός, <u>ἵνα καταισχύνῃ τοὺς σοφούς</u>.

God chose the fools of the world <u>in order that he might shame the wise</u>.
(1 Cor 1:27)

οὐκ ἐστὲ ἐν σκότει, <u>ἵνα ἡ ἡμέρα ὑμᾶς ὡς κλέπτης καταλάβῃ</u>.

You are not in darkness <u>so that</u> [i.e., with the result that] <u>the day should catch you as a thief</u>. (1 Thess 5:4)

word, or (3) their being pure and spotless. Given that Paul is emphasizing community relations throughout this section of the letter, it seems likely that the third option is preferable because it allows Paul's boast to be more closely related to their conduct within the community. The λόγον (masc. acc. sg. ["word"]) ζωῆς (fem. gen. sg. ["life"]) refers to the gospel. One might view ζωῆς as what Wallace (106) calls a genitive of production, a genitive that indicates what the noun it is related to produces. O'Brien (298) seems to have this understanding in mind when he calls it a genitive of origin. This is Paul's only use of this expression.

εἰς καύχημα ἐμοὶ–This prepositional phrase expresses purpose. A similar construction with εἰς appears in Rom 10:1 (for other examples of such constructions, see Moule, 70). For translation into English, this construction often requires a verb to be supplied. If the implied verb is active, the dative noun (here, ἐμοὶ [dat. sg.]) serves as its subject, while it is the indirect object if a passive verb is used. In Paul's writings the noun καύχημα (neut. acc. sg.) often designates a reason or ground for boasting. This is a relatively common meaning in Paul's writings, but LSJ has no examples of this meaning outside the NT until the second century C.E. In other writers it refers to the boast itself rather than its grounds, but given Paul's usage of the word, we render the clause (with an active verb) "that I might have something to boast of."

εἰς ἡμέραν Χριστοῦ–See 1:10.

ὅτι οὐκ εἰς κενὸν ἔδραμον–This ὅτι clause expresses purpose, just as the immediately preceding εἰς does. Thus this is a parallel clause that expresses the same point but from the opposite perspective; this phrase expresses what Paul does not want to happen rather than what he hopes does hold true. Paul uses the metaphor of running (ἔδραμον [aor. act. indic. 1 sg. of τρέχω, "to run") often to speak of the conduct of his ministry or the progress that others are making in the Christian life (e.g., Gal 5:7). Κενὸν is the neut. acc. sg. of κενός and has the basic meaning "empty"; so in contexts such as this it means "in vain, to no purpose" (see BDAG). Idiomatically, we may render it "for nothing."

οὐδὲ εἰς κενὸν ἐκοπίασα–This phrase is a restatement of the previous phrase, and so ἐκοπίασα (aor. act. indic. 1 sg. of κοπιάω, "to work, labor") is related to the ὅτι of that phrase. The verb κοπιάω and its cognates are another way Paul commonly refers to his ministry and the work of other Christians.

2:17   **ἀλλὰ εἰ καὶ σπένδομαι**–Σπένδομαι, the pres. pass. indic. 1 sg. of σπένδω ("to offer a libation"), in the NT is found only here and in 2 Tim 4:6. There is considerable disagreement among interpreters as to what ἀλλὰ stands in opposition to. The option closest at hand, and therefore most likely, is that it draws a contrast between the metaphors "run" and "work" in the preceding verse and the sacrifice envisioned with σπένδομαι. Εἰ καὶ σπένδομαι begins the protasis of a simple conditional sentence. The καὶ has a sense of concession, and so the beginning of this sentence may be rendered "But even if . . ."

ἐπὶ τῇ θυσίᾳ καὶ λειτουργίᾳ–The word λειτουργία can refer to any sort of service rendered to someone (Paul uses the word this way
in 2:30), but here λειτουργία (fem. dat. sg.) refers to religious or cultic service, a common
meaning for the word. This is seen from the
close connection that it has with θυσίᾳ (fem.
dat. sg. ["offering, sacrifice"]), a connection
seen from both words being governed by a single article, τῇ (fem. dat. sg.). Thus it may be hendiadys (for similar examples see BDF §442[16])
and so understood as the altar of sacrifice or
perhaps as a sacrificial or sacred service. Perhaps the extension of the metaphor
begun with the mention of the libation favors the rendering "altar of service."

> **epexegetical genitive (genitive of apposition)**
>
> The common use of a word in the genitive case to explain or clarify the word it modifies.
>
> καὶ σημεῖον ἔλαβεν περιτομῆς.
>
> *And he received the sign of [which is] circumcision.* (Rom 4:11)
>
> τὸν ἀρραβῶνα τοῦ πνεύματος
>
> *the down payment of [which is] the Spirit* (2 Cor 5:5)

τῆς πίστεως ὑμῶν–Many commentators construe τῆς πίστεως (fem. gen. sg.
["faith"]) as an **epexegetical genitive;** that is,
the Philippians' faith is the sacrifice and service
with which Paul is willing to allow his sacrifice to count. But since Paul has clearly distinguished himself from the Philippians (ὑμῶν
[gen. pl.]) here, the context makes it more probable that this is an objective genitive. Thus Paul
is willing to be poured out for the faith of the
Philippians.

χαίρω καὶ συγχαίρω πᾶσιν ὑμῖν–This
clause is the central portion of the apodosis of
the simple conditional sentence begun at the
start of v. 17. Both χαίρω ("to rejoice") and συγχαίρω ("to rejoice with") are pres.
act. indic. 1 sg. verbs. Πᾶσιν (masc. dat. sg.) ὑμῖν (dat. pl.) is a **dative of accompaniment or association,** as the prefix συν
joined to συγχαίρω signals. What Paul seems
to be rejoicing about is the identity of the Philippians as children of God who thus have the
characteristics noted in vv. 15 and 16. Alternatively, the thought may only go back to his
thought of their being his boast in "the day of
Christ."

> **dative of accompaniment or association**
>
> The use of the dative case to indicate that someone else accompanies or is associated with the subject in the action.
>
> συγχαίρω πᾶσιν ὑμῖν.
>
> *I rejoice with all of you.* (Phil 2:17)
>
> μὴ γίνεσθε ἑτεροζυγοῦντες ἀπίστοις.
>
> *Do not be unequally yoked with unbelievers.* (2 Cor 6:14)

> **accusative of respect**
>
> The rare use of the accusative case to supply a frame of reference within which the action of the verb is true or the extent to which it makes sense.
>
> Πιστὸς ἀρχιερεὺς τὰ πρὸς τὸν θεὸν
>
> *a faithful high priest in things related to God* (Heb 2:17)
>
> ἄνθρωπος πλούσιος . . . τοὔνομα Ἰωσήφ
>
> *a rich man . . . Joseph by name* (Matt 27:57)

τὸ δὲ αὐτὸ–In this expression αὐτὸ is neut.   2:18
acc. sg. On this idiom see BDF §154; Moule,
33–34. Moule identifies it as an **accusative of
respect** and renders it "in the same way."

καὶ ὑμεῖς χαίρετε καὶ συγχαίρετέ μοι—This construction is parallel with the preceding clause. The same verbs in the same tense and voice are used, though now they are in the second-person plural imperative. So Paul both states that he rejoices and exhorts them to do the same. This strengthens the case for understanding the rejoicing to be about the Philippians' identity as God's children, because this identity is a ground for rejoicing about them, as well as with them. Maintaining the parallels in the phrases, μοι (dat. sg.) is a dative of accompaniment. The presence of ὑμεῖς (nom. pl.) may be emphatic or may simply clearly mark the transition to the second person.

FOR FURTHER STUDY

Black, D. A. "Paul and Christian Unity: A Formal Analysis of Philippians 2:1-4." *Journal of the Evangelical Theological Society* 28 (1985): 299-308.

Brewer, R. R. "The Meaning of *politeuesthe* in Philippians 1:27." *Journal of Biblical Literature* 73 (1954): 76-83.

Fowl, S. E. *The Story of Christ in the Ethics of Paul: An Analysis of the Function of the Hymnic Material in the Pauline Corpus.* Journal for the Study of the New Testament: Supplement Series 36. Sheffield: JSOT, 1990. See especially pp. 49-101.

Hawthorne, G. F. "The Interpretation and Translation of Philippians 1:28b." *Expository Times* 95 (1983): 80-81.

Krentz, E. "Military Language and Metaphors in Philippians." Pp. 105-27 in *Origins and Method: Towards a New Understanding of Judaism and Christianity; Essays in Honour of John C. Hurd.* Edited by B. H. McLean. Journal for the Study of the New Testament: Supplement Series 86. Sheffield: JSOT, 1993.

Martin, R. P. *Carmen Christi: Philippians 2:5-11 in Recent Interpretation and in the Setting of Early Christian Worship.* Rev. ed. Downers Grove, Ill.: InterVarsity Press, 1997.

Martin, R. P., and B. J. Dodd, eds. *Where Christology Began: Essays on Philippians 2.* Louisville: Westminster John Knox, 1998.

Sanders, J. T. *New Testament Christological Hymns.* Society for New Testament Studies Monograph Series 15. Cambridge: Cambridge University Press, 1971.

Stowers, S. "Friends and Enemies in the Politics of Heaven: Reading Theology in Philippians." Pp. 105-21 in vol. 1 of *Pauline Theology.* Edited by J. M. Bassler. Minneapolis: Fortress, 1991.

Thekkekara, M. "A Neglected Idiom in an Overstudied Passage (Phil 2:6-8)." *Louvain Studies* 17 (1992): 306-14.

Wright, N. T. "ἁρπαγμός and the Meaning of Philippians 2:5-11." *Journal of Theological Studies* 37 (1986): 321-52.

Philippians 2:19-3:16

⟨⟨⟨⟨⟩⟩⟩⟩

Contrasting Examples of Responses
to the Gospel

2:19-30 Reports about Timothy and Epaphroditus, Who Serve as Good Examples of Living the Gospel

2:19-24 Paul's Sending of Timothy, Who Cares More for Others than for Himself

¹⁹Ἐλπίζω δὲ ἐν κυρίῳ Ἰησοῦ Τιμόθεον ταχέως πέμψαι ὑμῖν, ἵνα κἀγὼ εὐψυχῶ γνοὺς τὰ περὶ ὑμῶν. ²⁰οὐδένα γὰρ ἔχω ἰσόψυχον, ὅστις γνησίως τὰ περὶ ὑμῶν μεριμνήσει· ²¹οἱ πάντες γὰρ τὰ ἑαυτῶν ζητοῦσιν, οὐ τὰ Ἰησοῦ Χριστοῦ. ²²τὴν δὲ δοκιμὴν αὐτοῦ γινώσκετε, ὅτι ὡς πατρὶ τέκνον σὺν ἐμοὶ ἐδούλευσεν εἰς τὸ εὐαγγέλιον. ²³τοῦτον μὲν οὖν ἐλπίζω πέμψαι ὡς ἂν ἀφίδω τὰ περὶ ἐμὲ ἐξαυτῆς· ²⁴πέποιθα δὲ ἐν κυρίῳ ὅτι καὶ αὐτὸς ταχέως ἐλεύσομαι.

¹⁹Now I hope in the Lord Jesus to send Timothy to you quickly so that I might be encouraged by knowing about you. ²⁰For I have no one with his spirit, who genuinely cares about you, ²¹for they all seek their own affairs, not the affairs of Jesus Christ. ²²But you know his proof, that as a son with his father he served with me for the gospel. ²³He is the one that I hope to send to you as soon as I see how my affairs turn out, ²⁴and I am confident in the Lord that I myself will come soon.

In this paragraph Timothy embodies the manner of life that Paul calls the Philippians to adopt in 2:1-5 in particular, but also in all of 2:1-13.

Ἐλπίζω δὲ ἐν κυρίῳ Ἰησοῦ–Ἐλπίζω (pres. act. indic. 1 sg. ["to hope"]) expresses Paul's plans and seems to include rhetorically both warmth in his relationship with the Philippians and a warning that he will soon know whether they have been obedient. The prepositional phrase ἐν κυρίῳ (masc. dat. sg.) Ἰησοῦ (masc. dat. sg.) designates the sphere within which Paul expresses this hope.

Τιμόθεον ταχέως πέμψαι ὑμῖν–It is common for ἐλπίζω to be followed by an infinitive that indicates what is hoped for. This is the function of πέμψαι (aor. act. inf.

of πέμπω, "to send"). Τιμόθεον (masc. acc. sg.) serves as the direct object of πέμψαι and is in an emphatic position here. Timothy is a junior partner in Paul's work who is mentioned in 1 Cor 16:10 and 1 Thess 3:2 in connection with visits somewhat similar to that envisioned here. Timothy seems to have been with Paul from the beginning of Paul's work in Europe, because he is known to various churches in Macedonia and Greece. Acts 16 also has him join Paul just before the European mission begins. The pronoun ὑμῖν (dat. pl.) is the indirect object of the infinitive.

ἵνα κἀγὼ εὐψυχῶ–The ἵνα with the subjunctive εὐψυχῶ (pres. act. sub. 1 sg. of εὐψυχέω, "to be glad, have courage") shows that this clause expresses a purpose of Paul's sending of Timothy. The verb εὐψυχέω is a NT *hapax legomenon* but is not uncommon outside biblical texts. It is commonly found in the imperative in inscriptions on tombs where it seems to mean "farewell" or "be of good courage." It is also found in the greetings of letters of condolence. In other contexts it may refer to bravery in battle and to receiving comfort when in distress. Spicq notes that it often carries with it a "nuance of joy," citing its use in a letter to describe a father's reaction to receiving a letter from his son (*TLNT* 2:155–56; see also MM; LSJ). Building on this usage and the context of Paul's statement that he rejoices and of his call for the Philippians to rejoice, we can infer that knowing their circumstances will bring joy and encouragement to Paul.

γνοὺς τὰ περὶ ὑμῶν–Γνοὺς (aor. act. ptc. masc. nom. sg. of γινώσκω, "to know") is a circumstantial participle of cause that is the object of εὐψυχῶ. Once again the definite article τὰ (neut. acc. pl.) substantivizes the phrase extending through ὑμῶν, the genitive plural object of περὶ. Woodenly, it might be translated "the things concerning you," but more idiomatically, "about you" or "about your affairs."

2:20   οὐδένα γὰρ ἔχω ἰσόψυχον–The adjective ἰσόψυχον (masc. acc. sg.) modifies the substantivized οὐδένα (masc. acc. sg. ["no one"]), the object of ἔχω (pres. act. indic. 1 sg. ["to have"]). This is the only occurrence of ἰσόψυχος in the NT, and the adjective is rare in other literature. It probably means "of equal spirit," "having the same mind," or "like-minded," although some have suggested that it means "having much in common" (see BDAG; LSJ; MM).

ὅστις γνησίως τὰ περὶ ὑμῶν μεριμνήσει–The compound indefinite relative pronoun ὅστις (masc. nom. sg. ["who"]) often introduces qualities of the person under discussion (see BDAG). Serving as the subject of the verb μεριμνήσει (fut. act. indic. 3 sg. of μεριμνάω, "to care for, be concerned about, be anxious"), ὅστις designates Timothy (its clear antecedent) as the one who "genuinely" (γνησίως) cares about the Philippians. (On τὰ περὶ ὑμῶν see 2:19.)

2:21   οἱ πάντες γὰρ τὰ ἑαυτῶν ζητοῦσιν–This strong statement seems to condemn all others, οἱ πάντες (masc. nom. pl.), with whom Paul is associated (see the options cited in O'Brien, 321–22) because they seek (ζητοῦσιν [pres. act. indic. 3 pl. of ζητέω, "to seek"]) their own good. However, its rhetorical function in this immediate context is more to commend Timothy than to condemn others. Once again τὰ (neut. acc. pl.) substantivizes what follows, in this case ἑαυτῶν (masc. gen. pl.), and so here means "the things of themselves" or "their own affairs."

οὐ τὰ Ἰησοῦ Χριστοῦ–This construction is an opposing parallel to the preceding phrase. Thus the τὰ (neut. acc. pl.) serves the same function in both. B and the Majority Text have transposed the words Ἰησοῦ (masc. gen. sg.) Χριστοῦ (masc. gen. sg.) so that they appear in their more common Pauline order (Χριστοῦ Ἰησοῦ). The reading adopted by the text is found in 𝔓⁴⁶, ℵ, and A. The reading in the text may be the more difficult reading because it runs counter to the common Pauline usage, even though Ἰησοῦ Χριστοῦ appears elsewhere in Philippians (e.g., 1:19). Here Paul has identified the affairs of the Philippians with τὰ Ἰησοῦ Χριστοῦ.

τὴν δὲ δοκιμὴν αὐτοῦ γινώσκετε–The unexpressed subject of γινώσκετε (pres. act. indic. 2 pl. of γινώσκω, "to know") and of the sentence is the Philippians. Δοκιμὴν is the fem. acc. sg. of δοκιμή ("test, ordeal"), a term that appears only in Paul's writings (Rom 5:4; 2 Cor 2:9; 8:2; 9:13; 13:3) in the NT and is rare in Greek literature, found only in the Hellenistic era. There seem to be only three extant uses of the word outside the NT (see MM; LSJ; *TLNT* 1:360). In Paul's writings it can have the active sense of testing (2 Cor 8:2; 13:3), or the passive sense of having been tested or of proven character, as it has here. Of course, the antecedent of αὐτοῦ (masc. gen. sg.) is Timothy.

2:22

ὅτι ὡς πατρὶ τέκνον σὺν ἐμοὶ ἐδούλευσεν–The ὅτι that begins this clause may be epexegetical, making the clause modify δοκιμὴν, even though it usually has this function after a demonstrative pronoun rather than following a noun. Alternatively, the ὅτι may relate back to γινώσκετε, a verb that it is often found with, and so be a second idea working from the same verb (the first being the direct object δοκιμὴν). It is not uncommon for Paul to speak of his converts as his children, but here he uses the metaphor a bit differently, speaking of how Timothy has acted as a (good) "child" (τέκνον [neut. nom. sg.]) in relation to a "father" (πατρὶ [masc. dat. sg.]). As he began to write this sentence, Paul may have been envisioning the common way that a father taught his craft to his son. Several commentators assert that Paul seems to have changed the direction of this sentence in midstream so that Timothy serves (ἐδούλευσεν [aor. act. indic. 3 sg. of δουλεύω, "to serve"]) with Paul (σὺν ἐμοὶ [dat. sg.]) for the gospel rather than simply being under Paul's direction or even serving Paul. This apparent change of direction may have been intentional, albeit difficult to render in English. Thus Paul speaks from two perspectives in this sentence; Timothy serves with Paul as both his colleague and his child. A reasonable rendering of ὡς πατρὶ τέκνον would be "as a son with his father."

εἰς τὸ εὐαγγέλιον–In this place the preposition εἰς may function as something like a dative of advantage (see BDAG) or may simply indicate that the serving of Timothy and Paul has been done with reference to the gospel. The translation "for the gospel" (εὐαγγέλιον [neut. acc. sg.]) allows either understanding.

2:23   **τοῦτον μὲν οὖν ἐλπίζω πέμψαι**—Repeating ἐλπίζω (pres. act. indic. 1 sg.) with the same infinitive, πέμψαι (aor. act. inf. of πέμπω), dependent on it, Paul picks up the thought begun in v. 19. Τοῦτον (masc. acc. sg.) seems to be emphatic, coming first in the sentence. Paul is emphasizing that it is the one who cares for them and who has been faithful to Paul and the gospel who is coming to them.

    ὡς ἂν ἀφίδω τὰ περὶ ἐμὲ ἐξαυτῆς—When the aorist subjunctive (here ἀφίδω [aor. act. sub. 1 sg. of ἀφοράω, "to fix one's eyes on"]) appears with ὡς ἂν, it designates a future time, and the particles may be translated "when." The adverb ἐξαυτῆς ("immediately, at once") may indicate that Paul feels some urgency to come to them. The combination of ὡς ἂν with ἐξαυτῆς brings us to render the phrase "as soon as." The now familiar use of τὰ (neut. acc. pl.) substantivizes the prepositional phrase and here designates it as the object of ἀφίδω. Ἀφοράω here means "to see" or "to find out." To give a smooth reading of this verb, we again need to paraphrase a bit so that we render this clause "as soon as I see how my affairs turn out" or "as soon as I find out about my affairs." BDAG suggests "as soon as I see how things go with me." One might be more explicit than Paul about his affairs and render "my affairs" as "my case."

2:24   **πέποιθα δὲ ἐν κυρίῳ**—Whereas v. 23 makes it sound doubtful that Paul will be able to visit the Philippians, here he reassures them. The δὲ may indicate that this clause completes the thought begun with the μὲν in v. 23. In that case, Paul was not expressing doubt about his coming, but rather explaining his delay while being confident (πέποιθα [pf. act. indic. 1 sg. of πείθω, "to convince, be confident"]) that he would come. Ἐν κυρίῳ (masc. dat. sg. ["Lord"]) may indicate that Paul sees it as God's will that he return to Philippi, or simply that his confidence that he will return is grounded in the Lord.

    ὅτι καὶ αὐτὸς ταχέως ἐλεύσομαι—Ὅτι often follows πέποιθα, indicating what the writer is confident about. So Paul is confident that he will come (ἐλεύσομαι [fut. mid. (deponent) indic. 1 sg. of ἔρχομαι, "to come"]) to Philippi. Αὐτὸς (masc. nom. sg.) serves its function as an intensive pronoun here, and so we translate "I myself." Use of the intensive pronoun emphasizes that Paul not only is sending Timothy to Philippi, but also plans to come himself, and will do so as soon as he is able. The original hand of ℵ, along with A and C, adds πρὸς ὑμᾶς to the end of this verse. This expansion of the text is not found in 𝔓⁴⁶, B, or D, and a corrector of ℵ removed it.

2:25-30 The Coming of Epaphroditus, Who Cares Deeply for the Philippians and Risks His Life for the Gospel and to Serve Others

²⁵Ἀναγκαῖον δὲ ἡγησάμην Ἐπαφρόδιτον τὸν ἀδελφὸν καὶ συνεργὸν καὶ συστρατιώτην μου, ὑμῶν δὲ ἀπόστολον καὶ λειτουργὸν τῆς χρείας μου, πέμψαι πρὸς ὑμᾶς, ²⁶ἐπειδὴ ἐπιποθῶν ἦν πάντας ὑμᾶς καὶ ἀδημονῶν, διότι ἠκούσατε ὅτι ἠσθένησεν. ²⁷καὶ γὰρ ἠσθένησεν

παραπλήσιον θανάτῳ· ἀλλὰ ὁ θεὸς ἠλέησεν αὐτόν, οὐκ αὐτὸν δὲ μόνον ἀλλὰ καὶ ἐμέ, ἵνα μὴ λύπην ἐπὶ λύπην σχῶ. ²⁸σπουδαιοτέρως οὖν ἔπεμψα αὐτόν, ἵνα ἰδόντες αὐτὸν πάλιν χαρῆτε κἀγὼ ἀλυπότερος ὦ. ²⁹προσδέχεσθε οὖν αὐτὸν ἐν κυρίῳ μετὰ πάσης χαρᾶς καὶ τοὺς τοιούτους ἐντίμους ἔχετε, ³⁰ὅτι διὰ τὸ ἔργον Χριστοῦ μέχρι θανάτου ἤγγισεν παραβολευσάμενος τῇ ψυχῇ, ἵνα ἀναπληρώσῃ τὸ ὑμῶν ὑστέρημα τῆς πρός με λειτουργίας.

²⁵And I consider it necessary to send to you Epaphroditus, my brother, fellow-worker, and fellow-soldier, and your emissary who ministers to my need, ²⁶because he misses all of you and is distressed because you heard he was sick. ²⁷In fact, he was so sick he nearly died, but God had mercy on him, and not only on him but also on me, so that I might not have sorrow piled up on sorrow. ²⁸So I am sending him more quickly so that when you see him you might again rejoice and so that I also may be free from anxiety. ²⁹Therefore, receive him in the Lord with all joy and hold such people in high esteem, ³⁰because he came near death for the work of Christ, risking his life so that he might fill up your lack of service to me.

---

epistolary aorist

The use of the aorist tense to speak in the time frame or from the viewpoint of the reader, often describing what the author is doing in conjunction with writing a letter.

οὖν ἔπεμψα αὐτόν.

Therefore, I sent (i.e., am sending) him.
(Phil 2:28)

ἔγραψα ὑμῖν, παιδία.

I wrote (i.e., am writing) to you, children.
(1 John 2:14)

This paragraph gives a second example of the manner of life that Paul is calling for among the Philippians. Epaphroditus, like Timothy, is someone who puts the good of others before his own good. Just this attitude embodies Paul's solution to the community strife that they are experiencing. There is some debate about whether this Epaphroditus is the Epaphras (the shortened form of this name) mentioned in Philemon.

Ἀναγκαῖον δὲ ἡγησάμην—Ἡγησάμην (aor.   2:25
mid. [deponent] indic. 1 sg. of ἡγέομαι, "to consider, regard, think") is an **epistolary aorist** and thus may be translated as a present, "I consider." This verb is often followed by an infinitive, which here is delayed until the description of Epaphroditus is given. Although ἡγέομαι often has a **double accusative,** here it makes more sense of the passage if ἀναγκαῖον (neut. acc. sg. ["necessity"]) is the sole accusative attached to it, with Ἐπαφρόδιτον and its accompanying accusatives attached to the following infinitive as its objects. When used with an infinitive, ἀναγκαῖος often comes to mean "it is necessary."

---

double accusative

The use, with certain verbs, of two accusative direct objects, often a person and a thing.

ἤρξατο διδάσκειν αὐτοὺς πολλά.

He began to teach them many things.
(Mark 6:34)

ὑμεῖς αὐτὸν ἐποιήσατε σπήλαιον λῃστῶν.

You have made it a den of thieves.
(Luke 19:46)

Ἐπαφρόδιτον τὸν ἀδελφὸν καὶ συνεργὸν καὶ συστρατιώτην μου, ὑμῶν δὲ ἀπόστολον καὶ λειτουργὸν τῆς χρείας μου—This series of accusatives describes Epaphroditus from several different perspectives, emphasizing his importance to both Paul and the Philippians. The possessive pronoun μου (gen. sg.) following συστρατιώτην seems to modify all three preceding nouns, so that Epaphroditus is Paul's brother, co-worker, and fellow-soldier. Then the emphatic ὑμῶν (gen. pl.) identifies him as the Philippians' emissary just before calling him a servant of Paul's χρείας (fem. gen. sg. ["need"]). This arrangement may intend to designate the Philippians as the source of this service to Paul. In fact, many interpreters find this to be hendiadys, so that it would be rendered "your emissary who ministers to my need." This use of ἀπόστολος is a good example of the breadth of meaning that the term had in this period. Λειτουργός, one of the terms that Paul uses to describe Epaphroditus, originated in the context of working for the public good—that is, rendering service for the (national) community. By the second century B.C.E., it could designate someone who performs cultic duties. The LXX then uses λειτουργός and its cognates extensively to refer to cultic service, with it even becoming a technical term for the cult and its priests (see *TDNT* 4:215–22). Outside biblical use, the word also comes to refer to a personal assistant or aide (BDAG). It may carry both the cultic and the personal connotations here: Epaphroditus is a personal aide to Paul and also is performing a religious act in his service to Paul.

πέμψαι πρὸς ὑμᾶς—The preposition πρὸς takes ὑμᾶς (acc. pl.) for its object. Πέμψαι (aor. act. inf. of πέμπω, "to send") completes the thought begun with ἡγησάμην at the very beginning of v. 25. For the sake of smoothness and clarity, a translation should place this infinitive before its object (Epaphroditus) rather than after it, even though in the Greek text it appears after all the identities assigned to Epaphroditus in v. 25. Thus our rendering is "I consider it necessary to send to you."

2:26 ἐπειδὴ ἐπιποθῶν ἦν πάντας ὑμᾶς καὶ ἀδημονῶν—Ἐπειδὴ is an uncommon word in Paul's writings, appearing only four other times, all of them in 1 Corinthians (1 Cor 1:21, 22; 14:16; 15:21). It nearly always expresses cause in the NT, not just time (as ἐπεί often does [see BDF §§455, 456]). Here it tells why Paul was sending Epaphroditus back to them. Epaphroditus is then the understood subject of ἦν (impf. act. indic. 3 sg. of εἰμί, "to be"), and the participles ἀδημονῶν (pres. act. ptc. masc. nom. sg. of ἀδημονέω, "to be distressed, troubled") and ἐπιποθῶν (pres. act. ptc. masc. nom. sg. of ἐπιποθέω, "to long for, [strongly] desire") function as predicate adjectives here. The verb ἀδημονέω signifies serious distress. The only other times it appears in the NT are in the descriptions of Jesus' agony in the garden (Matt 26:37; Mark 14:33). Πάντας (masc. acc. pl.) ὑμᾶς (masc. acc. pl.) is the direct object of ἐπιποθῶν. The original hand of ℵ, along with A, C, and D, adds ἰδεῖν (aor. act. inf. of ὁράω, "to see") after ὑμᾶς. It seems a bit more likely that scribes would add the infinitive than delete it, especially since ἐπιποθεῖν ἰδεῖν is found in Rom 1:11 and 1 Thess 3:6. These copyists perceived that the thought seems a bit incomplete with only ἐπιποθῶν. One might fill the gap in translation with the rendering "he is missing all of you."

διότι ἠκούσατε ὅτι ἠσθένησεν–Kennedy (446) suggests that ἠσθένησεν (aor. act. indic. 3 sg. of ἀσθενέω, "to be sick, weak") be translated as an **ingressive aorist:** he had become ill. This clause is intimately related to the previous one, especially to ἀδημονῶν and διότι. The conjunction διότι often follows ἀδημονέω and introduces the reason for the distress. So Epaphroditus was distressed because they had heard (ἠκούσατε [aor. act. indic. 2 pl. of ἀκούω) of his illness.

> ### ingressive aorist
>
> The use of the aorist to refer to the beginning or becoming of an act.
>
> ἐπτώχευσεν πλούσιος ὤν.
>
> *Though he was rich, he became poor.*
> (2 Cor 8:9)
>
> χωρὶς ἡμῶν ἐβασιλεύσατε.
>
> *Without us you have begun to reign.*
> (1 Cor 4:8)

καὶ γὰρ ἠσθένησεν παραπλήσιον θανάτῳ–Καὶ γὰρ points to the following   2:27
phrase as an explication of the previous statement and might be translated "in fact." The adjective παραπλήσιον (neut. acc. sg. ["coming near"]) seems to function as an adverb modifying ἠσθένησεν (aor. act. indic. 3 sg. of ἀσθενέω, "to be sick, weak") in this, its only appearance in the NT. Παραπλήσιος often appears with a dative, as it does here (LSJ). BDF (§184) identifies its use here as an adverb used improperly as a preposition. Thus θανάτῳ (masc. dat. sg. ["death"]) serves as the object of a preposition. Read this way, the meaning of ἠσθένησεν παραπλήσιον θανάτῳ is "he was so ill that he nearly died" (see BDAG).

ἀλλὰ ὁ θεὸς ἠλέησεν αὐτόν–The verb ἐλεέω ("to have compassion, mercy") is often used by Paul to speak of God's acts to effect salvation (see its uses in Rom 9; 11; 1 Cor 7:25), but here (ἠλέησεν [aor. act. indic. 3 sg.]) its meaning conforms to that seen in other passages where healing is involved, particularly in the Synoptic Gospels (e.g., Mark 5:19; 10:47; Luke 17:13). God (ὁ θεὸς [masc. nom. sg.]) is explicitly given as the actor here. So it indicates that God's pity has been extended to Epaphroditus, who is the clear antecedent of αὐτόν (masc. acc. sg.), through the healing of a disease.

οὐκ αὐτὸν δὲ μόνον ἀλλὰ καὶ ἐμέ–Again αὐτὸν (masc. acc. sg.) refers to Epaphroditus, as does its adjective, μόνον (masc. acc. sg.), and these accusatives, along with ἐμέ (acc. sg.), are all direct objects of ἠλέησεν. So we may translate the first part of this phrase as "not only on him . . ." The form of this phrase expresses emphatically the level of feeling that Paul has for Epaphroditus, and perhaps for the Philippians who would have been troubled by his death, by including himself as a recipient of the mercy extended in the recovery of Epaphroditus.

ἵνα μὴ λύπην ἐπὶ λύπην σχῶ–As usual, a subjunctive (σχῶ [aor. act. sub. 1 sg. of ἔχω, "to have") follows the ἵνα, here with the negative particle, so that it means "so that I might not have . . ." In this context ἐπὶ may mean "in addition to"

(BDF §235[3]). The first λύπην (fem. acc. sg. ["sorrow"]) in this clause is the object of the verb σχῶ, and the second is the object of ἐπὶ. O'Brien (338 n. 60) cites a long history of interpreters who have found the initial sorrow to be Paul's imprisonment and/or his having so many adversaries. This is perhaps too literal, and so the expression rather should simply be understood to indicate intense sorrow.

2:28 **σπουδαιοτέρως οὖν ἔπεμψα αὐτὸν**—Beginning this new and short sentence with οὖν makes Paul's sending of Epaphroditus, again the antecedent of αὐτὸν (masc. acc. sg.), a result of his recognition of the Philippians' concern about him and so a show of Paul's care about the Philippians. The use of σπουδαιοτέρως, the comparative form of the adverb σπουδαίως ("with haste"), increases this impression. The main verb, ἔπεμψα (aor. act. indic. 1 sg. of πέμπω, "to send"), is an epistolary aorist and so is translated as a present, "I am sending." Its object is αὐτὸν (masc. acc. sg.), whose antecedent remains Epaphroditus.

ἵνα ἰδόντες αὐτὸν πάλιν χαρῆτε—This ἵνα with its accompanying subjunctive, χαρῆτε (aor. pass. [deponent] sub. 2 pl. of χαίρω, "to rejoice, be glad"), expresses purpose. Ἰδόντες (aor. act. ptc. masc. nom. pl. of εἶδον, a stem created from the second aorist of ὁράω, "to see") is a **circumstantial participle denoting time** (when) or cause. The subject of ἰδόντες is an understood "you," as is implied by χαρῆτε, and αὐτὸν (masc. acc. sg.), still referring to Epaphroditus, is its object.

κἀγὼ ἀλυπότερος ὦ—The verb ὦ (pres. act. sub. 1 sg. of εἰμί, "to be") is the second subjunctive governed by the same ἵνα as χαρῆτε, and thus it expresses a second purpose in Paul's sending of Epaphroditus: that Paul himself might be ἀλυπότερος (masc. nom. sg.), "more free from grief." This predicate adjective is another comparative, although here an adjective rather than an adverb as above. Paul's assertion that the joy that the Philippians experience will make him even more free from anxiety makes it seem more likely that the λύπην ἐπὶ λύπην of v. 27 conveys intensity rather than that there are other things that cause him grief or anxiety.

> **circumstantial participle of time**
>
> The action of the participle has a temporal relationship to that of the leading verb. It may be translated *when, while, after,* etc.
>
> εὐχαριστήσας ἔκλασεν.
> *when he had given thanks,* he broke [the bread]. (1 Cor 11:24).
>
> ἔτι ἁμαρτωλῶν ὄντων ἡμῶν Χριστὸς ὑπὲρ ἡμῶν ἀπέθανεν.
> *While we were* still sinners, Christ died for us. (Rom 5:8)

2:29 **προσδέχεσθε οὖν αὐτὸν ἐν κυρίῳ μετὰ πάσης χαρᾶς**—The close connection between this sentence and at least the preceding sentence is evidenced by the οὖν, so that what is found in this sentence is related to their joy about Epaphroditus. It seems probable that οὖν relates this sentence to everything since v. 25, the beginning of the paragraph with its description of Epaphroditus. They are instructed to receive (προσδέχεσθε [pres. mid./pass. (deponent) impv. 2 pl. of προσδέχομαι]) him. The most common meaning of προσδέχομαι in the NT is "to await," as Christians await the eschatological blessings (e.g., Titus 2:13) or those

who await the Messiah (Mark 15:43; Luke 2:25). However, Paul uses προσδέχομαι only one other time (Rom 16:2), and both times it has its other primary
meaning: "to welcome, receive" someone (here Epaphroditus, referred to with the
αὐτὸν [masc. acc. sg.], the direct object of the verb). Paul uses ἀπεκδέχομαι
(Rom 8:19, 23, 25; 1 Cor 1:7; Gal 5:5; Phil 3:20 [his only uses of it]), instead of
προσδέχομαι, to speak of Christians awaiting final salvation. The prepositional
phrase ἐν κυρίῳ (masc. dat. sg. ["Lord"]) functions adverbially and specifies the
manner in which they are to receive Epaphroditus. It seems to mean simply "as a
Christian" (for variations on this meaning see O'Brien, 340). Μετὰ πάσης (fem.
gen. sg.) χαρᾶς (fem. gen. sg. ["joy"]) is a second adverbial phrase of manner that
further designates how they are to receive him.

καὶ τοὺς τοιούτους ἐντίμους ἔχετε–This clause clarifies Paul's reasons for giving instructions about how to receive Epaphroditus and clarifies the reason the
sentence is connected to the former thought of Epaphroditus's illness in service to
the gospel with οὖν. Such a connection between Epaphroditus's illness and his
welcome and the imperative makes good sense when Epaphroditus is presented
as an example of the type of people they are to honor. Their welcome to him is to
be the pattern for how they welcome such people because τοὺς τοιούτους
(masc. acc. pl. ["of such a kind, such as this"]), not just Epaphroditus, is a direct object of ἔχετε (pres. act. impv. 2 pl. of ἔχω, "to hold"), and ἐντίμους (masc. acc. pl.
["honored, respected"]) is a predicate accusative attached to the same verb (see
BDF §157). Such constructions are translated "hold such persons as honored," or
less woodenly, "hold such people in high esteem" or "esteem such people highly."
This is Paul's only use of ἔντιμος, which appears only four other times in the NT
(Luke 7:2; 14:8; 1 Pet 2:4, 6). Here it implies that one is respected/honored for
qualities of character (BDAG).

ὅτι διὰ τὸ ἔργον Χριστοῦ–Χριστοῦ (masc. gen. sg.) modifies τὸ ἔργον (neut.   2:30
acc. sg. ["work"]), the object of διὰ. Διὰ with an accusative often indicates the reason for something (BDAG). This phrase may be placed at the beginning of the
clause for emphasis. The ὅτι that begins this clause indicates that what follows is
a further explication of the aspects of Epaphroditus's character that are to be
honored both in him and in others. There are a number of textual variants surrounding Χριστοῦ. C omits any genitive (and this option is favored by some commentators); κυρίου is found in ℵ, A, P, and others; and the reading in the text is
found in 𝔓46, B, F, D (τοῦ Χριστοῦ) and others. This latter reading has strong external support and is perhaps to be favored because the presence of κυρίου may
be explained by Paul's use of this phrase elsewhere (e.g., 1 Cor 15:58). However,
the uniqueness of the expression τὸ ἔργον Χριστοῦ seems to make it the more
difficult reading and thus more probable.

μέχρι θανάτου ἤγγισεν–This main verb of the clause, ἤγγισεν (aor. act. indic.
3 sg. of ἐγγίζω, "to come near"), is modified by the preceding prepositional phrase.

The preposition μέχρι ("to the point of") is not strictly necessary with ἐγγίζω, which could simply take a dative (e.g., Luke 15:1; Acts 9:3; Heb 7:19). Kennedy (447) notes that this is an unusual use of μέχρι. O'Brien (342-43) conjectures that the phrase μέχρι θανάτου (masc. gen. sg. ["death"]) is used here in deliberate imitation of its use in connection with Christ's self-sacrifice in 2:8.

παραβολευσάμενος τῇ ψυχῇ–Παραβολευσάμενος is the pres. mid. (deponent) ptc. masc. nom. sg. of παραβολεύομαι ("to risk"). This verb is a NT *hapax legomenon* and is uncommon in other literature. BDF (§108[5]) lists it as one of the verbs formed by adding -εύειν to a noun. Such verbs often carry the meaning of "having as a vocation the thing named by the noun on which the verb is based." One meaning of παράβολος is "exposing oneself to danger" (LSJ). The participial phrase here may repeat the assertion in the first part of the verse, or it may explicate how Epaphroditus drew near to death, risking his life (ψυχῇ [fem. dat. sg.]) in his service for the work of Christ. This may imply that he faced dangers other than the illness previously mentioned, or, as some have conjectured, his illness may have been a result of the conditions that he endured while carrying out his ministry.

ἵνα ἀναπληρώσῃ τὸ ὑμῶν ὑστέρημα τῆς πρός με λειτουργίας–The ἵνα introduces a purpose clause, giving a second reason why Epaphroditus, the understood subject of ἀναπληρώσῃ (aor. act. sub. 3 sg. of ἀναπληρόω), risked his life. Ἀναπληρόω can mean "to complete" or "to fill a gap"; thus, Epaphroditus's service has completed, or perhaps supplemented, the Philippians' service to Paul. Τὸ ὑστέρημα (neut. acc. sg. ["deficiency, lack"]) is the direct object of ἀναπληρώσῃ. Λειτουργίας (fem. gen. sg. ["service, sacrificial service"]) is the second genitive dependent on the noun ὑστέρημα. This is an unusual construction because the two genitives are to be construed differently, but it follows the pattern commonly seen with such constructions: the noun appears between the two genitives. Τῆς λειτουργίας is an objective genitive, designating what was lacking, so we may translate "your lack of service." Since πρός με (acc. sg.) stands in the attributive position, it defines λειτουργίας, perhaps even emphasizing that the service was to Paul (see BDF §270). Paul indicates here that this deficiency in service was the Philippians' (ὑμῶν) deficiency. However, Epaphroditus has now supplied what previously was lacking. Perhaps what Epaphroditus supplied was the comfort that Paul derives from the Philippians' personal presence, as Stephanas, Fortunatus, and Achaicus do for the Corinthians in 1 Cor 16:17 (BDAG). Some think, however, that the "thing lacking" included the monetary gift that the Philippians sent to Paul.

Timothy and Epaphroditus, along with Paul himself, have now been given as good examples of the attitudes that the Philippians should adopt. These examples not only model the behavior that Paul seeks, but also help him reject those spoken of in chs. 1 and 3 by making them the sharp contrast in comparison with the approved examples. So those mentioned in chs. 1 and 3 should be seen as bad examples, those whose behavior the Philippians should avoid.

3:1-16   Exhortation to Consider Those Who Require Gentile Christians to Be Circumcised to Be Christian as Bad Examples of Responding to the Gospel

3:1   Introduction and Transition

¹Τὸ λοιπόν, ἀδελφοί μου, χαίρετε ἐν κυρίῳ. τὰ αὐτὰ γράφειν ὑμῖν ἐμοὶ μὲν οὐκ ὀκνηρόν, ὑμῖν δὲ ἀσφαλές.

¹So, my brothers and sisters, rejoice in the Lord. For my part, to write these things to you is not troublesome, and it is safe for you.

Τὸ λοιπόν—This construction represents an idiomatic use whereby neuter accusative **adjectives function adverbially;** when used this way, they are commonly articular (Wallace, 293). Τὸ λοιπόν (neut. acc. sg.) is often used to draw to a conclusion; thus its use here has been interpreted as evidence that a fragment of a different letter is found in 3:2–4:3. However, this is not the only use for this word. In the Hellenistic period it is also used as a transitional particle in other parts of writings; thus it may simply introduce a new section.

> **adjective used as adverb**
>
> The use of the adjective, often in the accusative case and with an article, to function as an adverb.
>
> τὸ <u>λοιπόν</u>, ἀδελπηοί
> <u>Finally</u>, brothers (Phil 3:1)
>
> ὕπαγε <u>πρῶτον</u> διαλλάγηθι.
> Go <u>first</u> and be reconciled. (Matt 5:24)

3:1

See its use in 1 Thess 4:1, where it has this function and is accompanied by the vocative ἀδελφοί. So it is probably better not to translate the words "Finally, . . ."

ἀδελφοί μου—Use of μου (gen. sg.) with the vocative plural ἀδελφοί is fairly uncommon in Paul (Rom 7:4; 15:14; 1 Cor 1:11; 11:33; 14:39 [some manuscripts]; 15:58; Phil 3:1; 4:1). Perhaps it is an attempt to keep the attachment that Paul feels for the Philippians within the scope of the readers' vision as he moves to give them the following warnings.

χαίρετε ἐν κυρίῳ—The prepositional phrase ἐν κυρίῳ (masc. dat. sg. ["Lord"]) probably designates the basis for their rejoicing or the sphere within which their rejoicing takes place, but other meanings are possible. The case for viewing 3:1 as part of the closing of a letter is strengthened by the presence of this phrase, because Paul occasionally uses χαίρετε (pres. act. impv. 2 pl. of χαίρω, "to rejoice") near the end of his letters (e.g., 2 Cor 13:11, which also has λοιπόν).

τὰ αὐτὰ γράφειν ὑμῖν—Γράφειν (pres. act. inf. of γράφω, "to write") is a **substantival infinitive** that serves as the subject of the understood main verb of this sentence, ἐστί

> **substantival infinitive**
>
> The use of the infinitive in place of a noun as either the subject or object of a verb.
>
> οὐχ ἁρπαγμὸν ἡγήσατο <u>τὸ εἶναι</u> <u>ἴσα</u> Θεῷ.
> He did not consider <u>equality</u> with God something to be grasped. (Phil 2:6)
>
> νυνὶ δὲ καὶ <u>τὸ ποιῆσαι</u> ἐπιτελέσατε.
> And now complete <u>the deed</u>. (2 Cor 8:11)

(pres. act. indic. 3 sg. of εἰμί, "to be"). It is not clear whether τὰ αὐτὰ (neut. acc. pl.) refers to what has come before it in the letter or what comes after it in 3:2–4:1. But since Paul sometimes uses the preceding τὸ λοιπόν to begin a new section, it is more probable that it refers to what follows. It is also not clear whether Paul is repeating something from his teaching while in Philippi or, as some have suggested, from correspondence with them that is no longer extant. A few interpreters who identify 3:2–4:1 as a fragment of another letter have suggested that these words are the beginning of the exhortation to Euodia and Syntyche. The pronoun ὑμῖν (dat. pl.) designates the recipients of the letter, as it often does. If the following ἐμοὶ (dat. sg.) is more directly dependent on γράφειν, it is a **dative of agent,** sometimes used in **impersonal clauses** (Smyth, 1490) such as the present one.

> ### dative of agent or personal agency
>
> The use of the dative case, usually with a passive verb, to designate the person by whom the action of the verb is done.
>
> ὅσοι γὰρ <u>πνεύματι</u> θεοῦ ἄγονται
> *For as many as are led <u>by the Spirit</u> of God (Rom 8:14)*
>
> οὐδὲν ἄξιον θανάτου ἐστὶν πεπραγμένον <u>αὐτῷ</u>.
> *Nothing worthy of death had been done <u>by him</u>. (Luke 23:15)*

> ### impersonal clause
>
> A clause in which subject of the verb is impersonal and is not explicitly stated.
>
> καυχᾶσθαι δεῖ.
> *It is necessary to boast. (2 Cor 12:1)*
>
> Πάντα μοι ἔξεστιν.
> *All things are lawful for me. (1 Cor 6:12)*

ἐμοὶ μὲν οὐκ ὀκνηρόν—These words begin a μὲν . . . δὲ clause whose understood verb, ἐστί (pres. act. indic. 3 sg. of εἰμί, "to be"), includes the understood subject, "it." So ὀκνηρόν (neut. nom. sg. ["troublesome"]) is a predicate adjective. It is more probable that the ἐμοὶ introduces this clause than that it belongs to the previous clause, because it stands in parallel with the following ὑμῖν both formally and in balancing the thought.

ὑμῖν δὲ ἀσφαλές—The verb remains unexpressed as the second predicate adjective, ἀσφαλές (neut. nom. sg. ["safe, certain"]), is used to complete the clause. Many find this explanation of Paul's writing good evidence that "the same things" mentioned in the first part of the verse must refer to the warnings that follow, because it makes little sense to say that it is for their safety to be reminded to rejoice. If τὰ αὐτὰ does refer to what follows, this construction supports the letter's integrity at this point.

3:2-11 *Contrast Between Those Teachers and Paul*

3:2-4a True Circumcision

²Βλέπετε τοὺς κύνας, βλέπετε τοὺς κακοὺς ἐργάτας, βλέπετε τὴν κατατομήν. ³ἡμεῖς γάρ ἐσμεν ἡ περιτομή, οἱ πνεύματι θεοῦ λατρεύοντες καὶ καυχώμενοι ἐν Χριστῷ Ἰησοῦ καὶ οὐκ ἐν σαρκὶ πεποιθότες, ⁴ᵃκαίπερ ἐγὼ ἔχων πεποίθησιν καὶ ἐν σαρκί.

²Consider the "dogs," consider the evildoers, consider the mutilators! ³For we are the circumcision who serve God through the Spirit and boast through Christ Jesus and do not rely on the flesh, ⁴ᵃ even though I have reason to have confidence in the flesh.

Βλέπετε τοὺς κύνας, βλέπετε τοὺς κακοὺς ἐργάτας, βλέπετε τὴν κατα-   3:2
τομήν–The meaning of the repeated imperative βλέπετε is disputed. When used with an accusative, as it is here (τοὺς κύνας . . . τοὺς κακοὺς ἐργάτας . . . τὴν κατατομήν), it always means "look at, consider." But most interpreters opt against its use elsewhere and argue that its repetition and connection with derogatory descriptions here show that it should be translated "beware." Although there is some polemical intent conveyed with these imperative clauses, it is probably best to adhere to known usage of the verb as closely as context allows. So while translating βλέπετε "consider," we should recognize that this implies not only thinking about them, but also watching and avoiding them. This rendering may cohere with the reading of those recent interpreters who think that this verse is an example of Paul giving negative examples that are the opposite of the attitudes that he wants the Philippians to adopt. The derogatory terms used here indicate that those whom the Philippians are being warned about probably are Christian missionaries who urge Gentiles to be circumcised and perhaps to keep more of the law than Paul thinks is permissible for Gentile Christians. Calling them "dogs" (τοὺς κύνας [masc. acc. pl.]) is straightforward invective that tells the reader nothing about the identity of these other teachers other than that Paul considers them opponents. Given that early Christians commonly used the term ἐργάτης ("worker") for missionaries, τοὺς κακοὺς ἐργάτας suggests that those whom Paul is rejecting are Christian missionaries. The term τὴν κατατομήν (fem. acc. sg. ["mutilation, cutting in pieces"]) is a collective noun used here in place of "the circumcision," and so it probably indicates that these teachers are Jewish Christians.

> **paronomasia**
>
> A play on words performed by various means such as using the same or slightly different words in different senses.
>
> μηδὲν ἐργαζομένος ἀλλὰ περιεργαζομένους.
>
> not <u>busy</u> at all but <u>busybodies</u> (2 Thess 3:11)
>
> ἀπορούμενοι ἀλλ᾽ οὐκ ἐξαπορούμενοι
>
> *at a loss*, but not (utterly) <u>*lost*</u> (2 Cor 4:8)

ἡμεῖς γὰρ ἐσμεν ἡ περιτομή–With the predicate nominative ἡ περιτομή (fem.   3:3
nom. sg. ["circumcision"]), Paul includes the Philippian Gentiles among God's Israel, in opposition to those who are requiring literal circumcision–that is, τὴν κατατομήν (and perhaps all the derogatory terms) of v. 2. So this **paronomasia** clarifies whom Paul wants them to "consider." The ἡμεῖς (masc. nom. pl.) is emphatic, stressing the distinction between "us," meaning the Philippians and Paul (and presumably those who agree with Paul), and "the dogs."

οἱ **πνεύματι θεοῦ λατρεύοντες**–Λατρεύοντες (pres. act. ptc. masc. nom. pl. of λατρεύω, "to serve, worship") is a **substantival participle.** This participial phrase stands parallel with the next two participial phrases in this verse. Although πνεύματι (neut. dat. sg.) θεοῦ (masc. gen. sg.) does not have the ἐν found in the next two phrases, the dative serves the same function here. BDF (p. 100) notes that the function of the dative was being taken over by ἐν and εἰς in this period. Since πνεύματι is an instrumental dative (Moule, 46), its placement in parallel with ἐν phrases is not strange (see BDF §195). Some witnesses (a corrector of ℵ, and D, P, and other late manuscripts) replace θεοῦ with θεῷ, perhaps because the object of λατρεύω in the LXX is dative and so the copyists were afraid that the passage might be taken to mean "worship the Spirit" rather than "worship by the Spirit." Thus the reading that results from the change is clearly "worship God by the Spirit." 𝔓⁴⁶ lacks any form of θεός. Still, both the manuscript evidence (including ℵ, A, B, and C) and the internal evidence favor θεοῦ.

> **substantival participle**
>
> The use of the participle to function as a noun or adjective.
>
> ἤγγικεν <u>ὁ παραδιδούς</u> με.
> *The one who betrays me is near.*
> (Matt 26:46)
>
> εἰς τὸ δοκιμάζειν ὑμᾶς <u>τὰ διαφέροντα</u>
> *that you may approve <u>the things that are excellent</u>* (Phil 1:10)

καὶ καυχώμενοι ἐν Χριστῷ Ἰησοῦ–Καυχώμενοι is the pres. mid./pass. (deponent) ptc. masc. nom. pl. of καυχάομαι ("to boast"). Paul uses this verb frequently in constructions such as this one–that is, followed by ἐν with a dative. It designates what one takes pride in, almost "how one finds one's identity" in Paul's use, and can signify a good thing or a bad thing, depending on what follows it (for negative implications see 1 Cor 3:21; for positive implications see Gal 6:14). Paul implies here that finding one's identity ἐν Χριστῷ (masc. dat. sg.) Ἰησοῦ (masc. dat. sg.) is the contrary of the position advocated by those teachers about whom he is warning them.

καὶ οὐκ ἐν σαρκὶ πεποιθότες–Πεποιθότες (pf. act. ptc. masc. nom. pl. of πείθω, "to trust, depend") has a broader meaning than "being confident" here that is parallel to καυχώμενοι in the previous clause. Paul identifies Christians as those who do not base their identity or their place before God ἐν σαρκὶ (fem. dat. sg. ["flesh"]). From what follows we see that this phrase here refers to marks of Jewish identity.

3:4a   **καίπερ ἐγὼ ἔχων**–The participle ἔχων (pres. act. ptc. masc. nom. sg. of ἔχω, "to have") serves as the verb of this dependent clause (see Moule, 179) in which Paul sets himself apart from his Gentile converts. The distinction is emphasized with the insertion of ἐγὼ in an emphatic position. This is a rather sudden shift because the previous plural participle included all Christians, not just Gentile Christians. The conjunctive particle καίπερ, rare in the NT and found in Paul's writings only here, is always concessive and so indicates that the reader should understand ἔχων as a **circumstantial participle of concession.**

πεποίθησιν—While the noun πεποίθησις means simply "trust, confidence" (BDAG), the context and its presence in this concessive clause seem to require something of an expansion. As the statements that follow show, Paul does not place his confidence ἐν σαρκί; thus we must render πεποίθησιν (fem. acc. sg.) "reason for confidence," as most translations do.

> **circumstantial participle of concession**
>
> The circumstance described by the participle is presented as true despite the state or action of the leading verb. It may be translated *although, even though*.
>
> γνόντες τὸν θεὸν οὐχ ὡς θεὸν ἐδόξασαν.
>
> *Even though they knew God, they did not honor [God] as God.* (Rom 1:21)
>
> ὀφθαλμοὺς ἔχοντες οὐ βλέπετε;
>
> *Even though you have eyes, do you not see?* (Mark 8:18)

καὶ ἐν σαρκί—The concessive clause (v. 4a) that these words conclude also seems to end the sentence. Some punctuate the clause so that it serves as the introduction to what follows, but that seems unlikely because the next words begin a conditional sentence. The clause in v. 4a is transitional, providing the thought-bridge to the discussion that follows, but grammatically it fits more smoothly with the preceding. Thus for Paul, having confidence ἐν σαρκί (fem. dat. sg. ["flesh"]) seems to mean finding one's identity and one's value in something other than Christ.

3:4b-6 Paul's Earthly Credentials

⁴ᵝ εἴ τις δοκεῖ ἄλλος πεποιθέναι ἐν σαρκί, ἐγὼ μᾶλλον· ⁵περιτομῇ ὀκταήμερος, ἐκ γένους Ἰσραήλ, φυλῆς Βενιαμίν, Ἑβραῖος ἐξ Ἑβραίων, κατὰ νόμον Φαρισαῖος, ⁶κατὰ ζῆλος διώκων τὴν ἐκκλησίαν, κατὰ δικαιοσύνην τὴν ἐν νόμῳ γενόμενος ἄμεμπτος.

⁴ᵇ If anyone else thinks he or she has reason to be confident in the flesh, I have more: ⁵circumcised on the eighth day; from the people of Israel; of the tribe of Benjamin; a Hebrew of Hebrews; with respect to the law, a Pharisee; ⁶with respect to zeal, a persecutor of the church; with respect to righteousness that is through the law, spotless.

εἴ τις δοκεῖ ἄλλος—The subject of the protasis of this simple **relative conditional**   3:4b
sentence is the indefinite pronoun τις (masc. nom. sg. ["anyone"]), to which the adjective ἄλλος (masc. nom. sg. ["other"]) belongs. Alternatively, ἄλλος may be construed as a substantive, to be understood as ἄνθρωπος is in the phrase τις ἄνθρωπος. The meaning is not changed significantly either way. The singular τις does not refer to a specific person whom Paul has in mind, but rather to any and all who might think such (see Wallace, 690, 706). Δοκεῖ is the pres. act. indic. 3 sg. of δοκέω, meaning to "think" or "consider" when used in constructions such as that found here.

> **relative conditional sentence**
>
> A conditional sentence in which the protasis contains a relative clause.
>
> εἴ τις ὑμᾶς εὐαγγελίζεται παρ' ὃ παρελάβετε, ἀνάθεμα ἔστω.
>
> *If anyone proclaims a gospel to you other than what you have received, let him be cursed.* (Gal 1:9)
>
> ὃς ἂν θέλῃ μέγας γενέσθαι ἐν ὑμῖν ἔσται ὑμῶν διάκονος.
>
> *Whoever wants to be great among you shall be your servant.* (Mark 10:43)

πεποιθέναι ἐν σαρκί–An infinitive often follows δοκέω, as πεποιθέναι (pf. act. inf. of πείθω, "to convince, depend on") does here. The subject of such an infinitive is often not expressed when it is the same as the subject of δοκέω. (On ἐν σαρκί see 3:3, 4a.)

ἐγὼ μᾶλλον–These two words, the comparative adverb μᾶλλον and the preceding personal pronoun ἐγὼ, form the basic apodosis. What follows is simply a list of things that Paul thinks some put their trust in and that he has reevaluated in light of the gospel. Thus the indicative verb (probably ἔχω or perhaps πέποιθα) must be understood. This brief, even terse, apodosis probably makes this thought more emphatic.

3:5   **περιτομῇ ὀκταήμερος**–The best translation strategy here probably is to place a colon after "I have more" and supply an understood εἰμί ("I am"), thus considering ὀκταήμερος (masc. nom. sg. ["on the eighth day"]) to be a predicate adjective. This understood εἰμί then applies to each element in the list that continues through the end of v. 6. The list begins with a reference to "circumcision," περιτομῇ (fem. dat. sg.) (a dative of respect [BDF §197]). This strengthens the possibility that circumcision was an issue raised by those whom Paul warned the Philippians about in v. 2. By mentioning that he was circumcised on the eighth day, Paul may be asserting that he possesses a characteristic that the Philippians cannot match: he was circumcised just as the covenant instructs, on the eighth day. The members of the series of identification markers begun here all stand in **asyndeton.**

> **asyndeton**
>
> The literary device in which words or phrases are put together without the conjunctions that normally link them.
>
> Πάντοτε χαίρετε, ἀδιαλείπτως προσεύχεσθε, ἐν παντὶ εὐχαριστεῖτε.
>
> *Rejoice always; pray without ceasing; give thanks in every circumstance.*
> (1 Thess 5:16-18)
>
> ἐπίστηθι εὐκαίρως ἀκαίρως.
>
> *Be persistent in season, out of season.*
> (2 Tim 4:2)

ἐκ γένους Ἰσραήλ–Although Ἰσραήλ is indeclinable, it functions as an epexegetical genitive (or in the terminology of Wallace [95], a genitive of apposition) related to γένους (neut. gen. sg. of γένος ["descendant, nation"]), the object of the preposition ἐκ. When Paul used the term Ἰσραήλ, it probably has the implication of claiming to be one of God's chosen people. This word is not found in pagan literature, but only in Jewish materials, and when Jews communicated with non-Jews, this is not the word they typically used to refer to themselves. The use of Ἰουδαῖος in 1 Macc 13:42, within a book that uses Ἰσραήλ almost exclusively, seems to indicate this (see *TDNT* 3:360-89). The use of Ἰσραήλ here does not indicate that the recipients of this letter are Jewish, as Paul needing to assert that they are the circumcision (3:3) seems to show. Rather, his use of the term perhaps indicates that he thinks of Gentile Christians as at least a part of Ἰσραήλ. Interestingly, the word Ἰσραήλ is not found in LSJ, perhaps because of its absence in pagan writers.

φυλῆς Βενιαμίν–Βενιαμίν (masc. gen. sg. ["Benjamin"]) is another inde-clinable epexegetical genitive. We should either understand φυλῆς (fem. gen. sg. ["tribe"]) as a genitive of origin or supply an ἐκ so that this noun is its object. We do not know with any certainty why Paul makes a point of being of this tribe, al-though he does attach some significance to it, because he also mentions this in Rom 11:1.

Ἑβραῖος ἐξ Ἑβραίων–Ἑβραῖος (masc. nom. sg. ["Hebrew"]) functions as a predicate nominative with the understood εἰμί at the beginning of the verse. Wallace (103) notes that when a noun is repeated in the genitive, as it is here with Ἑβραίων (masc. gen. pl.), it shows that the noun that the genitive modifies is a member of the category par excellence. Ἑβραῖος is known in pagan authors, although it does not seem to appear as often as Ἰουδαῖος. Ἑβραῖος may have less religious content than Ἰουδαῖος. It is often claimed that this term designates Palestinians as opposed to Hellenistic Jews, but it is also found applied to non-Palestinian Jews. Thus it is difficult to determine whether Paul designates any-thing in particular with this term beyond simply a place within the Jewish people. Kennedy (451) notes with approval that the early Greek commentators Theodore of Mopsuestia and Theodoret assert that Paul uses this term because it is the an-cient name and so Paul can emphasize the purity of his ancestry by using it (simi-larly Loh and Nida, 95). In any case, Paul claims to be an outstanding example of such a person. Perhaps the combination of these first four claims functions some-thing like the list in 2 Cor 11:22, where the list seems to claim everything there is about being Jewish, both religiously and ethnically.

κατὰ νόμον Φαρισαῖος–Φαρισαῖος (masc. nom. sg. ["Pharisee"]) is another predicate nominative. The prepositional phrase κατὰ νόμον (masc. acc. sg. ["law"]) is the first in a series of three parallel constructions, each beginning with κατὰ and its anarthrous object followed by a predicate nominative or adjective. These three phrases constitute a distinct part of the list to which they belong. The first four elements focus on Paul's birth and ancestry; then these three members of the series describe Paul's own religious practice before joining the Christian movement. In this context κατὰ denotes a relationship and thus can be rendered "with respect to."

κατὰ ζῆλος διώκων τὴν ἐκκλησίαν–Τὴν ἐκκλησίαν (fem. acc. sg. ["church"]) is   3:6
the object of διώκων (pres. act. ptc. masc. nom. sg. of διώκω, "to pursue"). Ζῆλος (neut. acc. sg. ["zeal"]) is most commonly a masculine noun, but in a few places, as here, it is neuter (see BDAG; LSJ). A corrector of both ℵ and D changed it to the masculine. The masculine is also found in Ψ and the Majority Text; however, the stronger manuscript evidence favors the neuter, as does the internal evidence, since it is more probable that a scribe would change the gender to fit the common usage than vice versa. F and G are among the rare manuscripts that add θεοῦ after ἐκκλησίαν and so bring it into conformity with 1 Cor 15:9 and Gal 1:13.

κατὰ δικαιοσύνην–Δικαιοσύνην is the fem. acc. sg. of δικαιοσύνη ("righteousness"), which has several different shades of meaning in Paul's writings. Its most basic meaning outside the Bible is "justice." It can refer to correct behavior in various areas of life, including the political, ethical, and religious (*TDNT* 2:192–93). Paul sometimes uses it to refer to the justness and holiness of God in passages such as Rom 3:21–26. Elsewhere it can stand for a right relationship with God, uprightness, and several related ideas. Its meaning here is determined by the modifier that follows.

τὴν ἐν νόμῳ–The definite article τὴν (fem. acc. sg.) governs the prepositional phrase ἐν νόμῳ (masc. dat. sg.) so that it functions as an adjective that specifies the type of δικαιοσύνη that Paul has in mind. Since this is righteousness ἐν νόμῳ, Paul probably uses it to carry the sense of fulfilling the expectations found in the law.

γενόμενος ἄμεμπτος–Γενόμενος is the aor. mid. (deponent) ptc. masc. nom. sg. of γίνομαι ("to be born, to be"). This statement shows that Paul believed that he successfully fulfilled the law, indeed that he was "spotless" (ἄμεμπτος [masc. nom. sg.]) in this effort, before becoming a Christian. Such a statement should put to rest the theories that attribute great guilt as Paul's motivation for becoming a Christian. It also signals that Paul does not think it impossible to fulfill the demands of the law. Perhaps Paul uses the verb γίνομαι to emphasize that this is a status that he had gained and was able to maintain (see BDAG, meaning 7).

3:7–11 The Surpassing Value of Christ

⁷(ἀλλὰ) ἅτινα ἦν μοι κέρδη, ταῦτα ἥγημαι διὰ τὸν Χριστὸν ζημίαν. ⁸ἀλλὰ μενοῦνγε καὶ ἡγοῦμαι πάντα ζημίαν εἶναι διὰ τὸ ὑπερέχον τῆς γνώσεως Χριστοῦ Ἰησοῦ τοῦ κυρίου μου, δι' ὃν τὰ πάντα ἐζημιώθην, καὶ ἡγοῦμαι σκύβαλα, ἵνα Χριστὸν κερδήσω ⁹καὶ εὑρεθῶ ἐν αὐτῷ, μὴ ἔχων ἐμὴν δικαιοσύνην τὴν ἐκ νόμου ἀλλὰ τὴν διὰ πίστεως Χριστοῦ, τὴν ἐκ θεοῦ δικαιοσύνην ἐπὶ τῇ πίστει, ¹⁰τοῦ γνῶναι αὐτὸν καὶ τὴν δύναμιν τῆς ἀναστάσεως αὐτοῦ καὶ (τὴν) κοινωνίαν (τῶν) παθημάτων αὐτοῦ, συμμορφιζόμενος τῷ θανάτῳ αὐτοῦ, ¹¹εἴ πως καταντήσω εἰς τὴν ἐξανάστασιν τὴν ἐκ νεκρῶν.

⁷Though these things were beneficial to me, I consider them loss for the sake of Christ. ⁸Beyond those things, I consider all things a loss for the sake of the surpassing value of the knowledge of Christ Jesus my Lord, for whom I have lost all things, and I consider them excrement, so that I might gain Christ ⁹and be found in him, not having my righteousness that comes from the law, but the righteousness that comes from the faithfulness of Christ, the righteousness that God gives the person who has faith; ¹⁰to know him and the power of

his resurrection and participation in his sufferings, being conformed to his death, ¹¹so that I may perhaps attain the resurrection from the dead.

(ἀλλὰ) ἅτινα ἦν μοι κέρδη—Κέρδη (neut. nom. pl.) is a predicate nominative. **3:7** It is doubtful that ἀλλὰ was originally a part of the text. It is missing in 𝔓⁴⁶, the original hand of ℵ, and A. However, another hand added it to ℵ, and it is in B, D, Ψ, and the Majority Text. It is retained in the critical text (but in brackets to show that it is questionable) perhaps because it was seen to be the more difficult reading, even though it makes the turning point in the text more clear. It may be regarded as a more difficult reading because ἀλλὰ must be used in an unusual sense (see Smyth 2775, 2784, 2785). Overall, however, the text without it is both shorter and difficult. Fee (311) maintains that ἀλλὰ was not originally part of the text and was added by a copyist because the context seemed to require such a **contrastive particle.** On this reading, the ἀλλὰ functions to contrast vv. 7–11 with vv. 4–6 rather than having its primary function within its clause. The transition from v. 6 to v. 7 seems to beg for some contrastive particle—the probable reason that ἀλλὰ was added. In most translations this clause and its finite verb ἦν (impf. act. ind. 3 sg. of εἰμί, "to be") are given the sense of a concessive (or perhaps a temporal) participle (e.g., "[Nevertheless] the very things which I formerly regarded as gains…" [O'Brien, 381]; "Yet whatever gains I had …" [NRSV]). The obvious contrast with the second clause requires some concessive sense, but we may remain closer to the text by rendering the clause "Now these things that were beneficial…" The indefinite relative pronoun ἅτινα (neut. nom. pl.), of course, requires a singular verb. Κέρδη (neut. nom. pl. ["gain, profit"]) is a predicate nominative. Μοι (dat. sg.) is a dative of advantage.

> ### contrastive particle
>
> A word that signals a contrast or distinction between two or more elements in a sentence, but in a way less forceful than an adversative particle.
>
> οὐ γὰρ ὀφείλει τὰ τέκνα τοῖς γονεῦσιν θησαυρίζειν <u>ἀλλὰ</u> οἱ γονεῖς τοῖς τέκνοις.
>
> *For children should not save up for parents, but parents for children.* (2 Cor 12:14)
>
> Μὴ θησαυρίζετε ὑμῖν θησαυροὺς ἐπὶ τῆς γῆς … θησαυρίζετε <u>δὲ</u> ὑμῖν θησαυροὺς ἐν οὐρανῷ.
>
> *Do not store up for yourselves treasures on earth … <u>but</u> store up for yourselves treasures in heaven.* (Matt 6:19-20)

ταῦτα ἥγημαι διὰ τὸν Χριστὸν ζημίαν—This clause stands in obvious opposition to the preceding one and so probably needs an adversative particle in translation unless the contrast has been made clear in the preceding clause, as it is in many translations. Paul uses the perfect tense ἥγημαι (pf. mid./pass. [deponent] indic. 1 sg. of ἡγέομαι, "to consider") to show that he adopted this new perspective with which he reevaluates all the previously listed privileges in the past and that it continues to be the way he views them. Here the verb ἡγέομαι has, as it sometimes does, two objects (BDF §157[3]): ταῦτα (neut. acc. pl.) and ζημίαν (fem. acc. sg. ["loss, forfeit"]). Κέρδος and ζημία are commercial terms for "profit" and "loss." The only two uses of ζημία in the NT beyond its use here and in the following clause are in Acts 27:10, 21, where Luke has Paul use it to speak of the losses associated with a shipwreck. The commercial metaphor does not support the idea that Paul saw his former religious life legalistically. Διά with the accusative (here Χριστὸν) often gives a reason for something, and thus we may render it "for the sake of."

3:8   **ἀλλὰ μενοῦνγε**–The emphatic particle μενοῦνγε coupled with the adversative ἀλλὰ has something of a corrective sense. This clause offers such correction by strengthening the previous statement, expanding it beyond those things included in the ταῦτα of the previous clause.

καὶ ἡγοῦμαι πάντα ζημίαν εἶναι–Πάντα (neut. acc. pl.) is the object of ἡγοῦμαι (pres. mid./pass. [deponent] indic. 1 sg. of ἡγέομαι, "to consider"). The verb ἡγέομαι often is followed by an infinitive (here εἶναι [pres. act. inf. of εἰμί, "to be"]) with an accusative. This clause indicates that Paul has reevaluated not just Jewish privilege, but all things, and found them to be ζημίαν (fem. acc. sg. ["loss"]).

διὰ τὸ ὑπερέχον–The substantivized participle ὑπερέχον (pres. act. ptc. neut. acc. sg. of ὑπερέχω, "to surpass, excel") is unusual in that it conveys an abstract idea (BDF §263). BDF (§263) also asserts that using this participle makes the idea more graphic than use of the noun ὑπεροχή. Fee (317 n. 19) contends that this word is best understood in the light of the context of the commercial metaphors that Paul has been employing, an understanding reflected in the RSV and NRSV but not in the NIV or the note in BDAG. Διά with the accusative again appears to give a reason for something and so can be translated "for the sake of" or "on account of."

τῆς γνώσεως Χριστοῦ Ἰησοῦ τοῦ κυρίου μου–In this series of genitives the first, τῆς γνώσεως (fem. gen. sg. ["knowledge"]), is dependent on τὸ ὑπερέχον and seems to be epexegetical; that is, the surpassing value is the knowledge. In the accumulation of genitives that follows, Χριστοῦ Ἰησοῦ (masc. gen. sg.) is an objective genitive related to τῆς γνώσεως (i.e., knowledge that has Christ as its object), τοῦ κυρίου (masc. gen. sg.) is an appositive dependent on Χριστοῦ Ἰησοῦ, and μου (gen. sg.) is possessive, as the last genitive in such a series often is (BDF §168).

δι' ὃν τὰ πάντα ἐζημιώθην–Ἐζημιώθην (aor. pass. indic. 1 sg. of ζημιόω, "to suffer loss, damage") appears only in the passive voice in early Christian literature (BDAG). With this statement Paul indicates that his reevaluation of τὰ πάντα (neut. acc. pl.) has led to his loss of those things. The antecedent of ὃν (masc. acc. sg.) is Christ; thus it indicates that Paul suffers these losses for Christ. This helps clarify what Paul means by "knowledge of Christ Jesus" in the previous phrase.

καὶ ἡγοῦμαι σκύβαλα–This is harsh language. Σκύβαλα (neut. acc. pl.) means "excrement" or in some contexts refers to the parts of the carcass of an animal that are unusable (LSJ). Thus Paul's evaluation (ἡγοῦμαι, pres. mid./pass. [deponent] indic. 1 sg. of ἡγέομαι, "to consider") of the things that he has lost is that they are valueless, even unpleasant or repugnant, at least in comparison with what he has gained.

ἵνα Χριστὸν κερδήσω–As it often does, the ἵνα clause expresses purpose: Paul changed his evaluation of all these things for the purpose of gaining (κερδήσω [aor. act. sub. 1 sg. of κερδαίνω]) Christ. Although κερδαίνω is commonly used in commerce (see, e.g., Matt 25:16-17; Jas 4:13), Christians had adopted it to speak of bringing someone into Christianity or into proper relationship with the speaker (see, e.g., 1 Cor 9:19-22; Matt 18:15; 1 Pet 3:1). Its usage here in Philippians, however, is somewhat unusual. This is the only instance in which its object is Christ; elsewhere (when used in this specialized Christian sense) its object is the person being brought into the faith or into proper relationship with fellow Christians.

---

circumstantial participle of result

The participle designates an actual outcome of the action or state of the main verb. It is often translated *thus* or *as a result*. There is at times some overlap between this function and that of the purpose participle.

τοὺς . . . <u>πεποιθότας</u> τοῖς δεσμοῖς μου.

They . . . (as a result) <u>have been made confident</u> by my imprisonment. (Phil 1:14)

ἐγένετο νεφέλη <u>ἐπισκιάζουσα</u> αὐτοῖς.

A cloud came (<u>and as a result</u>) <u>covered them</u>. (Mark 9:7)

καὶ εὑρεθῶ–These words continue the purpose clause. Interestingly, with εὑρεθῶ (aor. pass. sub. 1 sg. of εὑρίσκω, "to find") Paul moves to the passive voice here. This seems more consistent with his understanding of salvation found elsewhere (cf. Gal 4:9).

ἐν αὐτῷ–What Paul means by this prepositional phrase has been understood in various ways. Some see a reference to end-time judgment, while others perceive a sort of mystical identification with Christ or identification of the believer with Christ. What follows in vv. 9-11 perhaps suggests that Paul sees himself incorporated into Christ (αὐτῷ [masc. dat. sg.]), not in a mystical way but more in terms of corporate personality, because he expects to share Christ's suffering, be conformed to Christ's death, and be raised as Christ was.

3:9

μὴ ἔχων ἐμὴν δικαιοσύνην–The **circumstantial participle** ἔχων (pres. act. ptc. masc. nom. sg. of ἔχω, "to have, hold") may express cause ("found in him because I do not have my own righteousness"), manner ("found in him as a person who does not have my own righteousness"), or **result** ("found in him so that I would not have my own righteousness"). It may be that we should not limit the meaning to any one of these options, but rather allow Paul's ambiguity to encompass hints of each. Paul here calls the type of righteousness (δικαιοσύνην [fem. acc. sg.]) that he is describing "my own," ἐμὴν (acc. sg.). The meaning of this becomes clearer with the next phrase.

τὴν ἐκ νόμου—The prepositional phrase ἐκ νόμου (masc. nom. sg. ["law"]) functions as an adjective modifying δικαιοσύνην, being governed by the definite article τὴν (fem. acc. sg.), functioning here as a relative pronoun (Wallace, 215), as it often does. So the righteousness that Paul does not have is that which comes from the law. It is just such righteousness, justness, that is "*my* righteousness." This description does not imply that righteousness gained by keeping the law is necessarily (or in the case of Paul) self-righteousness in an egotistic or legalistic sense; rather, it is a sense of accomplishing what the law expects and seeking forgiveness through prescribed means when the law is violated. This is not legalism, but faithful living in covenant. This was generally viewed as a good situation in which to find oneself; however, Paul has found something superior.

ἀλλὰ τὴν διὰ πίστεως Χριστοῦ—The adversative ἀλλὰ signals that the contrast with what has gone before is beginning. Once again, τὴν (fem. acc. sg.) allows the following prepositional phrase to modify δικαιοσύνην. By not repeating the noun, Paul emphasizes the differences between the two ways of attaining righteousness. Here πίστεως (fem. gen. sg. ["faith"]) is the object of διὰ, and Χριστοῦ (masc. gen. sg.) modifies πίστεως. A great deal has been written over the last twenty years on the meaning of πίστις Χριστοῦ. The primary questions involve the meaning of πίστις and the type of genitive that follows it. Πίστις may mean "trusting, having faith in someone or something," or it may mean "faithfulness, trustworthiness" (other meanings not relevant to the present discussion are also possible). Both meanings are well-attested. The genitive may be either objective (designating the object of one's faith/trust) or subjective (designating the one who is faithful or who has faith). There are two basic options for understanding πίστις Χριστοῦ: (1) faith (trust) in Christ (objective genitive), (2) the faithfulness of Christ that he demonstrated in his obedience to God (subjective genitive). In this place, the contrast with "my righteousness" seems to make the subjective genitive preferable (although this is not the case in all places the expression appears). So Paul contrasts the (spotless) righteousness that he attained through his own faithfulness to the law with the righteousness achieved by Christ's faithfulness. Furthermore, if πίστεως Χριστοῦ is rendered as an objective genitive, then ἐπὶ τῇ πίστει, the last phrase in this verse, is redundant.

τὴν ἐκ θεοῦ δικαιοσύνην—Paul now repeats the object of ἔχων to offer another description of the righteousness (δικαιοσύνην [fem. acc. sg.]) that he now has: it is ἐκ θεοῦ (masc. gen. sg.). This prepositional phrase is the contrasting parallel to the preceding ἐκ νόμου. So just as "my righteousness" came "from the law," "the righteousness based on the faithfulness of Christ" comes "from God."

ἐπὶ τῇ πίστει—This righteousness that is given by God comes to those with faith. This is the only instance in the NT where ἐπὶ τῇ πίστει (fem. dat. sg.) is found. Paul uses the article with πίστις here, while it was anarthrous just a few words earlier. Fee (325 n. 45) asserts that the article is anaphoric, referring to the previous occurrence of πίστις, which he takes as an objective genitive. However, the article could just as easily function to distinguish this use of the word from the immediately preceding use. Ἐπί with the dative may have a spatial, temporal, or causal meaning. It seems best to see it as spatial here, meaning "upon the faith." Perhaps it conveys the meaning of τῇ πίστει most clearly if the article is personified, and so speaks of the person with faith. Accordingly, here it is translated "the person who has faith."

τοῦ γνῶναι αὐτὸν—The pronoun αὐτὸν (masc. acc. sg.) is the first of three objects of the articular infinitive τοῦ γνῶναι (aor. act. inf. of γίνομαι, "to know"). The genitive articular infinitive often expresses purpose, but here its connection with the previous parts of the sentence is not clear. Some think that it is parallel to the ἵνα purpose clause with the two subjunctives in vv. 8–9. However, since the structure is not parallel and since that construction is rather distant, this suggestion seems unlikely. Others see it as related to τῆς γνώσεως Χριστοῦ of v. 8, but that is even more distant. Perhaps it is best to see it as dependent upon, but loosely attached to, what immediately precedes it (so BDF §400; Vincent, 103).

3:10

καὶ τὴν δύναμιν τῆς ἀναστάσεως αὐτοῦ—The second object of the articular infinitive τοῦ γνῶναι is τὴν δύναμιν (fem. acc. sg. ["power"]). This object is modified by τῆς ἀναστάσεως (fem. gen. sg. ["resurrection"]) αὐτοῦ (masc. gen. sg.). It is difficult to know whether Paul has in mind a present experience of the power seen in Christ's resurrection or Paul's own resurrection at the Parousia. Even though Paul's thought is moving toward that future resurrection, it seems more likely that the focus is on the present here, as that has been the emphasis in what precedes. Furthermore, he knows Christ in the present. Fee (329) suggests that this power is the means that enables Paul to share Christ's sufferings.

καὶ (τὴν) κοινωνίαν (τῶν) παθημάτων αὐτοῦ.—The two definite articles in this phrase probably are later insertions. They are absent in 𝔓⁴⁶, ℵ (original hand), A, and B. Although they are present in a majority of witnesses, those witness are later than the manuscripts that lack them. The articles may have been added to create symmetry with the preceding phrase, whereas there is little reason for a copyist to drop them out. If it is correct that these articles are not part of the original text, then the connection between this phrase and the preceding one is close because a single article governs both δύναμιν and κοινωνίαν (fem. acc. sg. ["fellowship, sharing, participation"]). This may also mean that the καὶ that comes before τὴν δύναμιν is epexegetic; that is, it signals that what follows explains what has just been said (see BDF §442). Thus "the power of his resurrection" and the "participation in his sufferings" fill out what it means "to know him [Christ]." In any case, the two phrases following τοῦ γνῶναι αὐτὸν are parallel. So Paul places in the closest of relationships the Christian's experience of God's power and endurance of suffering. He does not see his κοινωνίαν, "participation" or "sharing," in the παθημάτων (neut. gen. pl. ["suffering"]) of Christ (who is the antecedent

for the pronoun αὐτοῦ [masc. gen. sg.]) as contributing to the efficacy of that suffering, but rather as a participation in the same sort of experience. Just as Christ
was rejected, so also is Paul, and so are others who follow Christ. It is in the midst
of that experience of suffering, a suffering that Paul shares with Christ, that he also
experiences the power of the resurrected Christ–thus the close connection between the two phrases. This power does not exempt Paul from the sufferings, but
rather enables him to endure with faith while experiencing the joy that he speaks
of throughout this letter.

συμμορφιζόμενος τῷ θανάτῳ αὐτοῦ–Συμμορφιζόμενος is the pres. pass. ptc.
masc. nom. sg. of συμμορφίζω ("to take on the same form as"). According to
BDAG, συμμορφίζω is found only in Christian writings. This verb is a NT *hapax
legomenon* (and the only use of it cited in LSJ), but the cognate adjective σύμ-
μορφος is found in v. 21 and in Rom 8:29. It is difficult to locate the grammatical
function of συμμορφιζόμενος because there are no immediate nominatives for it
to modify. It is probably best to see it as attributive for the understood subject of "to
know" (in which case it should be in the accusative case), whose understood subject is that of εὑρεθῶ (v. 9), or to see it more directly attached to the subject of
εὑρεθῶ. Given this grammatical structure, this participial phrase could function
primarily as another definition of knowing Christ or as directly modifying the
subject of εὑρεθῶ so that "being conformed" goes with "being found." However,
most interpreters assert that it either further defines sharing Christ's sufferings or
modifies both phrases that follow "to know him." Perhaps this συμμορφιζόμενος
does not fit clearly into the sentence's grammatical structure because Paul has
simply let a long and complicated sentence get away from him.

3:11   **εἴ πως καταντήσω**–Καταντήσω may be either aor. act. sub. or fut. act. indic.
(BDAG) of καταντάω ("to arrive, attain"). Although rare in earlier Greek, in the
LXX and Hellenistic Greek the subjunctive is found with εἰ. Εἴ πως is uncommon
in the NT, appearing only here and in Rom 1:10; 11:14; Acts 27:12 (there are several vocabulary connections between Phil 3: 8–11 and Acts 27:12-26). Most interpreters of Philippians identify καταντήσω as a subjunctive, but in the other
two places where Paul uses εἴ πως, it is followed by a future. This perhaps indicates that καταντήσω is also a future. Identifying it as a subjunctive might tend to
make the assumption of attaining more certain (see Wallace, 450-51, 469-70).
Even though this clause begins with two particles that may express doubt, the
combination of the two sometimes introduces a clause in which the writer expects the future thing to happen. O'Brien (412) suggests that the aspect of doubt is
tempered here because εἰ sometimes introduces "conditional clauses of expectation." Any doubt Paul may express about attaining the resurrection here is not a
doubt in God's faithfulness to do what God has set out to do. Rather, he indicates
that attaining the resurrection is dependent on being conformed to Christ's death.
Still, the attaining of the resurrection is not a certainty. This "if perhaps" expresses
not only Paul's sense of dependence on God's grace but also fits well with his com-

mon thoughts about accountability in judgment. Further, it may help prepare for the introduction of the exhortations which follow.

εἰς τὴν ἐξανάστασιν—Ἐξανάστασιν is the fem. acc. sg. of ἐξανάστασις ("resurrection"), a NT *hapax legomenon*, although the form without the prefix (ἀνάστασις) is common. BDAG maintains that the compound form signals a fuller participation in the resurrection. When the preposition εἰς appears with καταντάω, as it commonly does, it designates the thing reached or attained.

τὴν ἐκ νεκρῶν—Both the definite article τὴν and the preposition ἐκ (especially since it is already part of ἐξανάστασις, the noun that this phrase modifies) are unnecessary and make the phrase unique and emphatic. What Paul is emphasizing, however, is difficult to specify. Of the three times ἐκ appears with ἀνάστασις in the NT, 1 Pet 1:3 offers little clarification; Luke 20:35, however, clearly designates the righteous among the dead when it uses the expression because the preceding phrase designates those who participate in "that age" as those who are worthy. Acts 4:2 may envision such a distinction as well and so mean a resurrection of the righteous "from among the dead." Both Luke 20:35 and Acts 4:2 also have the definite article introducing ἐκ νεκρῶν (masc. gen. pl. ["dead"]), immediately following ἀνάστασις. The most probable explanation for the preposition here in Phil 3 is that it designates this resurrection as a resurrection of the righteous, as opposed to a general resurrection. This does not mean that Paul rejects the idea of a general resurrection, but only that his point here is that he will participate in the resurrection of the saints; that is, he will be conformed to the nature of the resurrected Christ (see 1 Cor 15).

3:12-16 *Paul's Striving as He Lives in Accord with the Gospel*

¹²Οὐχ ὅτι ἤδη ἔλαβον ἢ ἤδη τετελείωμαι, διώκω δὲ εἰ καὶ καταλάβω, ἐφ᾽ ᾧ καὶ κατελήμφθην ὑπὸ Χριστοῦ (Ἰησοῦ). ¹³ἀδελφοί, ἐγὼ ἐμαυτὸν οὐ λογίζομαι κατειληφέναι· ἓν δέ, τὰ μὲν ὀπίσω ἐπιλανθανόμενος τοῖς δὲ ἔμπροσθεν ἐπεκτεινόμενος, ¹⁴κατὰ σκοπὸν διώκω εἰς τὸ βραβεῖον τῆς ἄνω κλήσεως τοῦ θεοῦ ἐν Χριστῷ Ἰησοῦ. ¹⁵Ὅσοι οὖν τέλειοι, τοῦτο φρονῶμεν· καὶ εἴ τι ἑτέρως φρονεῖτε, καὶ τοῦτο ὁ θεὸς ὑμῖν ἀποκαλύψει· ¹⁶πλὴν εἰς ὃ ἐφθάσαμεν, τῷ αὐτῷ στοιχεῖν.

¹²I do not say I have already received or have already been made perfect, but I pursue it so that I may obtain it, for that is the reason I have been obtained by Christ [Jesus]. ¹³Brothers and sisters, I do not think I myself have attained, but I do this one thing: I put from my mind the things that are behind me and I reach out to what is before me, ¹⁴I pursue the goal to obtain the prize of the upward calling of God in Christ Jesus. ¹⁵Therefore, everyone who is mature, let us think this. And if you think differently about anything, then God will reveal this to you. ¹⁶However, that which we have already attained, let us hold to it.

3:12 **Οὐχ ὅτι ἤδη ἔλαβον**–This sentence and the preceding paragraph are very closely related, and we should not see a break in the subject here. Οὐχ ὅτι is an idiom that requires an understood λέγω, "I say" (BDF §480[5]). In its several appearances in the NT οὐχ ὅτι is used to qualify what precedes it to avoid misunderstanding; this is different from its meaning in classical usage. There is no expressed object of ἔλαβον (aor. act. indic. 1 sg. of λαμβάνω, "to receive"). Many suggestions have been put forward, but the word's proximity to vv. 7–11 suggests that its object is all that is included in "knowing Christ." 𝔓[46] and other Western texts, including D, add ἢ ἤδη δεδικαίωμαι ("or have already been justified") after ἔλαβον. Although such a statement may have dropped out because it seemed to contradict Pauline theology as seen elsewhere, it seems more likely that it was added. The required meaning of the verb δεδικαίωμαι here certainly would be different from what we find elsewhere in Paul and thus is the more difficult reading. However, omissions based on that sort of theological acumen are rare (so Fee, 337), while it is a characteristic of the Western texts that they often include such additions. The reading in the text is supported by 𝔓[61vid], ℵ, A, and B among other uncials. This external evidence seems to tip the scales a bit in favor of the shorter reading.

expectation clause
A clause introduced by εἰ or εἰ πως that expresses the likelihood that an uncertain event will occur.
δεόμενος <u>εἴ πως</u> ἤδη ποτὲ εὐοδωθήσομαι
praying that <u>somehow</u> I will at last succeed (Rom 1:10)
τὴν διακονίαν μου δοξάζω, <u>εἴ πως</u> παραζηλώσω μου τὴν σάρκα.
I magnify my service <u>in the hope that</u> I will provoke my people to jealousy. (Rom 11:13-14)

ἢ ἤδη τετελείωμαι–Τετελείωμαι, the pf. pass. indic. 1 sg. of τελειόω, has a wide range of meanings including "to perfect," "to complete," "to accomplish," and "to fulfill [prophecy]." In connection with mystery religions, it meant "to initiate or consecrate," and its cognate in v. 15 (τέλειοι) can mean "the mature." Rather than employing "mirror reading" here to find some perfectionist opponents, as several interpreters do, we do best to see this as Paul continuing to avoid misunderstanding. Paul has neither completely been conformed to the death of Christ nor experienced the full power of the resurrection, which will come only at the Parousia.

διώκω δὲ–Δὲ has its full adversative force here. The most basic meaning of διώκω (pres. act. indic. 1 sg.) is "to pursue," although it is often used in the NT to mean "persecute." Again, the object remains unexpressed.

εἰ καὶ καταλάβω–In regard to καταλάβω (aor. act. sub. 1 sg. of καταλαμβάνω, "to obtain"), some interpreters note that καταλαμβάνω can mean "to aggressively seize," but if that is its meaning here, that connotation of the word seems to fade quickly as it is used repeatedly in the next few lines. The particle εἰ (often with πῶς) can introduce an expression of **expectation** (vs. doubt) related to an indirect question (BDF §375). Here the meaning would be, "I pursue (it) with the expectation that I may take hold of (it)." Fee (345 n. 30) suggests as a rendering "[to see] whether I might take hold of." Still, the object remains unexpressed in Greek, although it is supplied in the above translation. The antecedent of the supplied pronoun is the resurrection.

ἐφ' ᾧ καὶ κατελήμφθην ὑπὸ Χριστοῦ (Ἰησοῦ)—It is uncertain whether Ἰησοῦ (masc. gen. sg.) should be included in this text. It is present in 𝔓⁴⁶, ℵ, and A, but absent from B and D. Since both uses are found in Paul, and there is no difference in meaning, it is impossible to decide with certainty which reading is preferred. Fortunately, it makes little difference which is original. There are also variants that add a definite article before Χριστοῦ, but the evidence for this is relatively late. Paul uses the same verb in this clause that he had used in the previous one, but this time it is in the passive, κατελήμφθην (aor. pass. indic. 1 sg. of κατα-λαμβάνω, "to obtain"). As it often does, ὑπό with genitive denotes the agent acting when used with a passive verb. The prepositional phrase ἐφ' ᾧ (masc. dat. sg.) may be taken as causal or **consecutive.** The causal meaning is idiomatic Greek (see BDF §235), but there is some dispute about Paul's other uses of this phrase. Some interpreters argue that since all other Pauline uses of ἐφ' ᾧ are causal, this is the meaning here; thus the phrase should be translated "because" (see O'Brien, 425; Wallace, 342). Others, however, think that a straightforward causal sense is not so clear in other Pauline uses and is not the meaning in this context (see Fee, 346 n. 31). In this context it seems best to attach the phrase to the understood object of the previous clause. Thus what Paul is pursuing is the very thing for which Christ attained him.

> **consecutive (force)**
>
> When a word, phrase, or clause expresses a result.
>
> ὑμεῖς μιμηταὶ ἡμῶν ἐγενήθητε . . . <u>ὥστε γενέσθαι</u> ὑμᾶς τύπον πᾶσιν τοῖς πιστεύουσιν.
>
> *You became imitators of us . . . <u>so that [with the result that] <u>you became</u> an</u> example to all believers. (1 Thess 1:6-7)
>
> ἀποκατήλλαξεν . . . <u>παραστῆσαι</u> ὑμᾶς ἁγίους.
>
> *He reconciled you . . . <u>with the result that he may present</u> you (as) holy.* (Col 1:22)

ἀδελφοί—Paul may use the vocative ἀδελφοί (masc. voc. pl.) here to draw special attention to the point he is making. On translating ἀδελφοί as "brothers and sisters," see 1:12.   **3:13**

ἐγὼ ἐμαυτὸν οὐ λογίζομαι κατειληφέναι—The infinitive κατειληφέναι (pf. act. inf. of καταλαμβάνω, "to attain, seize") is dependent on λογίζομαι (pres. mid./pass. [deponent] indic. 1 sg. ["to think, consider"]). The reflexive pronoun ἐμαυτὸν (masc. acc. sg.) is the subject of κατειληφέναι. The presence of this pronoun at the beginning of the clause with ἐγὼ makes the reference to Paul emphatic. This emphatic mention of himself is not sufficient reason to claim that he is contrasting himself with others who claim to have attained perfection. This phrase repeats the thought of the first phrase in v. 12, although with a bit different perspective. This is the third use of forms of καταλαμβάνω in three lines. Paul's selection of this word allows him to show that he knows that he has not yet attained the resurrection, to acknowledge his dependence on Christ for attaining it (perhaps continuing the theme of having a righteousness that comes from Christ), and to indicate that he himself must strive to live as he is called to live. This is a helpful lead into the call in v. 17 for the Philippians to imitate him. In 𝔓16.61, ℵ, D, and P the οὐ has been replaced by οὔπω ("not yet"). This change clearly fits the meaning of the passage, since Paul seems to be thinking within the framework of his eschatology. But since there is no reason to change from οὔπω to οὐ, and since οὔπω seems to clarify the sense, it is probably not the original reading. Additionally, οὐ has much stronger external support, including 𝔓46, B, a corrector of D, and other uncials.

ἓν δέ–The ellipsis here makes the clause so short that it is appropriate to call it an interjection. It may be left in this abrupt form and be rendered "but one thing," or it may be expanded to read more smoothly and so be translated "but I do this one thing." The content of ἓν (neut. acc. sg. ["one"]) is filled out in the rest of this verse and v. 14.

τὰ μὲν ὀπίσω ἐπιλανθανόμενος–Ἐπιλανθανόμενος (pres. mid./pass. [deponent] ptc. masc. nom. sg. of ἐπιλανθάνομαι, "to forget") marks the only use of this verb in Paul's writings. Besides simply meaning "to forget" (e.g., Mark 8:14), ἐπιλανθάνομαι can mean "to care nothing about," although this is usually expressed with a genitive (BDAG). Clearly, the latter meaning is in view here. Τὰ (neut. acc. pl.), modified by the adverb ὀπίσω ("behind"), is the object of ἐπιλανθανόμενος.

τοῖς δὲ ἔμπροσθεν ἐπεκτεινόμενος–Ἐπεκτεινόμενος is the pres. mid./pass. (deponent) ptc. masc. nom. sg. of ἐπεκτείνομαι ("to reach for"), a NT *hapax legomenon*. This participial clause is the second part of the μέν . . . δέ construction begun in the previous clause and so gives the second part of the basic content of the "one thing" that Paul does. This clause is not precisely parallel with the previous one because ἐπεκτείνομαι takes the dative τοῖς (neut. dat. pl.). The dative designates that which the subject of ἐπεκτείνομαι is stretching or straining toward. The dative article is modified by the adverb ἔμπροσθεν ("ahead, in front"), just as an adverb modified τὰ in the previous clause.

3:14 **κατὰ σκοπὸν διώκω**–It seems fairly unusual to find the preposition κατὰ governing the object of διώκω (pres. act. indic. 1 sg. ["to pursue"]). Perhaps κατὰ is present to show that Paul has a clear sense of the direction in which he is going (see Kennedy, 458; O'Brien, 429–30). Perhaps part of the reason this construction seems strange to NT interpreters is because this verb is often rendered "persecute" when found in the NT. This is a very uncommon meaning of the verb outside Christian literature, and perhaps readers of the NT are too hasty to read this as persecution. Clearly διώκω does not have that meaning here, and perhaps we are too quick to assign it that meaning in other places. It is also interesting to note that this verb appears in conjunction with καταλαμβάνω in other writers (see BDAG). The basic meaning of σκοπός is "a lookout." From that meaning it comes to connote a goal, the object on which one fixes one's eye, and the point at which one shoots in a contest (for this and other meanings see LSJ). Although it is common for interpreters to understand this word to designate the finish line of a race here, that metaphor is probably too specific. Since σκοπός is a NT *hapax legomenon*, we have no evidence from Pauline usage to lead us to render it as "finish line." Nor do the few uses of the cognate verb σκοπέω (only six in the NT, including Phil 2:4; 3:17) give any basis for such an understanding, because they all revert to the basic meaning of "watching out." So here we should render σκοπὸν (masc. acc. sg.) with the common and broader meaning "goal."

εἰς τὸ βραβεῖον—Perhaps it is the use of βραβεῖον (neut. acc. sg. ["prize"]) that has led so many to assert confidently that Paul is using the metaphor of a runner. The same word is used in connection with a runner in a race in 1 Cor 9:24, its only other occurrence in the NT; however, this is not sufficient reason to narrow the metaphor to runners. Although it need not be limited to races, Paul may well have the athletic games in mind when he uses this word. Even though this is not the most common noun used for a prize at the games (BDAG), it is used for such, and its cognates are often associated with the games. But this word is also used to refer simply to a reward. However, in a context that deals with receiving salvation there are good reasons not to render the word "reward," so it is probably better to translate it "prize." Once again, instead of a simple accusative, Paul places a preposition before this second object of διώκω. It is probably intended to convey that its object specifies the purpose of the pursuit.

τῆς ἄνω κλήσεως τοῦ θεοῦ ἐν Χριστῷ Ἰησοῦ—With the exception of ἐν Χριστῷ (masc. dat. sg.) Ἰησοῦ (masc. dat. sg.) and the adverb ἄνω, all the words here are genitive singular. While it is often suggested that τῆς κλήσεως is a genitive of apposition (see Fee, 349 n. 47, rejecting this view), others see Paul continuing his use of the athletic metaphor by identifying "the upward call" as the call to come forward and receive from the officials the prize for winning. However, those who hold this view have produced no instances in which κλῆσις is used for this ceremony (see O'Brien, 430–33). Perhaps it is better to see it as either a genitive of source (thus the prize has the call of God as its source) or as an epexegetical genitive (in which case it defines the prize). Designating this call as the "upward calling" may help Paul prepare the readers for his assertion that their "citizenship is in heaven," in opposition to those who think about earthly things (3:19–20). Τοῦ θεοῦ modifies τῆς κλήσεως and is either a genitive of source or a subjective genitive. The prepositional phrase ἐν Χριστῷ Ἰησοῦ modifies τοῦ θεοῦ rather than κλήσεως. It is the call of God, a call received in Christ.

Ὅσοι οὖν τέλειοι—Paul begins to move more toward hortatory instruction with   3:15
this phrase that must be rendered somewhat paraphrastically; this use of ὅσοι

means "all who" (cf. Rom 8:14). The οὖν indicates that what follows builds on vv. 12-14. There is no evidence that τέλειοι (masc. nom. pl. ["complete, perfect, mature"]) is a title that any Christians in Philippi have taken for themselves or that Paul is drawing on the word's use in mystery cults for an initiate. It probably simply means "mature" here. Its contrast with v. 12 is interesting because Paul includes himself among the mature here in v. 15, while in v. 12 he confessed that he had not been τετελείωμαι. Thus he has shifted the nuance from "full attainment" (v. 12) to "mature" (v. 14). This is fully within the semantic range of these terms.

> **hortatory subjunctive**
>
> The use of the subjunctive mood to encourage, exhort, or command oneself and others.
>
> ὅσοι οὖν τέλειοι, τοῦτο <u>φρονῶμεν</u>.
>
> <u>Let</u> those of <u>us</u> who are mature <u>think</u> this way. (Phil 3:15)
>
> <u>ἀγαπῶμεν</u> ἀλλήλους.
>
> <u>Let us love</u> one another. (1 John 4:7)

τοῦτο φρονῶμεν—Grammatically, there is no clear antecedent for τοῦτο (neut. acc. sg.), the object of the **hortatory subjunctive** φρονῶμεν (pres. act. sub. 1 pl. of φρονέω, "to think"). However, τοῦτο seems to refer back to what Paul has said about the way he thinks in vv. 12-14, or perhaps as far back as v. 4. ℵ and L are among the few manuscripts that have the indicative φρονοῦμεν in place of φρονῶμεν here. This change may have been inadvertent, or it may have been an attempt to make the text read a bit smoother. The external evidence overwhelmingly favors the subjunctive.

καὶ εἴ τι ἑτέρως φρονεῖτε—The second part of this compound-complex sentence could stand alone as a simple present conditional sentence, with this clause as the protasis. Although some have suggested that τι (neut. acc. sg.) should be understood adverbially with the adverb ἑτέρως and so read "somewhat differently," it is probably functioning in its usual capacity as an indefinite pronoun—thus the rendering "if you think [φρονεῖτε (pres. act. indic. 2 pl.)] differently about anything." Here τι seems to refer to understanding the Christian life in ways other than that just described by Paul; that is, it includes whatever is not part of the τοῦτο in the previous clause.

καὶ τοῦτο ὁ θεὸς ὑμῖν ἀποκαλύψει—Ἀποκαλύψει is the fut. act. indic. 3 sg. of ἀποκαλύπτω ("to reveal"). With this apodosis Paul expresses his confidence that God (ὁ θεὸς [masc. nom. sg.]) will bring the Philippians (ὑμῖν [dat. pl.]) to agree with him on this matter, and that this is, in turn, a sign of their maturity. The τοῦτο (neut. acc. sg.) of this clause perhaps has the same content as the first τοῦτο in this verse.

3:16 **πλὴν εἰς ὃ ἐφθάσαμεν**—Ἐφθάσαμεν is the aor. act. indic. 1 pl. of φθάνω, whose basic meaning is "to come to something first or before others." Coupled with εἰς. the word comes to mean "to reach" or "to attain" something (BDAG; MM 667). Although the comparative aspect is not pronounced here, the meaning is clearest if "already" is included as part of the translation, so we may translate "that which we have already attained." The adversative adverb that begins this clause, πλήν, is often used to conclude a discussion and to emphasize what follows it. Once again, discerning the content of the pronoun (ὅ [neut. acc. sg.]) is difficult because the antecedent is unclear. Some suggest that it is righteousness by faith or the Philippians' stage of spiritual growth, but the context suggests that it is the manner of life outlined in the preceding verses. Thus the content of this pronoun is close to that of the other pronouns in v. 15. If so, Paul is encouraging them to hold to whatever progress they have made in viewing life as he has described it.

τῷ αὐτῷ στοιχεῖν–Στοιχεῖν, the pres. act. inf. of στοιχέω, is commonly used to speak of going in military formation; thus it means "to conform one's behavior to a norm." That norm is named with the dative, as it is here with αὐτῷ (neut. dat. sg.). Most interpreters understand στοιχεῖν as an **imperatival infinitive** (e.g., BDF §389; Wallace, 608). However, Fee (360 n. 35) notes that such a construction does not fit well here because the preceding clause has a first-person verb, and imperatives are either second or third person. Thus Fee suggests that it has a hortatory force that is appropriate to the first person: "let us." The number of textual variants of this phrase is evidence of its unusual nature. Most of these take the form of explanatory additions, demonstrating that the present reading is the more difficult. Thus the difficulty of this reading and the diversity of these variants, along with the early witnesses (including 𝔓[16, 46], the original hand of ℵ, A, and B) for the reading given here, clearly make it the most probable.

> **imperatival infinitive**
>
> The use of the infinitive to express a command or exhortation.
> χαίρειν μετὰ χαιρόντων.
> *Rejoice with those who rejoice.*
> (Rom 12:15)

FOR FURTHER STUDY

Bloomquist, L. G. *The Function of Suffering in Philippians*. Journal for the Study of the New Testament: Supplement Series 78. Sheffield: JSOT, 1993.

Dunn, J. D. G. "Once More, ΠΙΣΤΙΣ ΧΡΙΣΤΟΥ." Pp. 730-44 in *Society of Biblical Literature 1991 Seminar Papers*. Edited by E. H. Lovering Jr. Atlanta: Scholars Press, 1991.

Funk, R. W. "The Apostolic *Parousia:* Form and Significance." Pp. 249-68 in *Christian History and Interpretation: Studies Presented to John Knox*. Edited by W. R. Farmer, C. F. D. Moule, and R. R. Niehbuhr. Cambridge: Cambridge University Press, 1967.

Furnish, V. P. "The Place and Purpose of Phil III." *New Testament Studies* 10 (1963-1964): 80-88.

Garland, D. E. "The Composition and Unity of Philippians III." *Novum Testamentum* 27 (1985):141-73.

Hays, R. B. *The Faith of Jesus Christ. An Investigation of the Narrative Substructure of Galatians 3:1-4:11*. Society of Biblical Literature Dissertation Series 56. Chico, Calif.: Scholars Press, 1983.

——. "ΠΙΣΤΙΣ and Pauline Christology: What Is at Stake?" Pp. 714-29 in *Society of Biblical Literature 1991 Seminar Papers*. Edited by E. H. Lovering, Jr. Atlanta: Scholars, 1991. Pp. 714-29.

Hooker, M. "ΠΙΣΤΙΣ ΧΡΙΣΤΟΥ." *New Testament Studies* 35 (1989): 321-42.

Kilpatrick, G. D. "ΒΛΕΠΕΤΕ in Phil 3,2." Pp. 146-48 *In Memoriam Paul Kahle*. Edited by M. Black and G. Fohrer. Beihefte zur Zeitschrift für die alttestamentliche Wissenschaft 103. Berlin: Töpelmann, 1968.

Kim, C.-H. *Form and Structure of the Familiar Greek Letter of Recommendation*. Society of Biblical Literature Dissertation Series 4. Missoula, Mont.: Society of Biblical Literature, 1972.

Koester, H. "The Purpose of the Polemic of a Pauline Fragment." *New Testament Studies* 8 (1961-62): 317-32.

Mullins, T. Y. "Visit Talk in New Testament Letters." *Catholic Biblical Quarterly* 35 (1973): 350-58.

Reed, J. T. "Philippians 3:1 and the Epistolary Hesitation Formulas: The Literary Integrity of Philippians, Again." *Journal of Biblical Literature* 115 (1996): 63-90.

Stroumsa, G. G. "Form(s) of God: Some Notes on Metatron and Christ." *Harvard Theological Review* 76 (1983): 269-88.

Sumney, J. L. *"Servants of Satan," "False Brothers," and Other Opponents of Paul*. Journal for the Study of the New Testament: Supplement Series 188. Sheffield: Sheffield Academic Press, 1999. See especially pp. 160-87.

Watson, D. "A Rhetorical Analysis of Philippians and Its Implications for the Unity Question." *Novum Testamentum* 30 (1988): 57-88.

Weidmann, F. W. "An (Un)accomplished Model: Paul and the Rhetorical Strategy of Philippians 3:3-17." Pp. 245-47 in *Putting Body and Soul Together: Essays in Honor of Robin Scroggs*. Edited by V. Wiles, A. Brown, and G. F. Snyder. Valley Forge, Pa.: Trinity Press International, 1997.

Philippians 3:17–4:9

~∞~

Application of Examples of Living in Accord with the Gospel with Explicit Exhortations

3:17–4:1 Exhortation to Imitate the Faithful and Avoid the Conduct of the "Enemies of the Cross"

¹⁷Συμμιμηταί μου γίνεσθε, ἀδελφοί, καὶ σκοπεῖτε τοὺς οὕτω περιπατοῦντας καθὼς ἔχετε τύπον ἡμᾶς. ¹⁸πολλοὶ γὰρ περιπατοῦσιν οὓς πολλάκις ἔλεγον ὑμῖν, νῦν δὲ καὶ κλαίων λέγω, τοὺς ἐχθροὺς τοῦ σταυροῦ τοῦ Χριστοῦ, ¹⁹ὧν τὸ τέλος ἀπώλεια, ὧν ὁ θεὸς ἡ κοιλία καὶ ἡ δόξα ἐν τῇ αἰσχύνῃ αὐτῶν, οἱ τὰ ἐπίγεια φρονοῦντες. ²⁰ἡμῶν γὰρ τὸ πολίτευμα ἐν οὐρανοῖς ὑπάρχει, ἐξ οὗ καὶ σωτῆρα ἀπεκδεχόμεθα κύριον Ἰησοῦν Χριστόν, ²¹ὃς μετασχηματίσει τὸ σῶμα τῆς ταπεινώσεως ἡμῶν σύμμορφον τῷ σώματι τῆς δόξης αὐτοῦ κατὰ τὴν ἐνέργειαν τοῦ δύνασθαι αὐτὸν καὶ ὑποτάξαι αὐτῷ τὰ πάντα. ⁴·¹Ὥστε, ἀδελφοί μου ἀγαπητοὶ καὶ ἐπιπόθητοι, χαρὰ καὶ στέφανός μου, οὕτως στήκετε ἐν κυρίῳ, ἀγαπητοί.

¹⁷Be fellow imitators of me, brothers and sisters, and observe those who live in the same manner; in this way you have us for an example. ¹⁸For many, whom I have spoken about to you many times, and even now I say it with tears, live as enemies of the cross of Christ; ¹⁹their end is destruction, their god is the belly, and their honor is in their shame; they are those whose minds are focused on the things of the earth. ²⁰For our commonwealth is in heaven, from which we eagerly await the savior, the Lord Jesus Christ, ²¹who will transform our body of humiliation, giving it the same form as his body of glory according to the divine power so that he also is able to subject all things to him. ⁴:¹Therefore, my loved and desired brothers and sisters, my joy and crown, in that way stand in the Lord, beloved.

Συμμιμηταί μου γίνεσθε–Συμμιμηταί (masc. nom. pl. ["one who imitates, follows an example") is the object of γίνεσθε (pres. mid./pass. [deponent] impv. 2 pl. of γίνομαι, "to be, become"). The noun συμμιμητής is a NT *hapax legomenon* and may be a word formed by Paul, as this is its only appearance in ancient Greek literature. The verb cognate is, however, found in Plato. Since the Philippians are being called on to imitate Paul (μου [masc. gen. sg.]), it cannot mean that they are to imitate *with* Paul (see Wallace, 130); rather, they as a church are to imitate Paul. Calls for imitation of the writer or speaker were common in ancient Greek hortatory material, so Paul is employing a well-known and highly respected admonitory device.

ἀδελφοί–The vocative probably introduces a slight break in the flow of thought, but 3:17–4:1 is intimately related to what has come just before it. On translating ἀδελφοί (masc. voc. pl.) as "brothers and sisters," see 1:12.

καὶ σκοπεῖτε τοὺς οὕτω περιπατοῦντας–A second imperative, σκοπεῖτε (pres. act. impv. 2 pl. of σκοπέω, "to pay careful attention to, notice" [see its cognate noun in v. 14]), is the main verb of this clause, with the participle περιπατοῦντας (pres. act. ptc. masc. acc. pl. of περιπατέω, "to live") serving as its object. The adverb οὕτω refers to the manner of life that Paul lives. Περιπατέω literally means "to walk about/around," but the NT often uses it to speak of the manner of one's life or the way one conducts one's life.

καθώς–This word probably functions here as it does elsewhere with οὕτω, correlatively. So it may be rendered something like "in this way" (see BDAG on οὕτω). The meaning is that the Philippians are to observe carefully those who live as Paul does and in that way continue to have Paul as a model (see O'Brien, 448–49).

ἔχετε τύπον ἡμᾶς–Fee (365, n. 14) notes that ἡμᾶς (acc. pl.) is an "editorial we," one of only a few in this letter. It is probably useless to try to identify precisely who is included in this "us" (e.g., only those mentioned in the salutation or all of Paul's associates). Paul probably has chiefly himself in mind, although the switch to the plural indicates that he is not limiting the reference to himself, especially since the singular would have fit more smoothly with τύπον (masc. acc. sg. ["model, pattern"]). This is another case of a double accusative with ἔχετε (pres. act. indic. 2 pl. of ἔχω, "to have").

3:18   πολλοὶ γὰρ περιπατοῦσιν–Περιπατοῦσιν is the pres. act. indic. 3 pl. of περιπατέω ("to live"). The πολλοὶ (masc. nom. pl. ["many"]) of whom Paul speaks have been the subject of much discussion. Interpreters have used the description that follows to identify them as those mentioned in 3:2–gnostic libertines, antinomians, perfectionists, and even docetists. It seems more probable, however, that the hortatory context renders all such identifications misguided. These characteristics are given as the contrast to the model that the Philippians have in Paul. These characteristics make explicit what they are not to be. We may infer that those whom Paul describes claim to be Christian because they are possible models for the Philippians.

οὓς πολλάκις ἔλεγον ὑμῖν—The relative pronoun οὓς governs the following clause and is the object of ἔλεγον (impf. act. indic. 1 sg. of λέγω, "to say, tell, speak"). The antecedent of this pronoun is πολλοί at the beginning of the verse. This is not the first time Paul has mentioned such people to the Philippians, but rather πολλάκις ("many times, often") ἔλεγον. The distinction between the Philippians (ὑμῖν [acc. pl.]) to whom Paul has spoken and those about whom (οὓς) he is talking may show that he does not see this latter group as a part of the Philippian congregation.

---

circumstantial participle of manner

The participle describes the manner in which the action of the main verb is accomplished. It is often translated *by* or *with*.

κλαίων λέγω
I tell you <u>with weeping</u> (Phil 3:18)
τρέμουσα ἦλθεν
she came <u>trembling</u> (Luke 8:47)

νῦν δὲ καὶ κλαίων λέγω—Paul repeats his former warning about such people now, using a **circumstantial participle of manner** to show greater emotion, κλαίων (pres. act. ptc. masc. nom. sg. of κλαίω, "to cry, weep"). It is often said that this emotion is expended on behalf of those whom Paul is describing, but it is perhaps more likely that he is concerned about the detrimental influence that such people could have on the Philippians or on the cause of the gospel.

τοὺς ἐχθροὺς τοῦ σταυροῦ τοῦ Χριστοῦ—The accusative τοὺς ἐχθροὺς (masc. acc. pl. ["enemy"]) is a direct object of περιπατοῦσιν. These are not simply people who opposed Paul or the Philippians; Paul identifies them as "enemies τοῦ σταυροῦ [masc. gen. sg.] τοῦ Χριστοῦ [masc. gen. sg.]." This is the only place this expression is found in the NT, but BDAG gives Acts 13:10 (entry for ἐχθρός), Eph 5:15, and 1 Thess 4:1 (entry for περιπατέω) as comparable constructions. With this reading, we translate the phrase "(they live) . . . as enemies of the cross." Alternatively, τοὺς ἐχθροὺς may be the object of ἔλεγον ("I have told you," or with this object, "whom I have identified as enemies of the cross"). Whichever verb we attach, we cannot identify anything about the theology of these people from this statement (e.g., they specifically reject the suffering of Jesus), because this is a polemical evaluation, perhaps even an accusation. That it was understood in this manner by early readings is seen in the strange insertion of βλέπετε by 𝔓⁴⁶. It is hard to understand how this insertion improves the syntax, as O'Brien (443) contends (see comments to the opposite effect in Fee, 362).

ὧν τὸ τέλος ἀπώλεια—The antecedent of the relative pronoun ὧν (masc. gen. pl.) is the plural τοὺς ἐχθρούς. Τὸ τέλος (neut. nom. sg. ["end, outcome, result"]) has the sense of "goal." Fee (370 n. 34) finds a play on words as Paul contrasts the τέλος of these people with uses of its cognates in vv. 12-16. The ἀπώλεια (fem. nom. sg. ["destruction"]) that Paul has in mind here is their ultimate destiny. Ἐστί is the understood verb of this relative clause.

3:19

ὧν ὁ θεὸς ἡ κοιλία—The relative pronoun here has the same antecedent and understood verb as in the previous clause. Again, the description is too vague and polemical to use as a way of identifying some specific teaching that such people advocate. It seems to be more of a broad accusation about their primary commitments; their god (θεὸς [masc. nom. sg.]) is lower things, the κοιλία (fem. nom. sg. ["belly"]). Just as the immediately preceding clause was an evaluation, so is this one.

καὶ ἡ δόξα ἐν τῇ αἰσχύνῃ αὐτῶν—This continuation of the relative clause may be a form of a proverb of that time (see Kennedy, 462). The linguistic evidence does not support understanding this expression to mean that they are proud of shameful things (as the TEV translates) or that they take delight in such things. The meaning of δόξα (fem. nom. sg.) as it is used here is "reputation" or "that for which they are held in honor" (see also TLNT 1:368 n. 38). So, since their only claim to honor is αἰσχύνη (fem. dat. sg. ["shame"]) αὐτῶν (masc. gen. pl.), they are wholly despicable, especially within a culture in which shame and honor were crucially important. Again, although many have used this expression to do so, we cannot characterize with any specificity those whom Paul is castigating with these words. Fee (373-74) successfully argues that it does not refer to circumcision.

οἱ τὰ ἐπίγεια φρονοῦντες—The substantival participle φρονοῦντες (pres. act. ptc. masc. nom. pl. of φρονέω, "to think, consider, hold an opinion") resumes the πολλοὶ of v. 18. Whereas the two relative clauses modified "enemies of the cross," this description stands somewhat separate, even as it speaks of the same people. Use of τὰ ἐπίγεια (neut. acc. pl. ["earthly"]) as the object of φρονοῦντες sets up the contrast that comes in the next verse.

3:20   **ἡμῶν γὰρ τὸ πολίτευμα**—Πολίτευμα (neut. nom. sg.) is a NT *hapax legomenon*. Translators render this noun "citizenship" (NIV, NRSV) and "commonwealth" (RSV). Spicq asserts that its basic meaning is "an organization of citizens from the same place . . . in the midst of a foreign state" (TLNT 3:130). This seems an apt description of the community, especially since Paul is in the middle of contrasting the earthly (v. 19) and the heavenly (v. 20). This is also a particularly appropriate word to use when writing to Philippi because a colony of veterans was sometimes called a πολίτευμα, and associations of veterans were often called πολιτεύματα. Such associations were present and well-known in Philippi. However, since their πολίτευμα is in heaven, in this verse the word seems to refer to the place of their true allegiance; thus "commonwealth" is probably the best translation. The γὰρ probably goes back to the exhortation to imitate Paul and those who live as he does in v. 17. Lexically, γάρ does not have an adversative sense. Despite this, the RSV, NIV, and NRSV translate it as "but" here. This rendering misses the connection that this sentence has with its broader context. Beginning the sentence with ἡμῶν, however, makes the pronoun emphatic (BDF §284) and thus highlights the sharp distinction Paul makes between those described in vv. 18-19 and those to whom this pronoun refers, including at least the Philippian recipients of the letter and Paul and his company. Based on style, rhythmic patterns, and vocabulary similar to that of the hymnic material in 2:6-11, some interpreters identify vv. 20-21 as hymnic material.

ἐν οὐρανοῖς ὑπάρχει–Paul perhaps uses ὑπάρχει (pres. act. indic. 3 sg. of ὑπάρχω, "to exist, be present") rather than ἐστί ("is") to emphasize the reality of the existence of the alternative πολίτευμα. Given the cosmology of the time, the plural οὐρανοῖς (masc. dat. pl. ["heaven"]) is not unexpected.

ἐξ οὗ–Identifying the antecedent of this singular genitive relative pronoun is something of a problem because οὐρανοῖς is plural and seems the most likely candidate. Some identify οὗ as neuter rather than masculine and so find πολίτευμα as its antecedent. Despite the difference in number, οὐρανοῖς makes the best sense of the passage. Paul refers to heaven in both the singular and the plural, so such a reference does not violate his patterns of usage. In addition, such constructions are not unknown (see BDF §§134, 296, with reference to relatives), even in Philippians (see 2:15, where the noun is singular and the relative pronoun is plural).

καὶ σωτῆρα ἀπεκδεχόμεθα κύριον Ἰησοῦν Χριστόν–Ἀπεκδεχόμεθα is the pres. mid./pass. (deponent) indic. 1 pl. of ἀπεκδέχομαι ("to await eagerly"), a verb that is fairly rare. It appears only eight times in the NT, only two of which are outside of Paul's writings (Heb 9:28; 1 Pet 3:20). Fee (380 n. 22) asserts that its use in Paul's writings is its first extant use, and probably it was coined by Paul or another early Christian to express eagerness for the coming of the Parousia. Many interpreters note that adding ἀπό as a prefix intensifies the meaning of expectation. This expectation is directed toward σωτῆρα (masc. acc. sg. ["savior, one who rescues"]). This word is not as common in the NT as one might expect. It appears only twenty-four times, ten of which are in the Pastoral Epistles. In some of these places the term refers to God; in others it refers to Christ. Here it clearly applies to Christ. The fact that σωτῆρα is anarthrous leads some to translate "a savior," which is then specified with the nouns following the verb. Others assert that it increases the emphatic force of σωτῆρα even beyond its placement before the verb. In any case, κύριον Ἰησοῦν Χριστόν stands in apposition to σωτῆρα.

ὃς μετασχηματίσει–Μετασχηματίσει is the fut. act. indic. 3 sg. of μετασχηματίζω ("to change, transform"), a verb used only by Paul in NT. Here it means "to transform," although it has a somewhat different meaning when Paul uses it in the only other two places we find it, 1 Cor 4 and 2 Cor 11. The relative pronoun ὅς (masc. nom. sg.) refers back to the whole of the object of ἀπεκδεχόμεθα.

3:21

τὸ σῶμα τῆς ταπεινώσεως ἡμῶν–As always for Paul, τὸ σῶμα (neut. acc. sg. ["body"]) will be transformed or changed, not done away with. In this context, this change is that which takes place at the Parousia. The singular here serves as a collective, since the plural ἡμῶν seems to attach to it. The NIV translates τῆς ταπεινώσεως (fem. gen. sg. ["humiliation"]) as "lowly" and thus the phrase as "our lowly bodies." Most interpreters reject this interpretation of the meaning of this expression, in part because its function in this context is to be the contrast to the following τῷ σώματι τῆς δόξης αὐτοῦ. Thus the humiliation is perhaps a reference to mortality or, more likely, to the present body as the means by which we presently experience suffering and weakness. So perhaps it is what Wallace (127–30) calls a **genitive of reference** or of association.

> **genitive of reference**
>
> The use of the genitive case to further specify something about the modified noun.
>
> τὸ σῶμα <u>τῆς ταπεινώσεως</u> ἡμῶν
> *the body <u>that endures humiliation</u>*
> (Phil 3:21)
>
> ἄξιον <u>τῆς μετανοίας</u>
> *worthy <u>of repentance</u>* (Matt 3:8)

σύμμορφον τῷ σώματι τῆς δόξης αὐτοῦ–The adjective σύμμορφον (neut. acc. sg. ["similar in form, like"]) probably stands in apposition with the previous τὸ σῶμα. The difficulty experienced in finding its place grammatically is evidenced by the textual variant εἰς τὸ γενέσθαι αὐτὸ. This attempt to smooth out the difficult syntax is clearly not the original reading, because the longer reading is found only in later manuscripts (e.g., a corrector of D, Ψ, the Majority Text), and because the current text is the more difficult reading. The reading adopted here is found in א, A, B, and D, among many other witnesses. In the NT σύμμορφον is found only here and in Rom 8:29 (another passage dealing with eschatology). Τῷ σώματι (masc. dat. sg. ["body"]) is a dative of accompaniment or association of the sort sometimes found with compounds with σύν (BDF §194[2]). BDF (§165) identifies both τῆς ταπεινώσεως (fem. gen. sg. ["humble state, humiliation"]) and τῆς δόξης (fem. gen. sg. ["glory"]) as **genitives of quality** (see also Wallace, 87). However, as noted above, perhaps a genitive of reference fits the context better. Since the two phrases are parallel, a translation should try to keep that parallel apparent. The expressions "body of humiliation" and "body of glory" seem to achieve this. Just as the body is the means through which our humiliation is experienced, so also Christ's resurrected body is the means through which his glory is seen and experienced. It is his body that models the coming existence for Christians.

> **genitive of quality**
>
> The use of the genitive to describe a quality or characteristic of the noun it modifies.
>
> ἐκ τοῦ μαμωνᾶ <u>τῆς ἀδικίας</u>
> *from the mammon <u>of unrighteousness</u>*
> (i.e., unrighteous mammon)
> (Luke 16:9)
>
> τὸ σῶμα <u>τῆς ἁμαρτίας</u>
> *the body <u>characterized by sin</u>* (Rom 6:6)

κατὰ τὴν ἐνέργειαν τοῦ δύνασθαι αὐτὸν– The pronoun αὐτὸν (masc. acc. sg.) is the subject of the articular infinitive τοῦ δύνασθαι, and its antecedent is Christ. The NIV and NRSV translate κατά with "by" here, thus giving it an instrumental sense, but this is not a sense in which κατά is used. Rather, its sense is "according to," referring to the norm by which our bodies are transformed (see BDAG). Τὴν ἐνέργειαν (fem. acc. sg. ["working"]) is found only in the Pauline corpus in the NT, and in all those instances ἐνέργεια refers to divine power. This noun is the object of κατά. Δύνασθαι is the pres. mid. [deponent] inf. of δύναμαι ("to be able, capable"). In the NT the genitive articular infinitive sometimes has a consecutive sense ("so that") that approaches the meaning of a ἵνα (BDF §400; Kennedy, 464), and this seems to be the sense of τοῦ δύνασθαι here.

καὶ ὑποτάξαι αὐτῷ τὰ πάντα—The pronoun πάντα (neut. acc. pl. ["each, every"; plural, "all"]) is the object of ὑποτάξαι (aor. act. inf. of ὑποτάσσω, "to subject, subordinate") and stands for the whole of the cosmos. Ὑποτάξαι is a complement to τοῦ δύνασθαι. There has been discussion about whether the breathing mark of αὐτῷ (masc. dat. sg.) should be rough or smooth. A smooth breathing mark makes it the simple pronoun "he," while a rough breathing mark makes it the contracted form of the reflexive pronoun "himself." Of course, the accents were not present in the earliest texts, so such marks are later interpretations. However, correctors of ℵ and D, along with other manuscripts, felt the difficulty of having αὐτῷ and so changed it to the reflexive ἑαυτῷ. BDF (§283) asserts that much of the work of reflexives had been taken over by the simple personal pronouns by the time of the NT. Thus, determining whether this pronoun is simple or reflexive becomes more a matter of context and Paul's theology than of grammar alone. Since ἐνέργεια is always used by Paul to refer to divine power, having God as the antecedent of αὐτῷ is not as difficult as it might otherwise be. This statement would then be consistent with Paul's statements in 1 Cor 15 (especially v. 27 there, which alludes to Ps 8:6, as this verse in Philippians seems to do). However, most interpreters find a more christocentric focus here and so treat αὐτῷ as a reflexive.

Ὥστε—This conjunction makes a connection between the foregoing eschatological affirmations and the exhortation found in this sentence. There is some question about the boundaries of this passage. Phil 4:1 may introduce a section that runs through v. 9 or that includes only vv. 1-3, the exhortation to Euodia and Syntyche. Alternatively, it may serve as the conclusion to the preceding section. This arrangement follows a pattern sometimes found in Paul of concluding a section on eschatology with exhortation (e.g., 1 Thess 4:18; 5:11). If this verse is more closely related to the end of ch. 3, it is not without connection to the various exhortations that follow.

4:1

ἀδελφοί μου ἀγαπητοὶ καὶ ἐπιπόθητοι—This series of masculine plural vocative nouns beginning with ἀδελφοί signals Paul's affection for the Philippians. They are used as collectives and thus are intended to refer to all the Philippian Christians, not just the males. The adjectives ἀγαπητοί (masc. nom. pl. "loved, beloved") and ἐπιπόθητοι (masc. nom. pl. "longed for, desired") are either used as substantives or are simply attributive; there is no real difference in meaning. More balance is brought to the phrase if these adjectives have a parallel function rather than having the first one more closely joined to ἀδελφοί. The pronoun μου (gen. sg.) seems more closely attached to ἀδελφοί, but it may attach to all three substantives.

χαρὰ καὶ στέφανός μου—These two vocative nouns are singular and thus obviously collective. These words have an eschatological orientation that ties this verse to those that precede it. In its literal uses στέφανος ("crown") is the wreath given to the victors of athletic contests and holders of certain offices. In early Christian literature it came to stand for eschatological rewards (1 Cor 9:25), and in Revelation it is a symbol of the high status/office of some heavenly beings (Rev 4:4). In 1 Thess 2:19 it refers to Paul's converts, as it does here. So it seems that the χαρὰ ("joy") Paul has in view is that which he will experience on the last day.

οὕτως στήκετε ἐν κυρίῳ—Only now does Paul give the exhortation, στήκετε (pres. act. impv. 2 pl. of στήκω, "to stand, be steadfast"). According to BDAG, the verb στήκω is first found in the NT. It is a new verb formed from the perfect of ἵστημι. Interpreters have suggested that the adverb οὕτως links this command to Paul's example in 2:17, to all of ch. 2, or to what follows. This last suggestion is the least likely, given the common usage of οὕτως, which is to link what follows to material that immediately preceded it. Given the ὥστε that begins this sentence, the emphasis seems to be on 2:17-21—that is, Paul's example and the eschatological perspective and hope given in those verses. The prepositional phrase ἐν κυρίῳ (masc. dat. sg. ["Lord"]) designates the sphere in which they are to locate themselves and to strive to remain.

ἀγαπητοί—This final vocative plural noun renews the sense of Paul's extraordinary affection for the Philippians. It is also an excellent rhetorical transition to dealing with specific problems in the following verses. A few, mostly Western manuscripts omit this word, perhaps seeing it as redundant. Retaining the word in the text is almost certainly correct, since there would be no reason to add it if it were not present, and since the manuscript evidence overwhelming favors it. B adds μου after ἀγαπητοί ("loved, beloved"), perhaps through assimilation to the initial vocative of the sentence; but again, this is clearly not the earlier reading.

4:2-3 Exhortation to Euodia and Syntyche for Unity

²Εὐοδίαν παρακαλῶ καὶ Συντύχην παρακαλῶ τὸ αὐτὸ φρονεῖν ἐν κυρίῳ. ³ναὶ ἐρωτῶ καὶ σέ, γνήσιε σύζυγε, συλλαμβάνου αὐταῖς, αἵτινες ἐν τῷ εὐαγγελίῳ συνήθλησάν μοι μετὰ καὶ Κλήμεντος καὶ τῶν λοιπῶν συνεργῶν μου, ὧν τὰ ὀνόματα ἐν βίβλῳ ζωῆς.

²I beseech Euodia and I beseech Syntyche to think the same thing in the Lord. ³And in fact, I ask you, genuine yokefellow, to help them because they are among those who struggled together for the gospel with me and with both Clement and the rest of my co-workers, whose names are written in the Book of Life.

Εὐοδίαν παρακαλῶ–Παρακαλῶ (pres. act. indic. 1 sg. of παρακαλέω, "to be- **4:2** seech, implore, encourage") often appears in Paul's hortatory sections. It is un- usual to find it directed to single individuals, as in this instance, rather than to the church as a whole, or at least to a segment of the community. Εὐοδία seems to have been a leader in the Philippian congregation. For comments on the unusual phenomenon of Paul giving the name of someone who is being corrected, see Fee, 389-90. Calling her by name indicates, at least, that Paul does not consider her an opponent.

καὶ Συντύχην παρακαλῶ–Paul repeats the verb παρακαλῶ and thus com- poses a precisely parallel phrase here, perhaps to be certain that he treats these women equally. There is no information about the conflict between Εὐοδία and Συντύχη. Some have thought that their disagreement was a large part of the reason for the writing of Philippians, and that perhaps they were leaders of groups within the Philippian congregation between which there were signifi- cant tensions.

τὸ αὐτὸ φρονεῖν–The pronoun αὐτό (neut. acc. sg.) serves as the object of the in- finitive φρονεῖν (pres. act. inf. of φρονέω, "to think"). Αὐτός appears with φρονέω two other times in Philippians (2:2; 3:16). Including those uses, φρονέω is used eleven times in Philippians. It is used only twenty-six times in the undis- puted Paulines (twenty-eight in the whole corpus). The only other similar concen- tration in its use is in Rom 12 and 14. It appears a total of eight times in those chapters. Thus this verb and its use in this phrase probably point us to an impor- tant part of the message of Philippians. So the problem between these two leaders may be the cause of the lack of unity that Paul addresses in this letter. (For further comments on φρονέω see 2:2.)

ἐν κυρίῳ–Some interpreters take this phrase, which modifies the previous three words, to mean that these women are to have the same attitude as that seen in the hymnic material in ch. 2. Others think that it means that they are to come to agreement because they recognize their common membership in Christ. This in- terpretive matter cannot be resolved on the basis of grammar or syntax. However, ἐν κυρίῳ (masc. dat. sg. ["Lord"]) at least designates the sphere in which they are to work toward better relations.

ναὶ ἐρωτῶ καὶ σέ–Since the pronoun σέ (acc. sg.) is singular, this request is di- **4:3** rected to the person mentioned next in the text, not the two women previously named. The Textus Receptus replaces ναὶ, the affirmative particle, with καὶ; however, since all other manuscript families read ναὶ, it is fairly certain that ναὶ is the correct reading. Its presence with the following καὶ gives a certain urgency to this matter. Here it is rendered "in fact" to give expression to that sense of urgency. The καὶ that follows ἐρωτῶ (pres. act. indic. 1 sg. of ἐρωτάω, "to ask") probably has more of an adverbial force ("also") than simply a copulative force ("and").

γνήσιε σύζυγε—Interpreters have ventured many a guess about the identity of this σύζυγε (masc. voc. sg. ["yokefellow, comrade"]). Some have even suggested that this is Paul's wife because σύζυγος is often used of wives. However, it is commonly also used more broadly of comrades. Others have asserted that this is a proper name. As of now, however, there are no extant examples of such a use. It seems more likely that Paul has returned to his usual habit of not referring to people by name. The adjective γνήσιε (masc. voc. sg.) should be rendered by its basic meaning "true" or "genuine" (so in the RSV) rather than "loyal," as the NIV and NRSV translate it. The point here is not that the addressee is loyal to Paul, but that this person may truly perform the task at hand. Σύζυγε is the first of four words with συν prefixes in this verse. This seems to emphasize the importance of these women coming together.

συλλαμβάνου αὐταῖς—Συλλαμβάνου, the pres. mid. impv. 2 sg. of συλλαμβάνω, can in the middle voice mean "to aid" or "to help" (BDAG), and that is the sense here. For help in understanding the difficult task that Paul has set out for this genuine yokefellow who is to aid these women (αὐταῖς [fem. acc. pl.]), see P. Marshall, *Enmity in Corinth: Social Conventions in Paul's Relations with the Corinthians*, 40–47.

αἵτινες ἐν τῷ εὐαγγελίῳ συνήθλησάν—The antecedent of αἵτινες (fem. nom. pl. of ὅστις) includes the two women of v. 2. This pronoun may simply substitute for ὅς or it may emphasize that something or someone possesses certain characteristics or belongs in a certain class. The latter usage seems more likely here because Paul specifies what sort of people they are in the words that follow. This pronoun is the subject of συνήθλησάν (aor. act. indic. 3 pl. of συναθλέω, "to contend, struggle along with"). The prepositional phrase ἐν τῷ εὐαγγελίῳ (neut. dat. sg. ["gospel"]) may designate the sphere in which they struggled together (Vincent, 132), or it may be instrumental, indicating that for which they struggled (see BDF §219[2]). Loh and Nida (126) render the phrase "to spread the gospel," which makes this latter meaning clearer.

μοι μετὰ καὶ Κλήμεντος καὶ τῶν λοιπῶν συνεργῶν μου—Using μου (masc. gen. sg.) within the prepositional phrase that begins with μετὰ and referring to himself (μοι [masc. dat. sg.]) before and outside that phrase, Paul seems to make a significant distinction between his co-workers, συνεργῶν (masc. gen. pl.), and himself. BDF (§442[13]) identifies the first καὶ in this phrase as **pleonastic**, although it may function to help set off Κλήμεντος (masc. gen. sg. ["Clement"]) from τῶν λοιπῶν (masc. gen. pl. ["others, rest of"]) and so be translated "both."

> **pleonasm, pleonastic**
>
> The use of more words than are necessary to convey an idea, often for greater emphasis or clarity.
>
> εἰς πᾶν πλοῦτος τῆς πληροφορίας τῆς συνέσεως, εἰς ἐπίγνωσιν τοῦ μυστηρίου τοῦ θεοῦ
>
> *to all the wealth of the fullness of understanding, to the knowledge of the mystery of God (Col 2:2)*
>
> τὸ πλήρωμα τοῦ τὰ πάντα ἐν πᾶσιν πληρουμένου
>
> *the fullness of the one who fills everything in every way (Eph 1:23)*

We have no information about this Clement or why Paul singles him out from his other co-workers at Philippi. The tradition of identifying him with Clement of Rome (which began at least as early as Origen) has no good evidence to support it. The original hand of ℵ and 𝔓¹⁶ (third/fourth century) have καὶ συνεργῶν μου καὶ τῶν λοιπῶν (i.e., "my fellow-workers and the others") after the name of Clement. This reading does not have enough support to challenge that found in 𝔓⁴⁶, ℵ's corrector, A, B, and D, among others. So the accepted reading is found in several families of manuscripts. Moreover, there would be little reason for a scribe to change the text to the less inclusive reading accepted here.

ὧν τὰ ὀνόματα ἐν βίβλῳ ζωῆς—The relative pronoun ὧν (masc. gen. pl.) governs all of this phrase. Grammatically, its antecedent includes Clement and the other co-workers, but Paul may intend those whose τὰ ὀνόματα (neut. nom. pl. ["name"]) are recorded to include Euodia and Syntyche as well. Reference to the βίβλῳ (fem. dat. sg. ["book"]) ζωῆς (fem. gen. sg. ["life"]) puts this matter in an eschatological perspective. This image is known from apocalyptic writings (e.g., 1 En 47:3; 90:20). This very expression is found four times in Revelation (Rev 3:5; 13:8; 20:15; 22:19; elsewhere in Revelation the noun βιβλίον is used rather than βίβλος), but nowhere else in the NT except here. It signals that they are participants in the eschatological blessings, and more specifically it is a metaphor for judgment. Use of this metaphor shows that even in a discussion such as the one here in Philippians, Paul always thinks within an apocalyptic framework. Since no verb is expressed, one should supply ἐστί (singular since a neuter plural subject normally takes a singular verb).

4:4-7 Exhortation to Eschatological Preparedness

⁴Χαίρετε ἐν κυρίῳ πάντοτε· πάλιν ἐρῶ, χαίρετε. ⁵τὸ ἐπιεικὲς ὑμῶν γνωσθήτω πᾶσιν ἀνθρώποις. ὁ κύριος ἐγγύς. ⁶μηδὲν μεριμνᾶτε, ἀλλ' ἐν παντὶ τῇ προσευχῇ καὶ τῇ δεήσει μετὰ εὐχαριστίας τὰ αἰτήματα ὑμῶν γνωριζέσθω πρὸς τὸν θεόν. ⁷καὶ ἡ εἰρήνη τοῦ θεοῦ ἡ ὑπερέχουσα πάντα νοῦν φρουρήσει τὰς καρδίας ὑμῶν καὶ τὰ νοήματα ὑμῶν ἐν Χριστῷ Ἰησοῦ.

⁴Rejoice in the Lord always. Again I say, Rejoice! ⁵Let your kindness be known to all people. The Lord is near. ⁶Do not be overly concerned about anything, but let your requests about everything be made known to God through prayers and requests made with thanksgiving. ⁷So the peace of God that surpasses all understanding will guard your hearts and your minds in Christ Jesus.

Χαίρετε ἐν κυρίῳ πάντοτε—Although Goodspeed translates χαίρετε (pres. act. impv. 2 pl. of χαίρω, "rejoice, be glad") as a farewell greeting, this seems rather unlikely because it is modified by πάντοτε ("always"). Additionally, its repetition immediately following makes little sense if it is a farewell greeting. Ἐν κυρίῳ

4:4

(masc. dat. sg. ["Lord"]) may designate the object of their rejoicing or the sphere within which their rejoicing takes place. Perhaps these should not be separated. This short statement, a complete sentence in itself, begins a series of short imperatival statements with no grammatical connection made between them— that is, in asyndeton. Such brief exhortations often appear at the end of Paul's letters. The larger context (verses 4–6) also provides an example of **parataxis,** the connection of a series of coordinate clauses or sentences with conjunctions or other connectives rather than using subordination to creare more complex sentences. Wallace (525) identifies the present-tense verbs in these sentences as **gnomic**— that is, giving a general precept. Understood in this way, they are sometimes used as evidence that 4:10–20 is part of a separate letter; however, their presence here may grow out of the exhortations that Paul issues with respect to the conflict between Euodia and Syntyche. The encouragement to rejoice makes an excellent contrast to the disagreement that they have been having, and it follows well the assertion of their place in the Book of Life.

> **parataxis**
>
> The practice of connecting one or more simple sentences with conjunctions or other connectives rather than creating more complex sentences with subordinate clauses.
>
> ἦν δὲ ὥρα τρίτη καὶ ἐσταύρωσαν αὐτόν.
>
> *And it was the third hour. And they crucified him.* (Mark 15:25)
>
> οὐ γὰρ ἔστιν ἐξουσία εἰ μὴ ὑπὸ θεοῦ, αἱ δὲ οὖσαι ὑπὸ θεοῦ τεταγμέναι εἰσίν
>
> *For no authority exists unless [it is] from God. And those that exist are appointed by God.* (Rom 13:1)

> **gnomic expression**
>
> An expression stating what is generally known to be the case.
>
> Φθείρουσιν ἤθη χρηστὰ ὁμιλίαι κακαί.
>
> *Evil associates corrupt good morals.* (1 Cor 15:33)
>
> ἱλαρὸν δότην ἀγαπᾷ ὁ θεός.
>
> *God loves a cheerful giver.* (2 Cor 9:7)

πάλιν ἐρῶ, χαίρετε—When Paul explicitly repeats χαίρετε (pres. act. impv. 2 pl. of χαίρω) and makes note of the repetition with πάλιν (adverb ["again"]) ἐρῶ (fut. act. indic. 1 sg. of εἶπον, "to say, tell"), he emphasizes yet again this common theme of Philippians.

4:5   **τὸ ἐπιεικὲς ὑμῶν γνωσθήτω πᾶσιν ἀνθρώποις**—Paul's choice of the passive imperative γνωσθήτω (aor. pass. impv. 3 sg. of γινώσκω, "to know"), in contrast to an active sense such as "show kindness," is interesting. Perhaps it indicates that he wants or expects this characteristic to be part of the Philippians' nature as Christians. This does not, however, weaken the imperatival force; Paul makes this a command (see Wallace, 486). The adjective ἐπιεικὲς (neut. nom. sg. ["gentleness"]) is used as a substantive here, as it is by other writers of the period. However, it appears only here in the undisputed Paulines, although it is found in the Pastoral Epistles (1 Tim 3:3; Titus 3:2). The only other NT occurrences are in Jas 3:17; 1 Pet 2:18. The cognate noun ἐπιείκεια is also rare in the NT, being found only in Acts 24:4; 2 Cor 10:1.

ὁ κύριος ἐγγύς—The understood verb of this statement is again ἐστί. This assertion of the nearness (ἐγγύς) of the Parousia seems to stand as a broad sanction for the various exhortations that both precede and follow it. This statement returns us to the eschatological outlook alluded to in 3:3, and so all the exhortations are given with the Parousia in view. Since this is the case, ὁ κύριος (masc. nom. sg.) clearly refers to Christ here.

μηδὲν μεριμνᾶτε–Given that Paul is in prison as he writes this, this exhortation to be overly anxious (μεριμνᾶτε [pres. act. impv. 2 pl. of μεριμνάω]) about nothing (μηδὲν [neut. acc. sg.]) should carry special weight. Perhaps its placement immediately after the reminder (and perhaps warning) that the Lord is near is intended to give a perspective from which to view any difficulties that one encounters.   4:6

ἀλλ᾽ ἐν παντὶ τῇ προσευχῇ –Παντὶ (neut. dat. sg.) is the opposite of the μηδὲν of the previous verse. This phrase and what follows in the rest of the verse give another sort of reason why the Philippians should not be overly concerned about anything. Not only is the Parousia certain, but also God is available in the present. The differing genders of παντὶ and προσευχῇ (fem. dat. sg. ["prayer"]) show that ἐν παντὶ should not be attached to the following words so that the phrase means "every kind of prayer" (see Fee, 408 n. 41); rather, παντί stands as the substantive "everything." Προσευχῇ is a dative of means: "by prayer."

καὶ τῇ δεήσει μετὰ εὐχαριστίας–Δεήσει is the fem. dat. sg. of δέησις, a less broad term than προσευχή. Δέησις refers to supplication or humble pleading, while προσευχή includes other ways of addressing God. Δέησις is found four times in Philippians (1:4 [twice]; 1:19; 4:6) and only three other times in the undisputed Paulines (Rom 10:1; 2 Cor 1:11; 9:14). Like προσευχή, δεήσει is a dative of means. In a letter that urges people to rejoice, it is not surprising that these prayers and pleadings are to be accompanied by thanksgiving (εὐχαριστίας [fem. gen. sg.]).

τὰ αἰτήματα ὑμῶν γνωριζέσθω πρὸς τὸν θεόν–The passive γνωριζέσθω (pres. pass. impv. 3 sg. of γνωρίζω, "to make known") may be parallel to that in v. 5, where the same verb is used in the passive. But here, rather than making something known to humans, the Philippians are to make requests known to God (τὸν θεόν [masc. acc. sg.]). Τὰ αἰτήματα (neut. nom. pl. ["request"]) can take the singular verb because it is a neuter plural. This is the only time αἴτημα appears in the Pauline corpus, and it appears elsewhere in the NT only in Luke 23:24; 1 John 5:15.

καὶ ἡ εἰρήνη τοῦ θεοῦ–The sentence that begins v. 7 is unusual in that it begins with καί, a construction rather uncommon in Paul. As it sometimes does, καί here seems to denote a result (see BDF §442[3]; BDAG). Thus the result of requests being known to God is εἰρήνη (fem. nom. sg. ["peace"]). Wallace (105-6) identifies τοῦ θεοῦ (masc. gen. sg. ["God"]) as a genitive of production, which seems rather similar to a genitive of source (see the distinction that Wallace [106]   4:7

draws with reference to this passage). The type of genitive that one identifies in this place depends on whether the emphasis of the passage is on the idea that this peace is produced by God (in the person) or has God as its source (i.e., it comes from God). There is little difference in the meaning. A few late witnesses (A, t [eleventh century], some Vulgate manuscripts, and a marginal note in a Syriac text) have changed θεοῦ to Χριστοῦ. Perhaps this was done to make it similar to Col 3:15 or for a liturgical setting.

> ### attributive (adjectival) participle
>
> A participle that stands in the attributive position, modifying a noun, often translated with a relative clause
>
> Ἰησοῦς <u>ὁ λεγόμενος</u> Ἰοῦστος
> *Jesus <u>who is called</u> Justus* (Col 4:11)
>
> τὴν <u>ἡτοιμασμένην</u> ὑμῖν βασιλείαν
> *the kingdom <u>prepared</u> for you* (Matt 25:34)

ἡ ὑπερέχουσα πάντα νοῦν–Νοῦν, the masc. acc. sg. of νοῦς, means either "the mind" or "understanding." The participle, ὑπερέχουσα (pres. act. ptc. fem. nom. sg. of ὑπερέχω, "to excel, surpass"), functions as an adjective standing in the **attributive** position with, and so modifying, εἰρήνη and at the same time has νοῦν as an object. Πάντα (masc. acc. sg.) modifies νοῦν so that the peace "surpasses all understanding."

φρουρήσει–Perhaps Paul uses φρουρήσει (fut. act. indic. 3 sg. of φρουρέω, "to guard") to express what the peace of God will do for them because of the circumstances in which he finds himself. However, he is not the only person to use this verb in a metaphorical sense (see BDAG).

τὰς καρδίας ὑμῶν καὶ τὰ νοήματα ὑμῶν–Νοήματα, the neut. acc. pl. of νόημα ("thought"), appears in the NT only in Paul's writings (here and five times in 2 Corinthians). When Paul gives τὰ νοήματα and τὰς καρδίας (fem. acc. pl. ["heart"]) as the objects of φρουρήσει, he may intend to distinguish between thinking processes and emotions. A few later manuscripts (e.g., 263 [thirteenth century]), some Vulgate manuscripts and lectionaries, and a few church fathers omit καὶ τὰ νοήματα ὑμῶν (gen. pl.). Perhaps it was overlooked through **homeoteleuton.** F and G (both ninth century) along with some Old Latin manuscripts substitute σώματα (neut. gen. pl. ["body"]). 𝔓16 (third/fourth century) combines the two readings so that it has καὶ τὰ σώματα after νοήματα; however, the overwhelming early evidence, including 𝔓46, ℵ, A, B, and D, is for the reading in the text.

> ### homeoteleuton
>
> A common mistake in copying in which a copyist omits a phrase or line because the eye jumps to an ending similar to that of the preceding line or phrase.
>
> οὐκ ἐρωτῶ ἵνα <u>ἄρῃς αὐτοὺς</u> [ἐκ τοῦ κόσμου, ἀλλ' ἵνα <u>τηρήσῃς αὐτοὺς</u>] ἐκ τοῦ πονηροῦ.
> I do not ask that you <u>take them</u> [out of the world, but that you <u>keep them</u>] from the evil one. (John 17:15)

ἐν Χριστῷ Ἰησοῦ–This prepositional phrase, with both nouns being dative singular, designates the sphere in which the Philippians experience the peace of God. 𝔓46 is alone in having κυρίῳ instead of Χριστῷ here.

4:8-9 Exhortation to Virtue

⁸Τὸ λοιπόν, ἀδελφοί, ὅσα ἐστὶν ἀληθῆ, ὅσα σεμνά, ὅσα δίκαια, ὅσα ἀγνά, ὅσα προσφιλῆ, ὅσα εὔφημα, εἴ τις ἀρετὴ καὶ εἴ τις ἔπαινος, ταῦτα λογίζεσθε· ⁹ἃ καὶ ἐμάθετε καὶ παρελάβετε καὶ ἠκούσατε καὶ εἴδετε ἐν ἐμοί, ταῦτα πράσσετε· καὶ ὁ θεὸς τῆς εἰρήνης ἔσται μεθ᾽ ὑμῶν.

⁸Finally, brothers and sisters, whatever is true, whatever is revered, whatever is just, whatever is holy, whatever announces the good, if there is any virtue and if any praise, consider these things. ⁹And those things you learned and received and heard and saw in me, practice them so that the God of peace will be with you.

Τὸ λοιπόν, ἀδελφοί–On the vocative ἀδελφοί (masc. voc. pl.), see 1:12. On τὸ λοιπόν (neut. acc. sg.), see 3:1. Here, however, there may be more justification for thinking that it is drawing this letter to a conclusion because the rest of this sentence reads more like a summary than a new topic.   **4:8**

ὅσα ἐστὶν ἀληθῆ–Ἀληθῆ (neut. nom. pl. ["true"]) is a predicate nominative. This clause sets the pattern for the following list of characteristics. Since ὅσα ("as many as, all that") is neuter nominative plural, it takes a singular verb, ἐστὶν (pres. act. indic. 3 sg. of εἰμί, "to be"). The ἐστὶν in this clause serves as the unexpressed verb for the other members of the list that this clause begins. The word ἀληθής is not as common in the NT as one might expect, appearing only three other times in the Pauline corpus. However, it appears relatively often in the Johannine materials (fourteen times in the Gospel of John, twice in 1 John, and once in 3 John). Perhaps this indicates that claiming to possess true doctrine was more pronounced in the Johannine community than in the Pauline communities.

ὅσα σεμνά–The substantivized predicate adjective σεμνά (neut. nom. pl. of σεμνός) is a *hapax legomenon* for the undisputed Paulines and is found elsewhere in the NT only in 1 Tim 3:8, 11; Titus 2:2. In those places it is one of the requirements of church leaders and their wives. Foerster suggests that it be rendered "serious" or "worthy" in its appearances in the Pastoral Epistles (*TDNT* 7:195; similarly BDAG); however, its meaning in broader usage is "revered," "august," or "holy." It could be applied to gods, humans, or even things. Paul seems to use it as an abstract quality that one may contemplate here.

ὅσα δίκαια–The predicate adjective δίκαια (neut. nom. pl. of δίκαιος) has a range of meanings that includes "fitting," "good," "observant of duties" (to gods or humans), and "righteous," as well as "just." Among other places, Paul uses it in Rom 3:10 to describe God and in Rom 7:12 to describe the commandments of the law.

ὅσα ἀγνά–The predicate adjective ἀγνά (neut. nom. pl. of ἀγνός ["holy, pure"]) is used by Paul elsewhere in 2 Cor 7:11; 11:2. Its other NT occurrences are in

1 Tim 5:22; Titus 2:5; Jas 3:17; 1 Pet 3:2; 1 John 3:3. The more common adjective that is derived from the same verb is ἅγιος. In its NT uses ἁγνός refers to chastity, purity, and moral uprightness.

ὅσα προσφιλῆ–The predicate adjective προσφιλῆ (neut. nom. pl. of προσφιλής ["pleasing, lovely, amiable"]) is a NT *hapax legomenon*.

ὅσα εὔφημα–The final predicate adjective of this list, εὔφημα (neut. nom. pl. of εὔφημος ["worthy of praise"]), is another NT *hapax legomenon*. In other religious contexts this adjective means that one utters words of good omen and abstains from their opposite; thus it sometimes indicates religious silence. It often refers to good-sounding or auspicious words (LSJ). It is from this meaning of εὔφημος that we derive the word "euphemism." The list that ends with this word contains many terms used by moralists of the first century. Since it contains so many words that Paul does not use elsewhere or uses very seldom, it may be that Paul has included a preformed list here.

εἴ τις ἀρετὴ καὶ εἴ τις ἔπαινος–This is the two-part protasis of a present conditional sentence, with the present indicative verb ἐστί understood. See the comments of Fee (416 n. 13), rejecting the idea that ἀρετὴ (fem. nom. sg. ["virtue"]) and ἔπαινος (masc. nom. sg. ["praise"]) summarize the preceding list. If it is correct that the understood verb is a present indicative, then this protasis affirms the existence of these two things. The presence of τις (masc. nom. sg.) seems to confirm that Paul does not doubt their existence. It is interesting to note that Paul used six substantivized adjectives in the previous list, and now he switches to nouns. This may be further evidence that the prior list had already been formed. Still, this is the only place Paul uses ἀρετή (the only other NT uses are in 1 Pet 2:9; 2 Pet 1:3, 5 [twice]), so he may still be drawing on other written material. Ἀρετή was the primary word used by first-century philosophers and moralists for "virtue." Paul would have given this well-known concept distinctly Christian qualities, as he often does when he adopts language from other contexts. Ἔπαινος is not extraordinarily common in Paul's writings, appearing only five other times (one of which is Phil 1:11), but it seems to have been more a part of his vocabulary than the other qualities mentioned in this verse. Some important Western manuscripts (D, F, G, and some Old Latin texts) add ἐπιστήμης so that the phrase reads "praise of the truth." Fee (413) speculates that this may have been a scribal attempt to keep the whole sentence a statement about the mind. The reading in the text is supported by ℵ, A, B, the corrector of D, and many other witnesses.

ταῦτα λογίζεσθε–Λογίζεσθε is the pres. mid./pass. (deponent) impv. 2 pl. of λογίζομαι ("to think") (on the use of the imperative in the apodosis of a present conditional sentence, see Smyth, 2364). The context seems to indicate that the antecedents of ταῦτα (neut. acc. pl.) are the six members of the prior list.

4:9

polysyndeton

The repetition of conjunctions in a series, particularly when not all of them are necessary or expected.

ὧν ἡ υἱοθεσία καὶ ἡ δόξα καὶ αἱ διαθῆκαι καὶ ἡ νομοθεσία καὶ ἡ λατρεία καὶ αἱ ἐπαγγελίαι

they have the adoption and the glory and the covenants and the giving of the law and the worship and the promises (Rom 9:4)

ἡμέρας παρατηρεῖσθε καὶ μῆνας καὶ καιροὺς καὶ ἐνιαυτούς.

You observe days and months and times and years. (Gal 4:10)

ἃ καί–The relative pronoun ἃ (neut. acc. pl.) serves as the object for all four verbs that follow. The καί here may introduce the sentence, or, more probably, it initiates the list of verbs that follow. This **polysyndeton** with the conjunction καί makes the list seem more extensive and encompassing (see BDF §460).

ἐμάθετε–Ἐμάθετε (aor. act. indic. 2 pl. of μανθάνω, "to learn") appears only seven times (including twice in Philippians) in the undisputed Pauline letters, and in these places it often seems to connote tradition that is handed on. Compare its use in the Pastoral Epistles, where it appears another six times. However, in its usage outside the NT it does not seem to have this connotation.

καὶ παρελάβετε–Παρελάβετε, the aor. act. indic. 2 pl. of παραλαμβάνω ("to receive, take over"), is used by Plato to describe the relationship of student to teacher. The student receives, while the teacher passes on (παραδίδωμι). It also stood for the rites received in some mystery religions (TDNT 4:11, 14). Paul may be using it because he has in mind passing on set traditions (cf. its use in 1 Cor 11:23). Given these uses of παραλαμβάνω, it seems unwise to attribute its appearance here solely or even primarily to its use in rabbinic Judaism (as, e.g., O'Brien 509–10).

καὶ ἠκούσατε καὶ εἴδετε ἐν ἐμοί–Both ἠκούσατε (from ἀκούω, "to hear") and εἴδετε (from εἶδον, "to see") are aor. act. indic. 2 pl. The prepositional phrase ἐν ἐμοί (masc. dat. sg.) may relate primarily to the final verb rather than the whole list, but this seems unlikely. Paul wants the Philippians to recall what he taught and said among them, as well as what he did. Allowing ἐν ἐμοί to modify the whole list gives a better sense to the following imperative and its place in this sentence's structure. The clause that constitutes v. 9 is parallel in its construction to v. 8: as v. 8 contained an imperative following a list, so in v. 9 an imperative follows a list (for other parallels see Fee, 413–14). Verse 9 is a call for the Philippians to imitate Paul. Such calls for imitation were common and seen as appropriate, even necessary, in the moral exhortation of this period.

ταῦτα πράσσετε–The antecedent of ταῦτα (neut. acc. pl.) is the ἃ that begins v. 9. Thus it includes all the things that the Philippians learned, received, heard, and saw. This clause is also part of the sentence that began at v. 8. After listing the qualities found in v.8, things that were also seen as profitable by the broader culture, Paul tells the Philippians to think about those things. Now, after the references to the Christian teaching that they had received from Paul, they are told to do (πράσσετε [pres. act. impv. 2 pl. of πράσσω]) them.

καὶ ὁ θεὸς τῆς εἰρήνης—It is probably no accident that this section, which began with a call to end a dispute, ends with a reference to the God (ὁ θεὸς [masc. nom. sg.]) of peace (τῆς εἰρήνης [fem. gen. sg.]). The connection of this appellation with the argument between Euodia and Syntyche is supported by the reference to the "peace of God" in v. 7. It is perhaps best to describe εἰρήνης as a qualitative genitive, so that it describes a characteristic of God, or as a genitive of production (so Wallace, 106-7), so that it makes God the source from which peace comes.

ἔσται μεθ᾽ ὑμῶν—This sentence does not fit any of the patterns of conditional sentences commonly cited; however, it seems to fit what Wallace (489-91) identifies as a **conditional imperative.** Functioning as a conditional sentence, it asserts that the God of peace will be with them *if* they practice those things received through the various avenues mentioned previously in the verse. Since this is the case, ἔσται

> ### conditional imperative
>
> The use of the imperative in an implied conditional sentence to assert that something will occur if the mandate of the imperative is fulfilled.
>
> Πίστευσον ἐπὶ τὸν κύριον Ἰησοῦν καὶ σωθήσῃ.
>
> *Believe on the Lord Jesus and you will be saved.* (Acts 16:31)
>
> ἀντίστητε τῷ διαβόλῳ καὶ φεύξεται ἀφ᾽ ὑμῶν.
>
> *Resist the devil and he will flee from you.* (Jas 4:7)

(fut. mid. indic. 3 sg. of εἰμί, "to be") is somewhat emphatic. See BDAG for καὶ being used to introduce a result (see also Loh and Nida, 136; O'Brien, 511-12). If this analysis is correct, this final clause of v. 9 (and that of v. 7) is probably not simply a peace wish, but rather a more integral part of the exhortation. In that case, the καὶ can be rendered "so that."

FOR FURTHER STUDY

Cotter, W. "Our *Politeuma* Is in Heaven: The Meaning of Philippians 3:17-21." Pp. 92-104 in *Origins and Method: Towards a New Understanding of Judaism and Christianity.* Edited by B. H. McLean. Journal for the Study of the New Testament: Supplement Series 86. Sheffield: JSOT, 1993.

Dodd, B. J. "The Story of Christ and the Imitation of Paul in Philippians 2-3." Pp. 154-61 in *Where Christology Began: Essays on Philippians 2.* Edited by R. P. Martin and B. J. Dodd. Louisville: Westminster John Knox, 1998.

Fiore, B. *The Function of Personal Example in the Socratic and Pastoral Epistles.* Analectica biblica 105. Rome: Biblical Institute Press, 1986.

Marshall, P. *Enmity in Corinth: Social Conventions in Paul's Relations with the Corinthians.* Wissenschaftliche Untersuchungen zum Neuen Testament 23. Tübingen: Mohr-Siebeck, 1987.

Moiser, J. "The Meaning of *koilia* in Philippians 3:19." *Expository Times* 108 (1997): 365-66.

Reumann, J. H. "Philippians 3:20-21—A Hymnic Fragment." *New Testament Studies* 30 (1984): 593-609.

Philippians 4:10-20

Paul's Thanksgiving to the Philippians for Their Gift to Him

4:10-14 Paul's Gratitude and Contentment

¹⁰Ἐχάρην δὲ ἐν κυρίῳ μεγάλως ὅτι ἤδη ποτὲ ἀνεθάλετε τὸ ὑπὲρ ἐμοῦ φρονεῖν, ἐφ' ᾧ καὶ ἐφρονεῖτε, ἠκαιρεῖσθε δέ. ¹¹οὐχ ὅτι καθ' ὑστέρησιν λέγω, ἐγὼ γὰρ ἔμαθον ἐν οἷς εἰμι αὐτάρκης εἶναι. ¹²οἶδα καὶ ταπεινοῦσθαι, οἶδα καὶ περισσεύειν· ἐν παντὶ καὶ ἐν πᾶσιν μεμύημαι, καὶ χορτάζεσθαι καὶ πεινᾶν, καὶ περισσεύειν καὶ ὑστερεῖσθαι ¹³πάντα ἰσχύω ἐν τῷ ἐνδυναμοῦντί με. ¹⁴πλὴν καλῶς ἐποιήσατε συγκοινωνήσαντές μου τῇ θλίψει.

¹⁰I was made very glad in the Lord that now finally you have renewed your concern for my affairs, about which you were concerned but had no opportunity to express it. ¹¹I do not say this because of need, for I have learned to be content in whatever circumstances I find myself. ¹²I know how to be humbled and I know how to abound; in any and every circumstance I have been taught this, whether full or hungry, whether abounding or needy. ¹³I am able to endure all things in the one who strengthens me. ¹⁴Nevertheless, you did well to participate together in my troubles.

Ἐχάρην δὲ ἐν κυρίῳ μεγάλως–The postpositive δὲ probably signals that a new 4:10
section has begun. It remains untranslated, as is often the case. Ἐχάρην (aor. pass. indic. 1 sg. of χαίρω, "to rejoice, be glad") is sometimes translated as an epistolary aorist. However, since it refers to a specific moment in the past, this seems unlikely. The way this phrase reflects Paul's exhortation of 2:4 with ἐν κυρίῳ (masc. dat. sg. ["Lord"]) supports finding vv. 10–20 as part of the same letter as vv. 2–9. The adverb μεγάλως ("greatly") is another NT *hapax legomenon*.

ὅτι ἤδη ποτὲ ἀνεθάλετε–Ὅτι is often used in conjunction with χαίρω to designate the reason for one's joy (BDAG). The word combination ἤδη ποτέ is an idiom that means "now at last" (see BDAG under both terms). The verb ἀνεθάλετε is the aor. act. indic. 2 pl. of ἀναθάλλω, a NT *hapax legomenon*. This verb is derived from agriculture and means "to bloom" or "to shoot up again."

However, it is sometimes used figuratively, as it is here, to mean "to (cause to) revive," "to renew," or "to flourish." Such usage is found in the LXX as well as in secular Greek (MM; LSJ).

τὸ ὑπὲρ ἐμοῦ φρονεῖν–Φρονεῖν is the pres. act. inf. of φρονέω, a word that has appeared often and in some rather significant places in this letter (e.g., 2:2, 3, 5; 4:2). Here it means "to express concern," "to take someone's side," or "to be kindly disposed toward," a somewhat different sense than elsewhere in Philippians. This meaning for φρονέω is found in other literature (BDAG; LSJ). The definite article τὸ (neut. acc. sg.) either serves to make the following prepositional phrase function as a substantive, "the things about me" (i.e., my affairs), and as the object of φρονεῖν, or makes φρονεῖν an articular infinitive and so the object of ἀνεθάλετε (so Wallace [601–2], who recognizes that this is an unusual construction). There is little difference in meaning. The first option allows τὸ ὑπὲρ ἐμοῦ (gen. sg.) to function as τὰ κατ' ἐμὲ (1:12), τὰ περὶ ὑμῶν (2:19), and other such phrases have throughout Philippians. This seems to fit the context quite well, since the subject is a gift of support for Paul, even though rendering ὑπὲρ ἐμοῦ as "for me" is its more common meaning. Furthermore, Wallace (602) notes that the infinitive does not require the article to function as the object of a finite verb. Thus, even if φρονεῖν is the object of ἀνεθάλετε, the article may still function as our first option suggests.

ἐφ' ᾧ καὶ ἐφρονεῖτε–Paul's use of the imperfect ἐφρονεῖτε (impf. act. 3 pl. of φρονέω, "to think, be concerned") may intend to make clear that he is not criticizing the Philippians, because it indicates that he recognizes that their concern was ongoing. The prepositional phrase ἐφ' ᾧ (masc./neut. dat. sg.) relates this clause to the preceding one, with the antecedent of ᾧ being Paul's affairs (τὸ ὑπὲρ ἐμοῦ). Since the phrase seems to express something much like a dative of respect (this is similar to the meaning given under ἐπί in BDAG 16; cf. Moule, 132), it perhaps strengthens the understanding of τὸ ὑπὲρ ἐμοῦ ("my affairs") given above.

ἠκαιρεῖσθε δέ–The conjunction δέ is adversative here. The verb ἠκαιρεῖσθε is the impf. mid./pass. (deponent) 2 pl. of ἀκαιρέομαι ("to have no opportunity, have no time"), another *hapax legomenon*–the third one in this sentence. Perhaps it is the unusual substance of this and the following verses that accounts for the concentration of vocabulary uncommon in the NT. To express the meaning of this rather cryptic statement, one may need to supply a phrase that indicates what the Philippians had no opportunity to do. The translation given above adds "to express it" (i.e., their concern).

4:11   **οὐχ ὅτι καθ' ὑστέρησιν λέγω**–This new sentence adds yet another qualifier to Paul's initial statement about the Philippians' renewing their support of him. So he asserts that he is not speaking (λέγω [pres. indic. act. 1 sg.]) καθ' ὑστέρησιν (fem. acc. sg. ["need, want, lack"]). BDAG lists this as an example of κατά being used to mean "because of" or "in accordance with." The noun ὑστέρησις appears only one other time in the NT (Mark 12:44). The word seems rather rare; LSJ gives only these two biblical references as instances of its use, although BDAG lists a few others.

ἐγὼ γὰρ ἔμαθον–The γὰρ indicates the reason why Paul is not speaking out of need, and so it can be translated "because." Ἔμαθον is the aor. act. indic. 1 sg. of μανθάνω ("to learn"). The ἐγὼ may be emphatic, but there is no indication from the context that it implies a contrast between Paul and the recipients of the letter.

ἐν οἷς εἰμι–This phrase is rather oblique, in part because there is no antecedent for οἷς (neut. dat. pl.). Some assert that it refers to Paul's present circumstances as he writes; others argue that it has a broader meaning, pointing to any and all circumstances. What follows in v. 12 seems to make the latter more likely, and so it may be rendered "whatever circumstances I am in," or "in whatever circumstances I find myself."

αὐτάρκης εἶναι–The infinitive εἶναι (pres. act. inf. of εἰμί, "to be") is dependent on ἔμαθον. The adjective αὐτάρκης (masc. nom. sg. ["content, self-sufficient"]) is a predicate adjective governed by the infinitive εἶναι. We usually expect the subject or object of an infinitive to be in the accusative case, but when an infinitive is accompanied by a predicate noun or adjective, the noun or adjective sometimes remains in the nominative case because of its relationship to the subject of the sentence (BDF §405). BDF (§405[1]) asserts that this is necessarily the case here because μανθάνω, the verb to which εἶναι is attached, is related in meaning to "be able," with which the accusative and infinitive is impossible. Αὐτάρκης appears only here in the NT, and its cognate noun αὐτάρκεια appears only twice in the NT (2 Cor 9:8; 1 Tim 6:6). This vocabulary was used by Stoics for inner imperturbability in the face of difficult external circumstances, but Paul probably is not simply drawing on the technical vocabulary of Stoicism. This language also had a broader and less technical usage (see MM). This does not mean that Paul's use of the language was not influenced by the Stoic use. His statement here sounds much like some Stoics, although he would have had a different basis for his contentment.

οἶδα καὶ ταπεινοῦσθαι–Ταπεινοῦσθαι is the pres. pass. inf. of ταπεινόω ("to lower, humiliate, humble"), a verb that appears only three other times in Paul's writings (Phil 2:8; 2 Cor 11:7; 12:21); also rare for Paul are the cognate adjective ταπεινός (only in Rom 12:16; 2 Cor 7:6; 10:1) and noun ταπείνωσις (only in Phil 3:21). It is interesting to note the concentration of Paul's use of this word group in Philippians and 2 Corinthians; both of these communities were experiencing strife. In 2 Cor 11:7 Paul uses the verb to speak of his taking on a craft to earn a living as a primary example of voluntarily taking on what was seen as demeaning (cf. 1 Cor 9:12–23), and in Phil 2:8 it refers to Jesus humbling himself. Here, however, the verb is in the passive. Paul does not state whether the abasement mentioned here is simply the result of a lack of funds or is a part of his ministry sent from God. It appears to be from lack of resources because it is set in

4:12

opposition to περισσεύειν (see below). The infinitive ταπεινοῦσθαι is dependent on οἶδα (pf. act. indic. 1 sg. of οἶδα, "to know" [perfect tense but with the sense of a present]). To offer a smoother, more idiomatic translation, one needs to add "how" between the two verbs: "I know how to be humbled." The καί probably is to be understood as a **correlative conjunction** (Wallace, 672) that pairs it with the following καί. Thus the two would be translated "both . . . and . . ." (see the slightly different nuance in BDF §444[3]).

correlative conjunctions

Paired conjunctions that may express several relationships: either . . . or, both . . . and, on the one hand . . . but on the other hand, etc.

<u>καὶ</u> ὁ λόγος μου <u>καὶ</u> τὸ κήρυγμά μου οὐκ ἐν πειθοῖ(ς) σοφίας (λόγοις).

<u>Both</u> my word <u>and</u> my proclamation were not [given] with persuasively wise words. (1 Cor 2:4)

τὸ <u>μὲν</u> σῶμα νεκρὸν διὰ ἁμαρτίαν τὸ <u>δὲ</u> πνεῦμα ζωὴ διὰ δικαιοσύνην.

The body [is] dead because of sin, <u>but</u> the spirit is alive because of righteousness. (Rom 8:10)

οἶδα καὶ περισσεύειν–Finding περισσεύειν (pres. act. inf. of περισσεύω, "to be more than enough, abound") here is somewhat surprising because one would have expected ὑψόω ("to exalt"), a common opposite of ταπεινόω. Paul's use of περισσεύω indicates that the primary meaning of ταπεινόω in this context relates to financial need. As in the immediately preceding phrase, the infinitive is dependent on the preceding οἶδα (pf. act. indic. 1 sg. of οἶδα, "to know"). As in the preceding clause, one needs to insert "how" between the verbs of this clause.

ἐν παντὶ καὶ ἐν πᾶσιν μεμύημαι–Μεμύημαι is the pf. pass. (deponent) indic. 1 sg. of μυέω ("to learn the secret of"), a NT *hapax legomenon*. It was used by mystery religions, even as part of their technical vocabulary, to speak of being initiated into the mystery, but it also had a more general meaning, "to instruct, teach" (LSJ; *TDNT* 4:828). The context gives us no reason to see it being used in any cultic sense here, although Paul may be using it metaphorically: he has been initiated by all the kinds of circumstances that follow. In the expression ἐν παντὶ (neut. dat. sg.) καὶ ἐν πᾶσιν (neut. dat. pl.), the prepositions with the datives probably function as datives of respect (for this function of ἐν see BDF §219; Wallace, 372). Thus the adjectives may be translated "in any and every circumstance."

καὶ χορτάζεσθαι καὶ πεινᾶν–Again, the first καὶ is correlative and thus paired with the second one. Read in this way in this sentence, they may be rendered "whether . . . or . . ." Alternatively, the first καὶ could be construed as epexegetical (see BDF §442). Thus it might be translated "that is to say, . . ." The verb χορτάζεσθαι (pres. pass. inf. of χορτάζω, "to feed, fill, be satisfied") is the opposite of πεινᾶν (pres. act. inf. of πεινάω, "to be hungry"). These verbs are also found as opposites in Matt 5:6. Thus the listing of pairs of opposites begun at the start of this verse is resumed. These opposites, especially those following ἐν παντὶ καὶ ἐν πᾶσιν μεμύημαι, give more concrete content to the "any and every circumstances" that Paul says he endures.

καὶ περισσεύειν καὶ ὑστερεῖσθαι—See the discussion of καὶ in the immediately preceding phrase. This is the second use of περισσεύειν (pres. act. inf. of περισσεύω, "to be more than enough, abound") in this sentence. In both instances it is employed with an opposite. Since it follows immediately a rather concrete pair of verbs, perhaps we should see ὑστερεῖσθαι (pres. pass. inf. of ὑστερέω, "to lack, be needy") to refer to economic needs, while ταπεινοῦσθαι points to a broader experience, that of being humiliated by need. Hebrews 11:37 uses the passive participle of ὑστερέω to speak of the destitution that some had to endure because of their faith; however, in the other place where Paul uses ὑστερέω and περισσεύω as opposites (1 Cor 8:8), the former seems to have a broader meaning than economic need. Still, we should not assume that Paul can use a term in only one way, and the context of Philippians weighs more heavily than the other Pauline usage in this case.

πάντα ἰσχύω—The adjective πάντα (masc. acc. sg. ["all"]) functions as a substantive and so as the object of the verb ἰσχύω (pres. act. indic. 1 sg. of ἰσχύω, "to be in good health, be able"). The "all" refers directly to various kinds of circumstances that Paul has been describing in vv. 11-12. In this context ἰσχύω means that Paul is able to endure. There is no room for triumphalism or claims that God removes difficult circumstances, as the following phrase shows.   4:13

ἐν τῷ ἐνδυναμοῦντί με—The participle ἐνδυναμοῦντί (pres. act. ptc. masc. dat. sg. of ἐνδυναμόω, "to strengthen") is the object of ἐν. This prepositional phrase sometimes has been taken as a dative of personal agency; however, Wallace (373-74) expresses doubt that such a construction is found in the NT. It seems better to understand the phrase in conjunction with the several ἐν Χριστῷ phrases in Philippians. Thus it comes closer to expressing the sphere within which Paul is able to endure. For reasons to reject an instrumental sense, see O'Brien, 526-27; Fee, 434. Fee, however, acknowledges that this is close to an instrumental usage of ἐν. Paul is able to endure hardship not because he has great power, but because he participates in the realm that he characterizes as ἐν Χριστῷ. A corrector of ℵ and one of D, along with some other later witnesses, add Χριστῷ here to specify who it is that strengthens Paul; however, the original hand of both these manuscripts, as well as A and B, have the reading in the text. Additionally, the internal evidence favors the shorter reading because there is no reason for a scribe to delete the reference to Christ, while there is some motivation for adding it. The pronoun με (acc. sg.) is the object of ἐνδυναμοῦντί.

πλὴν καλῶς ἐποιήσατε—Ἐποιήσατε is the aor. act. indic. 2 pl. of ποιέω ("to do"). Although some begin a new section with this sentence, it seems better to understand it as the conclusion of the present paragraph. This closer connection with what precedes is evidenced by the adversative πλὴν. BDAG cites this text as an example of this word being used to break off a discussion to emphasize what is important. BDAG and BDF assert that πλήν is the colloquial word for "however,   4:14

nevertheless." Although this term is common in Luke's Gospel, it is infrequent in Paul's undisputed writings, appearing only once outside Philippians (1 Cor 11:11), but three times in Philippians (1:18; 3:16; 4:14). With the sentences introduced by πλὴν, Paul brings closure to the thought begun in v. 10 by returning to the thought of their gift after emphasizing that he is not speaking out of need.

συγκοινωνήσαντές μου τῇ θλίψει—The dative designates that which one shares with the subject of the verb συγκοινωνέω; thus θλίψει ("affliction, trouble") is fem. dat. sg. The participle συγκοινωνήσαντές (pres. act. ptc. masc. nom. pl. of συγκοινωνέω, "to be connected, share") gives the Philippians a way of viewing their gift, describing it as "taking part in" or "having a joint share in" (see LSM) Paul's (μου [gen. sg.]) troubles. Fee (438–39) asserts that finding μου rather than μοι here emphasizes that they are sharing *Paul's* troubles. This use of the genitive, however, may simply follow a common pattern with this verb (see BDAG). This verb is used only three times in the NT, and only here in the undisputed Paulines. In its other two occurrences, Eph 5:11 and Rev 18:4, it is used for "participating in" evil works. These uses show that the idea of participation is central to its meaning.

4:15-20   The Philippians' Sweet-Smelling Offering

¹⁵Οἴδατε δὲ καὶ ὑμεῖς, Φιλιππήσιοι, ὅτι ἐν ἀρχῇ τοῦ εὐαγγελίου, ὅτε ἐξῆλθον ἀπὸ Μακεδονίας, οὐδεμία μοι ἐκκλησία ἐκοινώνησεν εἰς λόγον δόσεως καὶ λήμψεως εἰ μὴ ὑμεῖς μόνοι, ¹⁶ὅτι καὶ ἐν Θεσσαλονίκῃ καὶ ἅπαξ καὶ δὶς εἰς τὴν χρείαν μοι ἐπέμψατε. ¹⁷οὐχ ὅτι ἐπιζητῶ τὸ δόμα, ἀλλὰ ἐπιζητῶ τὸν καρπὸν τὸν πλεονάζοντα εἰς λόγον ὑμῶν. ¹⁸ἀπέχω δὲ πάντα καὶ περισσεύω· πεπλήρωμαι δεξάμενος παρὰ Ἐπαφροδίτου τὰ παρ' ὑμῶν, ὀσμὴν εὐωδίας, θυσίαν δεκτήν, εὐάρεστον τῷ θεῷ. ¹⁹ὁ δὲ θεός μου πληρώσει πᾶσαν χρείαν ὑμῶν κατὰ τὸ πλοῦτος αὐτοῦ ἐν δόξῃ ἐν Χριστῷ Ἰησοῦ. ²⁰τῷ δὲ θεῷ καὶ πατρὶ ἡμῶν ἡ δόξα εἰς τοὺς αἰῶνας τῶν αἰώνων, ἀμήν.

¹⁵Now you yourselves, Philippians, also know that from the beginning of the gospel, when I left Macedonia, no church shared with me in the matter of giving and receiving except you alone, ¹⁶and that even in Thessalonica you sent support to me for my needs time and again. ¹⁷I do not say this because I seek the gift, but I seek increasing fruit for your account. ¹⁸I am receiving all things and have more than enough; I have been filled because I have received from Epaphroditus the things from you, a sweet-smelling offering, an acceptable sacrifice that is pleasing to God. ¹⁹My God will fulfill your every need according to his riches that are in glory in Christ Jesus. ²⁰And the glory belongs to our God and Father forever and ever. Amen.

4:15   **Οἴδατε δὲ καὶ ὑμεῖς, Φιλιππήσιοι**—The vocative Φιλιππήσιοι may indicate that a new paragraph is beginning. Οἴδατε (pf. act. indic. 2 pl. of οἶδα) has the emphatic ὑμεῖς (nom. pl.) as its subject, with the vocative Φιλιππήσιοι (masc. voc. pl.) specifying its referent. The use of two conjunctions to begin this sentence may also add emphasis. Perhaps all these emphatic elements could be rendered "Now you yourselves, Philippians, also know . . ."

ὅτι ἐν ἀρχῇ τοῦ εὐαγγελίου—As it often does, ὅτι designates the content of what is known with verbs of thinking and knowing (BDAG). The meaning of ἐν ἀρχῇ (fem. dat. sg. ["beginning"]) with τοῦ εὐαγγελίου (masc. gen. sg. ["gospel, good news"]) has been discussed at length; its most probable meaning is "from the time of their conversion." However, given the phrase that follows, this should be qualified so that it points to the time after Paul left Philippi rather than while he was there.

ὅτε ἐξῆλθον ἀπὸ Μακεδονίας—The preposition ἀπὸ takes the genitive (Μακεδονίας [masc. gen. sg.]) and commonly appears with verbs denoting motion, such as ἐξῆλθον (aor. act. indic. 1 sg. of ἐξέρχομαι, "to go out, go away") here. This seems to point to Paul's first mission to Greece and probably includes the support that he mentions in 2 Cor 11:8-9.

οὐδεμία μοι ἐκκλησία ἐκοινώνησεν—᾽Εκοινώνησεν is the aor. act. indic. 3 sg. of κοινωνέω ("to share, contribute a share"), a verb that appears only four times in the undisputed Pauline letters and once in the disputed ones. In Rom 12:13 and Gal 6:6 it refers to financial matters, as it does here, while Rom 15:27 speaks of sharing spiritual gifts, and 1 Tim 5:22 instructs the reader not to share in sin. Since ἐκκλησία (fem. nom. sg. ["church"]) is the subject of ἐκοινώνησεν, οὐδεμία (fem. nom. sg. of οὐδείς ["no, no one"]) functions as an adjective that modifies the noun ἐκκλησία, the noun closest to the verb.

εἰς λόγον δόσεως καὶ λήμψεως εἰ μὴ ὑμεῖς μόνοι—Once again there is an emphatic reference to the Philippians signaled by the presence of both ὑμεῖς (nom. pl.) and μόνοι (masc. nom. pl.). When the particles εἰ and μή appear together, as they do here, and come after a negative (οὐδεμία at the beginning of the entire clause), they mean "except" or "if not." As the case is also here, they usually do not have a verb dependent on them (BDAG). The noun λόγον (masc. acc. sg.) has one of its more unusual meanings for the NT here. Λόγος is one of those words with a wide range of meanings (it takes up more than five columns in LSJ and nearly six in BDAG). In Gal 6:6 it appears with κοινωνέω, as it does here, and there as here it means "subject matter" or "topic." The subject matter of this discussion is δόσεως (fem. gen. sg. ["giving, gift"]) καὶ λήμψεως (fem. gen. sg. ["receiving"]). Δόσις is used commonly in discussion of financial matters, contexts in which λήμψις is also found (MM). However, it is also used in contexts of friendship, and probably this is the primary referent here. This does not mean that the financial element is denied or diminished, but rather nuanced, because friendships in the Greco-Roman world were understood to include such matters (see Marshall, *Enmity in Corinth*, 1-13, 160-64).

4:16   ὅτι καὶ ἐν Θεσσαλονίκῃ καὶ ἅπαξ καὶ δὶς–When the two adverbs ἅπαξ and δὶς are found together, BDAG gives the meaning as "again and again" or "more than once" rather than indicating a specific number. Fee (445) argues for a more narrow meaning for the idiom that allows that gifts were sent more than once, but does not show that there were more than three gifts. Paul's other use of the idiom in 1 Thess 2:18 suggests the former meaning. Thus the translation given above is "time and again." The ὅτι is dependent on the οἴδατε at the beginning of v. 15 and so gives content to what they know a second time. Strangely, Paul now speaks of gifts that he received in Thessalonica (Θεσσαλονίκῃ [fem. dat. sg.]) following his mention of gifts that he received after leaving Macedonia. Since Thessalonica is in Macedonia, Paul may mean to emphasize their giving to him repeatedly so soon after his departure. Fee (441–42) identifies the καὶ as ascensive (i.e., adding a final point or focus [see Wallace, 670–71]) and so argues that Paul began with gifts received beyond Macedonia to emphasize their long-term relationship with Paul and then added Thessalonica as a qualifier.

εἰς τὴν χρείαν μοι ἐπέμψατε–Μοι (dat. sg.) is the indirect object of ἐπέμψατε (aor. act. indic. 2 pl. of πέμπω, "to send"). Some suggest that since the article is present with χρείαν (fem. acc. sg. ["need, lack"]), Paul is referring to specific occasions or circumstances of need. Although this is possible, it may be over-specification. The εἰς seems to be one of reference/respect (for uses of εἰς see Wallace, 369). 𝔓⁴⁶ and D omit the preposition εἰς, either by accident because of its similarity to δὶς (i.e., homeoteleuton) or so that ἐπέμψατε has a direct object. D, P (eleventh century), and a few minuscules change μοι to μου, but the more uncommon and more difficult μοι has much stronger textual support.

4:17   οὐχ ὅτι ἐπιζητῶ τὸ δόμα–Δόμα (neut. acc. sg. ["gift"]) appears only four times in the NT. Luke (11:13) and Matthew (7:11) use it in the same saying of Jesus ("If you being evil know how to give good gifts to your children . . ."). The only other NT use is in Eph 4:8, where it is a part of a quotation from Ps 68:18. The word also seems to appear fairly infrequently in other literature where δόσις is more common. The sentence that opens v. 17 begins with an ellipsis (a place where something is omitted). The missing verb probably is λέγω (so BDF §480), although one might also supply εἰμί. Λέγω is preferable because of the parallel thought in v. 11. The first occurrence of ἐπιζητῶ (pres. act. indic. 1 sg. of ἐπιζητῶ, "to seek after, wish for") is not the main verb of the sentence, because it follows a causal ὅτι (Wallace, 460), indicating that this is a dependent clause.

ἀλλὰ ἐπιζητῶ τὸν καρπὸν τὸν πλεονάζοντα–Ἐπιζητῶ (pres. act. indic. 1 sg. of ἐπιζητέω) is the main verb of the second clause of this compound sentence. Paul's use of τὸν καρπὸν (masc. acc. sg. ["fruit"]) may point to eschatological reward, but probably he does not have just this meaning in view. In the present their gifts to him are the result, and so evidence, of their continuing faithfulness to God. Paul uses καρπός only seven other times (Rom 1:13; 6:21, 22, 15:28; 1 Cor 9:7;

Gal 5:9; Phil 1:11); in none of these places does it refer to eschatological reward. In Rom 6:22 Paul says that the fruit of being one who serves God is sanctification, which he distinguishes from "eternal life." He also uses it in connection with giving gifts in Rom 15:28, where it is used of the collection for Jerusalem. His less abstract, metaphoric use of the term comes in a discussion of financial maintenance for apostles, where he uses the vineyard worker as an example of one who lives from work (1 Cor 9:7). It is unlikely, therefore, that Paul uses καρπός here primarily for eschatological reward. Thus he wants the evidence of their faith to increase (πλεονάζοντα [pres. act. ptc. masc. acc. sg. of πλεονάζω, "to increase, become more"]).

εἰς λόγον ὑμῶν—Another of the less common uses of λόγος appears here in εἰς λόγον (masc. acc. sg.). It means "account." Given this usage with the εἰς of reference or perhaps advantage, some suggest that καρπός should be understood as "interest on an account." This is a known use for that noun.

ἀπέχω δὲ πάντα καὶ περισσεύω—The verb ἀπέχω (pres. act. indic. 1 sg.) is   **4:18** used in commercial documents to indicate that one has received payment or to mark something paid (BDAG). Paul may be drawing on this use here, saying that their debt to him is paid in full; however, when used by Stoics, ἀπέχω πάντα (neut. acc. pl.) had nearly the same meaning as αὐτάρκεια. This seems to make this expression similar to that in v. 11, where Paul speaks of αὐτάρκεια as well as of having plenty (see Fee, 450-51). As a result of receiving the gift that the Philippians had sent him, Paul says that he now has more than he needs (περισσεύω [pres. act. indic. 1 sg. of περισσεύω, "to have an abundance, abound"]).

πεπλήρωμαι δεξάμενος—Δεξάμενος (aor. mid. ptc. nom. sg. of δέχομαι, "to receive, take") is a circumstantial participle expressing cause, and it governs the remaining part of the sentence. It expresses the reason why Paul can say in a third way that he is fulfilled (πεπλήρωμαι [pf. pass. indic. 1 sg. of πληρόω, "to fill"]). The perfect tense may express the sense of being filled and remaining so. This third verb introduces the explanatory clause that ends the sentence (Vincent, 150).

παρὰ Ἐπαφροδίτου—As it often does, παρά with the genitive (Ἐπαφροδίτου [masc. gen. sg.]) expresses agency.

τὰ παρ' ὑμῶν—The other primary use of παρά with the genitive is to express the source from which something comes (see Wallace, 378). That is how it is used this second time, with ὑμῶν (gen. pl.) as its object. As we have seen several times in Philippians, the definite article can function to substantivize what follows—in this case, a prepositional phrase. So these words designate the direct object of δεξάμενος, and thus the phrase would read, fairly woodenly, "having received ... the things from you."

ὀσμὴν εὐωδίας–Neither of these words is common in Paul's writings. Εὐωδίας (fem. gen. sg. ["aroma, fragrance"]), a genitive of quality here, appears in the undisputed Paulines only here and in 2 Cor 2:15. Its only other use in the Pauline corpus is Eph 5:2, where it is used in the same relation with ὀσμή as it is here. It is also interesting to note that θυσία is also used there. In 2 Cor 2:15 ὀσμή and εὐωδία seem synonymous. Ὀσμή is a fairly rare word outside of Attic Greek, while ὀδμή is much more common. Ὀσμή is used three other times in the undisputed Paulines (2 Cor 2:14, 16 [twice]). It appears only two other times in the NT (John 12:3; Eph 5:2). Paul's use of the term in Philippians seems to draw on its use in the LXX, where it is used to speak of what ascends to God from sacrifices. In fact, ὀσμὴ ("fragrance") εὐωδίας is found as a description of acceptable sacrifices in Lev 1:9, 13, 17; 2:12 (LXX) among other places. So this expression ties this phrase to ideas of sacrifices to God and designates an offering pleasing to God (*TDNT* 5:493–95). It is interesting to note the aural resonance of εὐωδίας here and the name Εὐοδία in 4:2. This might well catch the attention of the listeners and draw them into the point that Paul is making, even if it was not what lead him to think of the language of Leviticus.

θυσίαν δεκτήν–Δεκτήν, the fem. acc. sg. of the adjective δεκτή ("acceptable, pleasing), is also rare in the NT, appearing only one other occasion within the Pauline corpus (2 Cor 6:2) and only three times elsewhere (Luke 4:19, 24; Acts 10:35). Θυσίαν, the fem. acc. sg. of θυσία ("sacrifice, offering"), although it is somewhat more common, appears only three times in the Pauline corpus outside Philippians (Rom 12:1; 1 Cor 10:18; Eph 5:2). It is used regularly only in Hebrews (fifteen times). Ephesians 5:2 has both θυσίαν and ὀσμὴν εὐωδίας. The use of these terms together in both Ephesians and Philippians seems to indicate that there is some deliberate echo of Lev 1:9, 13, 17, where we find κάρπωμά ἐστιν θυσία ὀσμὴ εὐωδίας τῷ κυρίῳ. The presence of the cognate of καρπός, which Paul used to speak of the Philippians' gift in the previous verse, supports the suggestion that Paul purposefully alludes to Leviticus. Whether or not he was conscious of the direct echo, he makes their gift to him an act of worship. If the echo is intentional (which seems most probable to me), he raises the Philippians' service to the level of offering a sacrifice to God.

εὐάρεστον τῷ θεῷ–Εὐάρεστον, the masc. dat. sg. of εὐάρεστος ("pleasing, acceptable"), appears only four more times in the undisputed Paulines (Rom 12:1, 2; 14:18; 2 Cor 5:9). Its uses in Rom 12 are again associated with the metaphor of sacrifice. In Rom 12:1 and 14:18, εὐάρεστος is followed by τῷ θεῷ, and clearly God is the one pleased in Rom 12:2. This usage tends to support making the less clear reference (κύριος) in 2 Cor 5:9 apply to God as well. Its three uses in the disputed Paulines are less clear (Eph 5:10; Col 3:20; Titus 2:9), but in Heb 13:21, its only other NT use, it is used with θεός (cf. the use of the cognate verb εὐαρεστέω in Heb 13:16 with θεός and θυσία).

ὁ δὲ θεός μου πληρώσει—The conjunction δὲ ties the following affirmation of **4:19**
God's blessing to the acceptable nature of their gift, but it should not be understood to establish some mechanical connection, as the translation "in return" suggests (*contra* Hawthorne, 207). Paul seldom refers to God as θεός (masc. nom. sg.)
μου (gen. sg.). With the exception of this passage and 2 Cor 12:21, Paul refers to
God as "my God" only in his opening thanksgivings, and then only in Rom 1:8;
1 Cor 1:4; Phil 1:3; Phlm 4. This may mean that we should understand what Paul
says here as something of a word of prayer; however, Fee (449) sees this statement
from within the framework of the reciprocity of friendship and so not as a prayer.
Its similarity to Paul's use of this language in prayer may be what led D, F, G, and
the Latin tradition to change the indicative πληρώσει (fut. act. indic. 3 sg. of
πληρόω, "to fill") to the optative πληρῶσαι. Clearly, the optative is the less problematic theologically, and so the reading of the text, beside having stronger external support (𝔓⁴⁶, ℵ, A, B, corrector of D), is preferable as the more difficult reading.

πᾶσαν χρείαν ὑμῶν—Paul's use of πᾶσαν (fem. acc. sg.) χρείαν (fem. acc. sg.
["need"]) seems to recall the language he used in vv. 16, 18, as did his immediately preceding use of πληρώσει. So Paul is using the same language to describe
God's care of them (ὑμῶν [gen. pl.]) as he used in talking about their gift to him.

κατὰ τὸ πλοῦτος αὐτοῦ—This prepositional phrase is adverbial, modifying
πληρώσει. It tells how God will supply what they need. Τὸ πλοῦτος (neut. acc.
sg. ["wealth, abundance"]) takes up the language of extravagance begun with
πληρώσει that Paul uses to describe God's blessing of them. This is continued in
the next prepositional phrase.

ἐν δόξῃ ἐν Χριστῷ Ἰησοῦ—Ἐν δόξῃ (fem. dat. sg. ["glory"]) modifies the previous prepositional phrase, with ἐν designating the sphere in which God's riches
are located. The NT uses of δόξα in connection with God seem to draw on its use in
the LXX, where it often refers to God's honor or power. More broadly, it speaks of
the divine nature (TDNT 2:244-48). Ἐν Χριστῷ (masc. dat. sg.) Ἰησοῦ (masc.
dat. sg.) indicates that the glory of God is located in Christ Jesus, so ἐν is again
locative (see Wallace, 372; Fee, 453-54).

τῷ δὲ θεῷ καὶ πατρὶ ἡμῶν ἡ δόξα—The unusual "my God" has now yielded to **4:20**
ἡμῶν (gen. pl.). This possessive pronoun probably modifies both θεῷ (masc. dat.
sg.) and πατρὶ (masc. dat. sg.) because both probably share the one definite article
τῷ (masc. dat. sg.). However, the article may designate God as the God who lav-
ishes blessing (v. 19), then adding that this God is also our Father. In both Gal 1:4
and 1 Thess 1:3, when these two titles are together with one article, it is preferable
to see them sharing it. In 1 Thess 3:11 the article seems to apply only to θεός, but
this is the case because αὐτός intensifies θεός in the predicate position. If the article and pronoun go with both nouns, the translation would be "our God and
Father" (see Wallace, 274). More than one meaning of the term δόξα (fem. nom.
sg.) is found in the NT. It may speak of divine glory or radiance, as it does in Luke

2:9; John 1:18 (and as it often does in the LXX). However, it is also used to speak of one's honor (1 Thess 2:6), and at times it seems somewhat synonymous with praise, as in John 9:24. When Paul uses δόξα in connection with God, it often refers to the divine glory or radiance, and thus to the divine nature. If this is its meaning here, the doxology does not imply that the divine glory is being conferred, but that it is being actively acknowledged (*TDNT* 2:248). As is the case with many doxologies in the NT, this one has no verb. Some suggest supplying the optative εἴη ("Glory be to God . . ."). If that is correct, then δόξα must refer to something akin to praise, or perhaps that the worshiper is giving God proper honor. This type of doxology is seen in Rev 5:13, where the multitudes of heaven say that the Lamb is worthy to receive various honors, and then the doxology confers those on God and the Lamb with the same type of construction that we find in Philippians. If δόξα refers to an attribute of God (see immediately above), then supplying the indicative ἐστί is more probable. The doxology in 1 Pet 4:11 is an example of this type of doxology. This 1 Peter doxology is one of the few in the NT that includes its verb, and that verb is the indicative ἐστιν. Given the common usage, honor and praise are the more likely meanings that the Philippians would hear, unless they had heard Paul use the language in a different way.

εἰς τοὺς αἰῶνας τῶν αἰώνων—This phrase would be translated literally as "to the ages of the ages" or "to the eternities of the eternities." The repetition of the noun τοὺς αἰῶνας (masc. acc. pl.), though with a change in case to the genitive (αἰώνων [masc. gen. pl.]), intensifies the meaning. According to O'Brien (550), this expression appears nowhere outside the NT; however, these words are used in this construction in the singular in the LXX (e.g., Ps 148:6).

Ἀμήν—Ἀμήν is an indeclinable particle. This expression is a transliteration of the Hebrew word for "surely." It is also used to join oneself to a doxology in Ps 41:13; 89:52, and by Symmachus and Theodotian in Deut 27:15, where the people accept an oath and the conditions of a curse. Among the other few places it is used similarly in the LXX are 1 Chron 16:36 and Neh 5:13; 8:6. The LXX usually, however, translates the Hebrew with γένοιτο. See, for example, Ps 41:13 (LXX 40:14), whose ending (ἀπὸ τοῦ αἰῶνος καὶ εἰς τὸν αἰῶνα. γένοιτο γένοιτο.) is very interesting to compare with the present doxology.

FOR FURTHER STUDY

Berry, K. L. "The Function of Friendship Language in Philippians 4:10–20." Pp. 107–24 in *Friendship, Flattery, and Frankness of Speech: Studies on Friendship in the New Testament World*. Edited by J. T. Fitzgerald. Supplements to Novum Testamentum 82. Leiden: Brill, 1996.

Fowl, S. E. "Know Your Context: Giving and Receiving Money in Philippians." *Interpretation* 56 (2002): 45–58.

Malherbe, A. J. "Paul's Self-sufficiency (Philippians 4:11)." Pp. 125–39 in *Friendship, Flattery, and Frankness of Speech: Studies on Friendship in the New Testament World.* Edited by J. T. Fitzgerald. Supplements to Novum Testamentum 82. Leiden: Brill, 1996.

Peterman, G. W. "'Thankless Thanks': The Epistolary Social Convention in Philippians 4:10-12." *Tyndale Bulletin* 42 (1991): 261–70.

Suggs, M. J. "Koinonia in the New Testament." *Novum Testamentum* 4 (1960-1961): 60-68.

Weima, J. A. D. *Neglected Endings: The Significance of the Pauline Letter Closings.* Journal for the Study of the New Testament: Supplement Series 101. Sheffield: Sheffield Academic Press, 1994.

Philippians 4:21-23

Epistolary Closing

²¹Ἀσπάσασθε πάντα ἅγιον ἐν Χριστῷ Ἰησοῦ. ἀσπάζονται ὑμᾶς οἱ σὺν ἐμοὶ ἀδελφοί. ²²ἀσπάζονται ὑμᾶς πάντες οἱ ἅγιοι, μάλιστα δὲ οἱ ἐκ τῆς Καίσαρος οἰκίας. ²³ἡ χάρις τοῦ κυρίου Ἰησοῦ Χριστοῦ μετὰ τοῦ πνεύματος ὑμῶν.

²¹Greet every saint in Christ Jesus. The brothers and sisters with me greet you. ²²All the saints greet you, especially those from the household of Caesar. ²³May the grace of the Lord Jesus Christ be with your spirit.

4:21   **Ἀσπάσασθε πάντα ἅγιον**—Paul's use of the singular πάντα (masc. acc. sg.) ἅγιον (masc. acc. sg. ["saint, holy one"]) is unusual. He seems to want to convey his greeting to "every single one" of the Philippians individually. This may be part of Paul's response to the division within this church. He may be calling each one to receive all the others. Ἀσπάσασθε, the aor. mid. (deponent) impv. 2 pl. of ἀσπάζομαι ("to greet, welcome"), is a standard word for conveying greetings in the epistolary closings of letters. Letters of this period commonly contained greetings to the recipient(s) from others who are in contact with the sender. It is not clear to whom the imperative ἀσπάσασθε is addressed. Perhaps it is the church leaders (bishops and deacons) addressed in the greeting, but since the letter is first of all addressed to the whole church, this imperative may simply be the way that Paul sends his greetings.

ἐν Χριστῷ Ἰησοῦ—On this phrase see 4:19.

ἀσπάζονται ὑμᾶς οἱ σὺν ἐμοὶ ἀδελφοί—These people who ἀσπάζονται (pres. mid./pass. [deponent] indic. 3 pl. of ἀσπάζομαι, "to greet") ὑμᾶς (acc. pl.), whom Paul designates as those σὺν ἐμοὶ (dat. sg.), seem to be Paul's co-workers because they are distinguished from "all the saints" who send their greeting in the next sentence. The prepositional phrase σὺν ἐμοὶ stands in the attributive position with respect to ἀδελφοί and so designates which "brothers" send their greeting. Just as Paul's use of ἀδελφοί (masc. nom. pl.) to refer to the Philippians does not mean that he is speaking only to the men of the congregation, so also when Paul calls his co-workers "brothers," it does not indicate that they all are men. After all, he has named Euodia and Syntyche co-workers in this letter.

ἀσπάζονται ὑμᾶς πάντες οἱ ἅγιοι–Now a wider group, πάντες (masc. nom. pl.) οἱ ἅγιοι (masc. nom. pl.), "all the saints," sends its greetings (ἀσπάζονται [pres. mid./pass. (deponent) indic. 3 pl. of ἀσπάζομαι, "to greet"]). So Paul conveys the greeting of all Christians who are in the place from which he writes.

4:22

μάλιστα δὲ οἱ ἐκ τῆς Καίσαρος οἰκίας–Οἰκίας (fem. gen. sg. ["household"]), with its definite article τῆς (fem. gen. sg.), is the object of the preposition ἐκ, and Καίσαρος (masc. gen. sg.) is a possessive genitive, indicating that this household belongs to Caesar. The definite article οἱ (masc. nom. pl.) substantivizes the prepositional phrase following it, which then is a second subject of ἀσπάζονται. The superlative adverb μάλιστα is found in only two other places in the undisputed Paulines (Gal 6:10; Phlm 16). It is uncommon in all the NT (appearing only twelve times) except for the Pastoral Epistles, where it is used five times. The mention of Caesar's household helps us identify where Paul was when he wrote this letter. It does not, however, limit the possibilities to one city. Caesar's household included soldiers, freed people, and slaves. The largest grouping of such people clearly was Rome, but there were other places, in particular Caesarea and Ephesus, that also had a contingent of members of the emperor's household.

ἡ χάρις τοῦ κυρίου Ἰησοῦ Χριστοῦ–The closing benediction found here is quite similar to most of Paul's closing benedictions, and it is almost identical to that found in Galatians. Most closing benedictions in the undisputed Pauline letters begin with ἡ χάρις (fem. nom. sg. ["grace, favor"]). Most also have κυρίου (masc. gen. sg.) Ἰησοῦ (masc. gen. sg.) Χριστοῦ (masc. gen. sg.). Given that this is a closing formula, it seems probable that an optative verb rather than an indicative one should be supplied here because the phrase expresses a wish.

4:23

μετὰ τοῦ πνεύματος ὑμῶν–The object of μετὰ is τοῦ πνεύματος (neut. gen. sg. ["spirit"]). This construction is most likely the **distributive singular.** Paul clearly intends to include all the Philippians because he uses ὑμῶν, the plural (genitive) pronoun. Paul more often writes simply μεθ' ὑμῶν, but we find μετὰ τοῦ πνεύματος in Galatians and Philemon as well as here (it is also in 1 Timothy). It may be discomfort with this distributive singular that led some copyists (a corrector of ℵ, K [ninth century], L [ninth century], Ψ [eighth/ninth century]) to replace it with πάντων, also found in 1 Cor 16:24; 2 Cor 13:13; 2 Thess 3:18; Titus 3:15. That this is assimilation to those closing benedictions is confirmed by the stronger attestation for the accepted reading, found in 𝔓⁴⁶, the original hand of ℵ, A, B, D, F, G, and

---

distributive singular

A singular noun or substantive used to refer to members of a group

πεπωρωμένην ἔχετε τὴν <u>καρδίαν</u> ὑμῶν;

Have you (plural) hardened your <u>heart</u>? (Mark 8:17)

Μὴ οὖν βασιλευέτω ἡ ἁμαρτία ἐν τῷ θνητῷ ὑμῶν <u>σώματι</u>.

Do not therefore let sin reign in your (plural) mortal <u>body</u>. (Rom 6:12)

several other witnesses. Perhaps Paul was drawn to express himself as he does here because he had already used the singular to speak of the Philippians (v. 21). While this may not account for its use in Galatians and Philemon, note that in Gal 6:17 Paul uses the singular μηδεὶς just before the same phrase, and in Phlm 23 Epaphras individually sends his greeting (with a third-person singular verb) just two verses above the other appearance of the phrase. It seems doubtful that Paul is making any theological point (beyond his usual μεθ' ὑμῶν) with this phrase. Still, this may be one last rejection of the divisions among them if πνεύματος is meant to refer to the spirit of the Philippian congregation.

A final ἀμήν is found in 𝔓46, ℵ, A, D, and other uncials and most minuscules. Although this reading has strong external attestation, it may have been added to cohere with liturgical practice. It is more difficult to account for its omission in B, F, and G than for its addition in the other manuscripts. ℵ, A, and B also add the subscription πρὸς Φιλιππησίους.

FOR FURTHER STUDY

Doty, William G. *Letters in Primitive Christianity*. Philadelphia: Fortress, 1973.

Weima, J. A. D. *Neglected Endings: The Significance of the Pauline Letter Closings*. Journal for the Study of the New Testament: Supplement Series 101. Sheffield: Sheffield Academic Press, 1994.

White, John L. *Light From Ancient Letters*. Foundations and Facets. Philadelphia: Fortress, 1986.

Conclusion: Philippians and Beyond

This book has tried to help beginning and intermediate readers work their way through a book of the New Testament in a way that shows the importance of working with the Greek text. Thinking through sentence and grammatical structures may not seem like exciting work, but often it influences interpretation in substantial ways. It is important, then, to look beyond the completion of your initial reading of Philippians to ways to continue and improve your work with the Greek text. As you continue to read Greek, it will become easier because you will have a larger vocabulary and remain familiar with a broader range of grammatical constructions.

Readers who are interested in more detailed study of Philippians will want to turn to both critical commentaries and studies that help with word studies and other historical and theological issues. The leading English-language commentaries on the Greek text of Philippians are listed below. Philippians is rich in its theology. Its Christology has been a focus of much study, and it continues to be an important source for our understanding of the earliest church's reflections on the nature and work of Christ. The poetic material in ch. 2 also gives us a window into the sources on which those first believers drew to think about Christ. Philippians also invites study of what it means to be a Christian. Its use of πολίτευμα signals a direction of thought that is significant for understanding Paul's theological thought. There are also resources in this letter for understanding Paul's view of apostleship and ministry, as well as how his theological affirmations not only lead to but also entail a commitment to a particular manner of life.

It is important that due care is taken with word studies. First, interpreters should remember that words change meanings over time. That a word had a particular nuance in the fourth century B.C.E. does not mean that it does, or even could have, that meaning in the first century C.E. Second, interpreters must take into account the cultural predispositions of those who do word studies. Many New Testament scholars recognize that the *TDNT* has something of an anti-Jewish or anti-Judaism bias, a product of the cultural environment in which it was produced. At the same time, there is no comparable tool for acquiring data quickly about many New Testament words. Readers must simply take into account the limitations of this (and all) work as they use it and go to multiple sources to seek balance in the interpretation of the evidence. Finally, word studies must take the context of their primary text into account. That a word has a particular meaning in one context does not mean that it has, or even can have, that meaning in all contexts. The word πίστις is a prime example. Besides meanings such as "faith," "faithfulness," and "assurance," it can also mean a "proof" or element in an argument when it appears in the writings of orators. It is rather clear that πίστις does not mean a "proof" when Paul uses it in Galatians. So context remains an important indicator of a word's meaning, no matter how broad that word's semantic range is.

Those who are ready to read another text and are interested in the Pauline letters may wish to continue their reading of Greek by turning to Galatians or 1 Thessalonians. These short letters will provide good practice and will give the student a sense of making genuine progress. Both are also letters that are important for understanding Paul and his theology. Those who tackle the longer letters may feel that they will never complete the task ahead and become discouraged. Staying within the Pauline corpus may present fewer problems than moving to the Catholic Epistles. Some of those letters are more difficult syntactically and sometimes will require more new vocabulary. In the long run this may have the reward of making less complex writings easier to read, but it may make daily reading less rewarding in the short run.

Those who prefer to move to a different genre may find the Gospel of John or the book of Revelation the best places to go. Both of these books are written in relatively simple Greek. Luke (along with Acts) is written in the most complex Greek in comparison with the other Gospels. Still, much of the New Testament is composed in relatively simple Greek. Moving to some other Hellenistic writers will prove more challenging. Noncanonical texts require you to work with texts that you are less familiar with (and so cannot guess as often what the phrase says) and will frequently move you to writings that are more grammatically and syntactically complex. Reading more difficult works outside the New Testament also will enhance your reading of those within the canon when those within are less complex. Such reading will also aid your reading of the New Testament by giving you a richer understanding of its historical context.

Perhaps the most probable way readers will continue faithfully to read their Greek text is if they are reading texts that they must interpret for some other reason. If you have a class on a group of texts or a paper on a particular text, or if in the context of church ministry you have a Bible study on a particular book, this may provide the best text to choose for your continuing study of Greek. In those cases, Greek study also serves as preparation for other, pressing obligations. Whatever option you chose, it is important to read Greek on a very regular basis, daily if possible. When you do not use a language, your facility in it will decrease rapidly. Constant, even brief, use will maintain and increase your ability to read the text. So find a text that intrigues you or that you must learn about and determine to understand it as clearly as possible.

Overview of the Syntactical Structure of New Testament Greek

$$\multimap\!\!\infty\infty\infty\!\!\multimap$$

The following summary of various syntactical features of New Testament Greek by no means exhausts the uses of the grammatical forms. This overview is intended only as a quick guide to enable an initial reading of Philippians, though there are notes on syntactical constructions here that do not appear in Philippians. Readers should consult standard grammars for more details and further examples. The primary grammars consulted for this summary, and from which some examples are taken, are BDF, Wallace, Smyth, Paine, Moule, and Dana and Mantey.

1. The Article

A. With modifiers. When an adjective or other modifier comes between the article and the noun, it is in the <u>attributive position</u>: ἀπὸ τῆς πρώτης ἡμέρας, *from the first day* (Phil 1:5). The modifier is also in the attributive position when it follows a noun and has its own article: Ἐπαφρόδιτον τὸν ἀδελφὸν ... μου, *Epaphroditus my brother* (Phil 2:25). Modifiers in the <u>predicate position</u> are anarthrous (that is, they are not preceded by an article): ἐπὶ πάσῃ τῇ μνείᾳ, *at every remembrance* (Phil 1:3).

B. With proper nouns or those designating persons. An article may accompany a proper name. This happens often with ὁ Χριστός, *Christ* (Phil 1:27) and ὁ Θεός, *God* (Phil 2:27), and in the Gospels with Ἰησοῦς, *Jesus*, but only rarely in Paul (however, διὰ τοῦ Ἰησοῦ, *through Jesus* [1 Thess 4:14]). In such instances, the article identifies the case of the noun, but usually does not alter its sense.

C. With abstract nouns. Nouns that denote abstractions or qualities often take the definite article: πληρώσατέ μου <u>τὴν χαρὰν</u>, *fulfill my joy* (Phil 2:2). The article is sometimes absent with an abstract noun, where one might expect it in English: ἐν σαρκί, *in the flesh* (Phil 1:22). With abstract nouns the article often makes no difference in the meaning; however, when it is used with ἅγιον πνεῦμα, the article sometimes indicates that the reference is to the Holy Spirit.

D. With a substantivizing force. An article sometimes substantivizes an adjective: οἱ <u>τὰ ἐπίγεια</u> φρονοῦντες, *who set their minds on <u>earthly things</u>* (Phil 3:19). They also can substantivize a prepositional phrase: τὰ κατ᾽ ἐμέ, *my affairs* (or more woodenly: *the things about me*; Phil 1:12; cf. 2:4, 19).

E. With appositives. An article sometimes appears with an appositive even when the other noun is anarthrous: Ἐπαφρόδιτον τὸν ἀδελφὸν καὶ συνεργὸν καὶ συστρατιώτην μου, *Epaphroditus, my brother and fellow-worker and fellow-soldier* (Phil 2:25).

2. Noun Cases

Nominative Case

A. Subject of the verb. The basic use of the nominative is to serve as the subject of finite verbs:

B. Predicate nominative. A nominative may also serve as the predicate of a verb of being, knowing, and thinking:

ἡμεῖς γὰρ ἐσμεν <u>ἡ περιτομή</u>.
For we are <u>the circumcision</u>. (Phil 3:3)

C. Nominative absolute. Nominatives are sometimes used not as the subject of a sentence, but in a way grammatically unconnected to a verb. This normally occurs in greetings, salutations, and titles of writings. According to Wallace (50–51), only nouns that are not parts of a complete sentence and that appear in the introductory sections are nominative absolutes. Other grammarians allow that the category may include nominatives that are part of a sentence, but are still grammatically unrelated to the rest of the sentence. In some uses the reader must supply an implied verb (e.g., Phil 1:2).

<u>Παῦλος ἀπόστολος</u> Χριστοῦ Ἰησοῦ
<u>Paul, apostle</u> of Christ Jesus (2 Cor 1:1)

Genitive Case

Genitives limit or describe the meanings of substantives, adjectives, and adverbs. They can appear in either the predicate or attributive position.

A. Epexegetical genitive. The genitive sometimes explains or clarifies the word it modifies. This is one of the broadest identifications of the use of a genitive.

B. Genitive absolute. See participles.

C. Genitive of apposition. A substantive in the genitive case may refer to the same person or thing as the substantive it modifies. Often the genitive word provides more specific information about a general or ambiguous word.

ἀρραβῶνα <u>τοῦ πνεύματος</u>

the guarantee, <u>that is the Spirit</u> (2 Cor 5:5)

D. Genitive of comparison. The genitive is sometimes used to denote comparison, often with a comparative adjective or adverb

ὁ πατὴρ μείζων <u>μού</u> ἐστιν.

The Father is greater <u>than I</u>. (John 14:28)

E. Genitive of content. The genitive sometimes specifies the contents of the word it modifies.

τὸ δίκτυον <u>τῶν ἰχθύων</u>

the net <u>of</u> [i.e., <u>containing</u>] <u>(the) fish</u> (John 21:8)

F. Genitive of means. The genitive may indicate the means or instrument by which the word it relates to is accomplished

τῆς δικαιοσύνης <u>τῆς πίστεως</u>

the righteousness <u>received by means of faith/faithfulness</u> (Rom 4:11)

G. Genitive of origin. See Genitive of relationship.

H. Genitive of place. The genitive sometimes designates a place in which the word it is related to is placed or situated.

I. Genitive of price or value. The genitive sometimes designates the value of the governing substantive.

<u>διακοσίων δηναρίων</u> ἄρτοι οὐκ ἀρκοῦσιν αὐτοῖς.

Loaves <u>worth two hundred denarii</u> are not enough for them. (John 6:7)

J. Genitive of production. On occasion, but rarely, the genitive designates what produced the noun that governs it, as perhaps in the following example. See Wallace, 105.

θανάτου δὲ <u>σταυροῦ</u>

death <u>produced by the cross</u> (Phil 2:8)

K. Genitive of quality. This genitive designates an innate quality or an attribute of the governing noun.

τῷ σώματι <u>τῆς δόξης</u> αὐτοῦ

his <u>glorious</u> body (Phil 3:21)

L. Genitive of reference. On rare occasions and usually with a substantive, the genitive is used to specify something about the governing noun it is related to. Perhaps there is a case in the following example.

τὸ σῶμα <u>τῆς ταπεινώσεως</u> ἡμῶν
our body <u>that endures humiliation</u> (Phil 3:21)

M. Genitive of relationship (origin). Genitives may specify the family one belongs to or a substantive's place of origin.

Μαρία ἡ <u>Ἰωσῆτος</u>
Mary, the <u>mother of</u> Joses (Mark 15:47)

καρπὸν <u>δικαιοσύνης</u>
fruit <u>that comes from righteousness </u> (Phil 1:11)

N. Genitive of source. Similar to the gen. of origin, this genitive identifies the source from which an object derives.

τοῦτό μοι καρπὸς ἔργου.
For me this is fruit <u>of labor</u> [that is, *fruit <u>that comes from work</u>*]. (Phil 1:22)

O. Objective genitive. The genitive case is used to designate the object of an action. In places where the phrase πίστις Χριστοῦ uses an objective genitive, it refers to faith directed to Christ, faith "in Christ."

P. Partitive genitive. Genitives may designate the group or the whole of which the substantive is a part.

τοὺς πλείονας <u>τῶν ἀδελφῶν</u>
the majority <u>of the brothers</u> (Phil 1:14)

Q. Possessive genitive. The genitive case is used to denote possession or ownership of objects or attributes.

οἱ ἐκ τῆς <u>Καίσαρος</u> οἰκίας
those of the household <u>of Caesar</u> (Phil 4:22)

R. Qualitative genitive. The genitive may make a noun function as an adjective so that it attributes a particular quality or characteristic to the term it modifies.

ἐν τῷ σώματι <u>τῆς σαρκός</u> αὐτοῦ
in his <u>fleshly</u> body (Col 1:22)

S. Subjective genitive. The genitive case is used to designate the subject of the action implied in the word it modifies. Thus "the love of Christ" would indicate the love Christ has for others.

Dative Case

A. Dative as indirect object. The most basic use of the dative is to designate an indirect object.

B. Dative of accompaniment (association). A dative is used with words that imply that others accompany the subject in the action (e.g., following a leader).

χαίρω καὶ συγχαίρω <u>πᾶσιν ὑμῖν</u>.
I rejoice, and I rejoice <u>with all of you</u>. (Phil 2:17)

C. Dative of advantage or disadvantage. The dative case is used to designate persons or things to whom the action or situation gives an advantage or disadvantage.

ἅτινα ἦν <u>μοι</u> κέρδη
these things that were <u>of benefit to me</u> (Phil 3:7)

D. Dative of agent. When the dative appears with a passive verb and designates a person, it sometimes designates the one by whom the action of the verb was done.

ὤφθη <u>ἀγγέλοις</u>
He was seen <u>by angels</u>. (1 Tim 3:16)

E. Dative of association. See Dative of accompaniment.

F. Dative of cause. Closely related to the dative of means, the dative may designate the cause of something. The phrase in Phil 1:14, identified in the text as an instrumental dative, may also be more narrowly defined in this way.

καὶ τοὺς πλείονας τῶν ἀδελφῶν ἐν κυρίῳ πεποιθότας <u>τοῖς δεσμοῖς</u> μου
and most of the brothers have been made confident in the Lord <u>because of</u> my <u>bonds</u> (Phil 1:14)

G. Dative of degree of difference. When it appears with comparatives, the dative may designate the degree of difference between (or among) things.

ἀλλὰ νῦν πολλῷ μᾶλλον <u>ἐν τῇ ἀπουσίᾳ</u> μου
but now much more <u>in my absence</u> (Phil 2:12)

H. Dative of manner. The dative may indicate the manner or method in which something was accomplished, a use closely related to the instrumental dative. It designates how something was done.

εἴτε <u>προφάσει</u> εἴτε <u>ἀληθείᾳ</u> Χριστὸς καταγγέλλεται
Whether <u>from false motives</u> or <u>from true</u>, Christ is preached. (Phil 1:18)

I. Dative of means. See Instrumental dative.

J. Dative of personal agency. See Dative of agent.

K. Dative of place. See Locative dative.

L. Dative of recipient. The use of the dative case in a verbless construction (such as the greeting of a letter) to designate the person(s) or thing(s) receiving the implied action.

πᾶσιν τοῖς ἁγίοις ἐν Χριστῷ Ἰησοῦ τοῖς οὖσιν ἐν Φιλίπποις
to all the saints in Christ Jesus who are in Philippi (Phil 1:1)

M. Dative of respect (relation). The dative is used to limit the statement in a predicate to the person named (Smyth, 1495) or to limit to whom a statement or perspective holds true. Often this dative is used when the statement might not be true otherwise, or in a different frame of reference.

ἐμοὶ . . . τὸ ζῆν Χριστὸς
From my perspective . . . *to live is Christ* (Phil 1:21)

N. Dative of space. See Locative dative.

O. Dative of time. See Temporal dative.

P. Ethical dative. The dative sometimes designates whose point of view is being expressed. Some consider this a subcategory under dative of reference.

ἀστεῖος τῷ θεῷ
precious to God (Acts 7:20)

ἄσπιλοι καὶ ἀμώμητοι αὐτῷ
pure and spotless before him [i.e., *from God's perspective*] (2 Pet 3:14)

Q. Instrumental dative (dative of means). The dative may designate the means or instrument by which an action is accomplished.

πεποιθότας τοῖς δεσμοῖς μου
being made confident by means of my bonds (Phil 1:14)

R. Locative dative (dative of place). Similarly to the dative of reference, sometimes the dative may designate the sphere in which something occurs.

τῷ πλοιαρίῳ ἦλθον.
They came in a boat. (John 21:8)

also more figuratively:

μακάριοι οἱ καθαροὶ τῇ καρδίᾳ.
Blessed are the pure in heart. (Matt 5:8)

S. Temporal dative (dative of time). The dative case is used to designate when something happens or how long it continues.

καὶ ὅτι ἐγήγερται <u>τῇ ἡμέρᾳ τῇ τρίτῃ</u>

and that he was raised <u>on the third day</u> (1 Cor 15:4)

Accusative Case

A. Accusative as direct object. The basic function of an accusative is to designate the direct object of the verb.

B. Accusative of content. The object of the verb indicates something implied within the verb itself, e.g., to fight a war. Such accusatives are often cognates of the governing verb. See the discussion of Phil 1:6 in the text.

<u>ἐφοβήθησαν φόβον</u> μέγαν

They <u>feared</u> with great <u>fear</u> (Mark 4:41)

C. Accusative of respect. On rare occasions, the accusative case supplies a frame of reference within which the action of the verb is true or the extent to which it makes sense.

<u>τὸ μυστήριον</u> τῶν ἑπτὰ ἀστέρων

<u>*regarding the mystery*</u> *of the seven stars* (Rev 1:20)

D. Cognate accusative. When an accusative appears with a verb from the same root, it is a cognate accusative. This construction may, but does not necessarily, convey emphasis.

ἀνθρώπῳ <u>οἰκοδομήσαντι οἰκίαν</u>

a man who <u>built a house</u> (Luke 6:49)

E. Double accusative. With verbs of teaching, reminding, asking, and other verbs that need two direct objects, often a person and a thing, both are in the accusative case.

ἐκεῖνος <u>ὑμᾶς</u> διδάξει <u>πάντα</u>

He will teach <u>you all things</u>. (John 14:26)

F. Predicate accusative. A double accusative is often used with verbs of having, designating, regarding, etc. The first accusative designates the object, while the second indicates what is said about the object.

<u>ἀλλήλους</u> ἡγούμενοι ὑπερέχοντας ἑαυτῶν

considering <u>others better</u> than yourselves (Phil 2:3)

G. With infinitives. Accusatives function as both the subject and the object of infinities, often with articular infinitives. In some cases it can be difficult to determine which accusative is the subject and which is the object (cf. Phil 1:7).

As subject:

μετὰ τὸ παθεῖν <u>αὐτὸν</u>

after <u>he</u> suffered (Acts 1:3)

As object:

τοῦ γνῶναι <u>αὐτὸν</u>

to know <u>him</u> (Phil 3:10)

As both subject and object:

εἰς τὸ δοκιμάζειν <u>ὑμᾶς</u> <u>τὰ διαφέροντα</u>

so that <u>you</u> may discern <u>the important things</u> (Phil 1:10)

Vocative Case

The vocative is used to designate those being addressed, and so is a form of direct address: ἀγαπητοί μου, *my beloved* (Phil 2:12). It may also indicate emphasis or appear in an appositive. It gives emphasis in Romans 2:3: ὦ ἄνθρωπε ὁ κρίνων, *O person, who judges.*

3. Pronouns

A. Demonstrative pronouns. These pronouns serve to point to a person or object in a particular way. Three such pronouns occur in the New Testament: οὗτος, *this* (pointing to something near) ἐκεῖνος, *that* (pointing to something more distant) and ὅδε, *this.*

B. Indefinite pronoun. The indefinite pronoun (τις, τι) refers to persons or things non-specifically, e.g., "whoever," "someone," "a certain [person]," "anyone" (Phil 3:4). In the New Testament, forms of τις and τι are distinguished from the interrogative pronouns τίς and τί only by the way they are accented.

C. Indefinite relative pronoun. See the discussion of ὅστις under Relative pronouns.

D. Intensive pronoun. When αὐτός appears with an anarthrous noun or in the predicate position, it makes the noun emphatic in the sentence. It may also have this force when it appears in a sentence where it is not needed.

αὐτὸς ταχέως ἐλεύσομαι.

I <u>myself</u> will come quickly. (Phil 2:24)

E. Interrogative pronouns. The interrogative pronouns (τίς, τί) (*who* or *what*), ποῖος (*what kind*), and πόσος (*how much*) ask questions. In the New Testament, forms of τίς and τί are distinguished from the indefinite pronouns τις and τι only by the way they are accented.

<u>τίς</u> ὁ κατακρινῶν;
<u>Who</u> is the one who condemns? (Rom 8:34)

F. Personal pronouns. The first, second, and third person personal pronouns (ἐγώ, σύ, and αὐτός [*I, you,* and *he/she/it*]) take the place of nouns. Beside their basic (anaphoric) use, personal pronouns may add emphasis or indicate possession.

χάρις <u>ὑμῖν</u> καὶ εἰρήνη
grace and peace <u>to you</u> (Phil 1:2)

G. Possessive pronouns. Possessive pronouns (also called possessive adjectives: ἐμός, σός, ἡμέτερος, ὑμέτερος) indicate ownership or possession, much like personal pronouns used in the genitive case.

ποιεῖτε εἰς τὴν <u>ἐμὴν</u> ἀνάμνησιν.
Do this in <u>my</u> memory. (1 Cor. 11:24)

H. Reflexive pronouns. The reflexive pronouns (ἐμαυτοῦ, σεαυτοῦ, ἑαυτοῦ) refer back to their antecedent, usually the subject of the sentence, and commonly make that person or thing both the subject and the direct or indirect of the verb at the same time.

<u>ἑαυτὸν</u> ἐκένωσεν.
He emptied <u>himself</u>. (Phil 2:7)

I. Relative pronouns. Relative pronouns (ὅς and ὅστις) typically relate their antecedent to an additional phrase or clause. Occasionally, they may appear with no grammatical antecedent and function as the subject of a sentence. They may appear in any case, as determined by their function in the relative clause, and often serve as the subject of the relative clause. Ὅστις, often referred to as an indefinite relative pronoun, has a more generic or qualitative sense than ὅς.

<u>ὅς</u> ἐν μορφῇ Θεοῦ ὑπάρχων
<u>who</u> being in the form of God (Phil 2:6)

4. Adjectives

A. Agreement with nouns. Adjectives agree in case, number, and gender with the noun or adjective they modify.

καὶ <u>πᾶσα γλῶσσα</u> ἐξομολογήσηται.
And <u>every tongue</u> shall confess. (Phil 2:11)

B. Predicate adjectives. With verbs of being, adjectives may function as predicates and in this way describe or add an attribute to their subject.

ἵνα γένεσθε <u>ἄμεμπτοι</u> καὶ <u>ἀκέραιοι</u>
so that you might be <u>blameless</u> and <u>pure</u> (Phil 2:15)

Adjectives may also function in this way when making an assertion about the subject.

παραστῆσαι ὑμᾶς <u>ἁγίους</u> καὶ <u>ἀμώμους</u> καὶ <u>ἀνεγκλήτους</u> κατενώπιον αὐτοῦ
to present you <u>holy</u> and <u>spotless</u> and <u>blameless</u> before him (Col 1:22)

C. Used as adverbs. On some occasions adjectives function as adverbs. When they do, they are often in the accusative case and appear with the article. Λοιπός is one of the group of adjectives that often has this function.

<u>τὸ λοιπόν</u>, ἀδελφοί μου
<u>Finally</u>, my brothers [and sisters] (Phil 3:1)

D. Used as substantives. Adjectives, and particularly frequently used ones, sometimes function as nouns in sentences. Usually such adjectives will be preceded by the article. Perhaps the most common such usage in the Pauline corpus and the New Testament is ἅγιος, which comes to denote *saints*, a common title by which Paul addresses his congregations.

πᾶσιν <u>τοῖς ἁγίοις</u> ἐν Χριστῷ Ἰησοῦ τοῖς οὖσιν ἐν Φιλίπποις
to all <u>the saints</u> in Christ Jesus who are in Philippi (Phil 1:1)

5. Verbs

Agreement with subject. Verbs agree in person and number with their subject. An important exception is that a neuter plural subject takes a singular verb.

Tense

In Greek, *tense* refers to both the *time* (past, present, or future) and the *state* or *aspect* (continuing, complete, or completed with continuing results) of a verb's action. The element of time is present in an absolute sense only in the indicative mood, and in a relative sense in the participle. In the other moods, aspect alone is communicated by a verb's tense.

A. Present. The present tense represents continuing action. In the indicative mood the action typically occurs in the present. The present participle usually represents action that occurs at the same time as that of the leading verb.

B. Imperfect. The imperfect tense represents continuous or repeated action in the past.

C. Future. The future tense denotes a complete or ongoing action that will take place in the future.

D. Aorist. The aorist tense refers to a complete action—an action as a whole—with no indication as to its progress. In the indicative mood, the aorist typically represents action that took place in the past. The aorist participle usually represents action that occurs prior to that of the leading verb.

E. Perfect. The perfect tense denotes an action performed in the past that has continuing results or effects that reach into the present. Depending on the context, the emphasis may either be on the completion of the action in the past or on the results of the action in the present.

F. Pluperfect. The pluperfect is the past tense of the perfect and thus denotes an action completed in the past that continued to have effects at a later time in the past.

Special Uses of the Tenses

A. Historical present. When the present is used in a narrative to refer to an action in the past, it is an historical present. It is fairly common in the Gospels.

Καὶ <u>λέγει</u> αὐτοῖς ὁ Ἰησοῦς
And Jesus <u>said</u> to them (Mark 14:27)

B. Iterative present or imperfect. Sometimes the present or the imperfect describes an event that occurs repeatedly.

καθ' ἡμέραν <u>ἀποθνῄσκω</u>.
I <u>die</u> daily. (1 Cor 15:31; see also 1 Tim 5:5; 2 Tim 1:3)

C. Perfective present. Sometimes the present has the significance of a perfect in that it denotes an action in the past that continues to have effects in the present. This is especially common with verbs of hearing and speaking, among others. Often this construction introduces a Scripture quotation.

<u>λέγει</u> γάρ, Καιρῷ δεκτῷ ἐπήκουσά σου.
For <u>he says</u>, at the favorable time I heard you. (2 Cor 6:2)

Compare this present with the use of the perfect verb γέγραπται throughout 1 Corinthians (e.g., 3:19). In Gal 4:27, 29 the first quotation is introduced with the perfect and the second with the perfective present.

D. Predictive future. This use of the future tense signifies that something is expected with certainty to take place in the future.

ὁ ἐναρξάμενος ἐν ὑμῖν ἔργον ἀγαθὸν <u>ἐπιτελέσει</u>.

The one who began a good work in you <u>will complete</u> it. (Phil 1:6)

E. Epistolary aorist. Sometimes the author of a letter uses the aorist indicative to speak in the time frame or with the viewpoint of the readers, describing as past an action that the author has not yet taken. This is most often used in describing what the author is doing in conjunction with writing the letter

οὖν <u>ἔπεμψα</u> αὐτόν.

Therefore, <u>I am sending</u> (lit. <u>I sent</u>) *him [Epaphroditus].* (Phil 2:28)

F. Ingressive aorist. This use of the aorist refers to the initiation or beginning of an act or state of being.

<u>ἐπτώχευσεν</u> πλούσιος ὤν.

Though he was rich, <u>he became poor</u>. (2 Cor 8:9)

Mood

A verb's mood indicates whether the verbal action is actual or merely potential.

A. Indicative. The indicative is used to present an assertion or to ask a simple question. The verb of the main clause of a sentence is usually in the indicative mood.

B. Subjunctive. The subjunctive acknowledges that there is some contingency about the action, but asserts that the action is probable. It is often translated with "might" before the verb.

1. Deliberative subjunctive. The subjunctive may express a real question or a rhetorical question that does not expect an answer because the answer is clear or the question rests on certain assumptions.

Real question:

τί <u>φάγωμεν</u>;

What <u>should we eat</u>? (Matt 6:31)

Rhetorical question:

<u>ἐπιμένωμεν</u> τῇ ἁμαρτίᾳ;

<u>Shall we continue</u> in sin? (Rom 6:1)

2. Hortatory subjunctive. The subjunctive may be used to encourage, exhort, or command others and oneself.

ὅσοι οὖν τέλειοι, τοῦτο <u>φρονῶμεν</u>·

<u>Let</u> those of <u>us</u> who are mature <u>think</u> this way. (Phil 3:15)

3. **Prohibiting subjunctive (Subjunctive of prohibition).** The subjunctive may express a prohibition, telling what one must not do.

Μὴ <u>ἅψῃ</u> μηδὲ <u>γεύσῃ</u> μηδὲ <u>θίγῃς</u>.

Do not <u>handle</u>, do not <u>taste</u>, do not <u>touch</u>. (Col 2:21)

C. **Optative.** The optative expresses a possibility or often a wish or desire. It is also used in indirect discourse and in some conditional sentences. It is rare in the New Testament.

μὴ <u>γένοιτο</u>·
<u>May it</u> never <u>be</u>! (Rom 3:4)

In Phil 4:19, some manuscripts (including D, F, and G) have an aorist optative verb, πληρῶσαι, in place of the future indicative verb πληρώσει. With the optative the statement reads as a prayer request ("<u>May</u> my God <u>supply</u> your every need") rather than as a straightforward assertion ("My God <u>will supply</u> your every need").

D. **Imperative.** The basic function of an imperative is to issue a command or entreaty:

<u>προσδέχεσθε</u> οὖν αὐτὸν ἐν κυρίῳ·
Therefore, <u>receive</u> him in the Lord. (Phil 2:29)

Sometimes, however, imperatives have more of a permissive implication:

εἰ δὲ ὁ ἄπιστος χωρίζεται, <u>χωριζέσθω</u>.
If the unbeliever leaves, <u>let him</u> (or <u>her</u>) <u>go</u>. (1 Cor 7:15)

Voice

The voice of a verb designates the way that the subject is related to the action of the verb.

A. **Active.** The subject performs the action of the verb:

<u>Εὐχαριστῶ</u> τῷ Θεῷ μου.
<u>I thank</u> my God. (Phil 1:3)

B. **Middle.** The subject who performs the action also in some way receives or participates in the action. Often the middle voice has a reflexive sense:

<u>ἐνδύσασθε</u> τὴν πανοπλίαν τοῦ Θεοῦ.
<u>Cloth yourselves</u> with the armor of God. (Eph 6:11)

The majority of middle verbs in the NT are deponent, in which the middle voice has an active meaning:

<u>συλλαμβάνου</u> αὐταῖς.

<u>Help</u> them. (Phil 4:3)

C. Passive. The passive voice denotes that the subject of the verb receives the action, or that the action is done to the subject.

Χριστὸς <u>καταγγέλλεται</u>.

Christ <u>is preached.</u> (Phil 1:18)

6. Infinitives

The infinitive is defined as a verbal noun. Like a noun, it can take the article and can serve as the object of a preposition. Although not itself declinable, an articular infinitive commonly has the force of a substantive: τὸ δὲ ἐπιμένειν (ἐν) τῇ σαρκὶ ἀναγκαιότερον, *but remaining in the flesh is more necessary* (Phil 1:24). Like a verb, it has tense and voice, can take a subject or an object, and can be modified by an adverb.

εἰς τὸ <u>δοκιμάζειν</u> ὑμᾶς τὰ διαφέροντα

so that you may <u>discern</u> what is important (Phil 1:10)

or as a complement of a verb:

<u>Γινώσκειν</u> δὲ ὑμᾶς βούλομαι.

I want you <u>to know.</u> (Phil 1:12; see also 2:19)

A. Epexegetical. The epexegetical infinitive clarifies or defines more clearly the noun or adjective it accompanies.

κατὰ τὴν οἰκονομίαν τοῦ Θεοῦ . . . <u>πληρῶσαι</u> τὸν λόγον τοῦ Θεοῦ

according to the commission of God . . . <u>to fulfill</u> the word of God (Col 1:25)

B. Imperatival. The infinitive sometimes gives a command.

τῷ αὐτῷ <u>στοιχεῖν</u>.

[Let us] <u>hold</u> to the same thing. (Phil 3:16)

<u>χαίρειν</u> μετὰ χαιρόντων.

<u>Rejoice</u> with those who rejoice. (Rom 12:15).

C. Purpose. The infinitive is commonly used to express the goal or purpose of the governing verb. The infinitive may be anarthrous, have the genitive article τοῦ, and/or have the preposition εἰς or πρός. On rare occasions it may follow ὥστε or ὡς.

ἀποκατήλλαξεν . . . <u>παραστῆσαι</u> ὑμᾶς ἁγίους καὶ ἀμώμους καὶ ἀνεγκλήτους κατενώπιον αὐτοῦ.

He has reconciled [you] . . . <u>to present</u> you holy and spotless and blameless before him. (Col 1:22)

D. Results. Infinitives may express the result that is produced by the governing verb. Such infinitives commonly follow ὥστε. This construction is less common in Paul, where it is often difficult to decide whether ὥστε with the infinitive expresses result or purpose, than in the Gospels.

ὁ δὲ Ἰησοῦς οὐκέτι οὐδὲν ἀπεκρίθη, ὥστε <u>θαυμάζειν</u> τὸν Πιλᾶτον.

But Jesus no longer answered anything, so that Pilate <u>was amazed</u>. (Mark 15:5)

Sometimes the infinitive has no particle or preposition and may be articular or anarthrous:

ἵνα ὁ Θεὸς ἀνοίξῃ ἡμῖν θύραν τοῦ λόγου <u>λαλῆσαι</u> τὸ μυστήριον

that God might open a door of utterance for us <u>to speak</u> the mystery (Col 4:3)

E. Substantival. Infinitives may be used in place of a noun as either the subject or object of a verb:

οὐχ ἁρπαγμὸν ἡγήσατο <u>τὸ εἶναι</u> ἴσα Θεῷ

He did not consider <u>equality</u> with God something to be grasped. (Phil 2:6; see also Phil 1:21, 2:13; 4:10)

7. Participles

Participles may function as nouns, adjectives, adverbs, or verbs. Participles have tense and voice, as do verbs; they also have gender, number, and case, as do adjectives. They may modify nouns, complete the action of verbs, or function independently, much as a relative clause functions.

A. Adverbial. A participle may qualify its governing verb:

<u>πεποιθὼς</u> οἶδα.

I know <u>confidently</u>. (Phil 1:25)

B. Attributive (Adjectival). A participle may stand in the attributive position and modify a noun. In this case it should often be translated as a relative clause:

Ἰησοῦς <u>ὁ λεγόμενος</u> Ἰοῦστος

Jesus <u>who is called</u> Justus (Col 4:11)

C. Circumstantial. A participle may be used in the predicate position to define the circumstances in which the main action takes place, or the state of affairs that exists in the context of that action. The following are some of the most common circumstances indicated:

1. *Attendant circumstances:* The action of the participle presents an additional fact or thought closely related to or coordinated with the action of the main verb. It is often translated as a finite verb connected to the main verb with "and."

   <u>πεσὼν</u> ἐξέψυξεν.

   He <u>fell down and</u> died. (Acts 5:5)

2. *Cause:* The participle provides a reason for the state or action of the main verb. It is often translated "because."

   καὶ τοῦτο <u>πεποιθὼς</u> οἶδα

   And being confident (<u>because I am confident</u>) of this, I know. (Phil 1:25; see also 1:6)

3. *Concession/Concessive:* The circumstance described by the participle is presented as true despite the state or action of the leading verb. It may be translated *although, even though.*

   διότι <u>γνόντες</u> τὸν θεὸν οὐχ ὡς θεὸν ἐδόξασαν

   Because <u>even though they knew</u> God they did not honor [God] as God. (Rom 1:21; perhaps also Phil 2:6 [so Wallace 634])

4. *Condition:* The participle gives the conditions under which the action of the main verb takes place or will take place. It is often translated as the protasis of a conditional sentence using "if."

   καιρῷ γὰρ ἰδίῳ θερίσομεν <u>μὴ ἐκλυόμενοι</u>.

   For at the right time we will reap <u>if we do not faint</u>. (Gal 6:9)

5. *Manner:* The participle describes the manner in which the action of the main verb is accomplished. It is often translated "by" or "with."

   νῦν δὲ καὶ <u>κλαίων</u> λέγω.

   And now I tell you with <u>weeping</u>. (Phil 3:18)

6. *Means:* The participle tells how or describes the means by which the action of the main verb takes place. It is often translated "by" or "by means of." The difference between means and manner is not always clear in translation, though sometimes it may be significant.

   ἀλλὰ ἑαυτὸν ἐκένωσεν μορφὴν δούλου λαβών.

   But he emptied himself (by) taking the form of a servant. (Phil 2:7; see also 1:30)

7. *Purpose:* The participle gives the purpose for which the action of the main verb takes place. It may be translated as "for the purpose of" or as an infinitive with "to."

> Οὐκ <u>ἐντρέπων</u> ὑμᾶς γράφω ταῦτα.

> *I do not write these things <u>for the purpose of shaming</u> (to shame) you.* (1 Cor 4:14)

8. *Result:* The participle designates an actual outcome of the action or state of the main verb. It is often translated "thus" or "as a result." There is at times some overlap between this function and that of the purpose participle.

> καὶ τοὺς πλείονας τῶν ἀδελφῶν ἐν κυρίῳ <u>πεποιθότας</u> τοῖς δεσμοῖς μου.

> *And (as a result) most of the fellow believers <u>have been made confident</u> in the Lord by my imprisonment.* (Phil 1:14)

9. *Time/Temporal:* The action of the participle has a temporal relationship to that of the leading verb. It may be translated "as," "when," "while," "after," etc. (See the section on Verbs, Tense above for more about the relationship between the participle's tense and its time of occurrence in relation to the leading verb.)

> <u>εὐχαριστήσας</u> ἔκλασεν.

> *When [after] he had given thanks he broke [the bread].* (1 Cor 11:24)

> ἔτι ἁμαρτωλῶν <u>ὄντων</u> ἡμῶν Χριστὸς ὑπὲρ ἡμῶν ἀπέθανεν

> *<u>while we were</u> still sinners, Christ died for us* (Rom 5:8)

D. Imperatival. The participle is used to express a command:

μὴ τὰ ἑαυτῶν ἕκαστος <u>σκοποῦντες</u>
<u>Do not (merely) look out for</u> your own affairs. (Phil 2:4)

E. Periphrastic. The participle is used in a periphrastic expression, normally in combination with the verb εἰμί, to express, sometimes more vividly, an action or situation that a single finite verb could also express:

ἐπειδὴ <u>ἐπιποθῶν ἦν</u> πάντας ὑμᾶς.
Indeed, <u>he was desiring</u> you all. (Phil 2:26)

F. Predicate. The participle functions as an object of a verb or as a predicate adjective or predicate nominative:

Θεὸς γάρ ἐστιν ὁ <u>ἐνεργῶν</u> ἐν ὑμῖν.
For God is the one who works in you. (Phil 2:13)

G. Substantival. The participle functions as a noun or adjective:

οἱ τὰ ἐπίγεια <u>φρονοῦντες</u>
those whose minds are focused in the things of the earth (Phil 3:19)

The Genitive Absolute

A genitive absolute is an independent clause composed of an anarthrous genitive participle, usually with a genitive subject (noun or pronoun) that often differs from the subject of the main verb. The participle may appear before or after its subject and may bear any nuance a circumstantial participle may bear. This construction appears relatively often in the Gospels and Acts and rarely in the New Testament letters:

Ταῦτα <u>αὐτοῦ λαλοῦντος</u> αὐτοῖς ἰδοὺ ἄρχων . . . προσεκύνει αὐτῷ.

<u>While he was saying</u> these things to them, behold, a ruler . . . bowed before him. (Matt 9:18)

8. Conditional Sentences

Conditional sentences set out a presupposed condition in the protasis and reach the conclusion on the basis of that supposition in the apodosis.

A. "Real" (Simple) conditional sentences. These assume that the state of affairs given in the protasis is true for the sake of argument, even though what it asserts may not be true (e.g., 1 Cor 15:13). This type of conditional sentence consists of a protasis formed with εἰ plus an indicative verb of any tense and an apodosis with any mood and tense.

εἴ τις ἀρετὴ καὶ εἴ τις ἔπαινος, ταῦτα λογίζεσθε.

If there is any virtue and if there is any praise, think on these things (Phil 4:8)

In the previous example (as in Phil 2:1–2), the verb ἐστίν in the protasis is understood, as is often the case in Greek.

B. Contrary-to-fact ("unreal") conditional sentences. These work on the premise that the statement in the protasis is false, but draw conclusions from the incorrect premise to make a point. This type of conditional sentence appears less often than the other types discussed here. The protasis of this type contains εἰ plus an indicative aorist (for past time) or imperfect (for the present) verb, while the apodosis also has an indicative aorist or imperfect.

εἰ ἔτι ἀνθρώποις ἤρεσκον, Χριστοῦ δοῦλος οὐκ ἂν ἤμην.

If I still sought to please humans, I would not be a servant of Christ. (Gal 1:10)

C. General conditional sentences. These give consequences in the apodosis that are not as certain as those of the real conditional sentences above. In these general conditionals, the asserted conclusion is logical and probable, but not certain. In a number of places, the apodosis contains instructions for what to do if something happens or once it has happened (e.g., Gal 6:1;

Col 3:13; 4:10). These sentences are formed by a protasis that has ἐάν plus the subjunctive in any tense and an apodosis with any mood or tense.

ἐὰν ἄδηλον σάλπιγξ φωνὴν δῷ, τίς παρασκευάσεται εἰς πόλεμον;
If the bugle gives an unclear sound, who will prepare for battle? (1 Cor 14:8)

ἐὰν ἔλθῃ πρὸς ὑμᾶς, δέξασθε αὐτόν.
If he should come to you, receive him. (Col 4:10)

D. Possible (less probable) future conditional sentences. These indicate that the outcome in the apodosis is possible but unlikely. They are formed with εἰ plus an optative verb in the protasis and ἄν plus an optative in the apodosis. This form does not appear fully in any New Testament text, though some sentences assume the apodosis (cf. 1 Pet 3:14) and others assume the protasis (Luke 1:62).

E. Relative conditional sentence. A relative clause may express the condition set out in the protasis.

ὅσοι δὲ ἔλαβον αὐτόν, ἔδωκεν αὐτοῖς ἐξουσίαν τέκνα θεοῦ γενέσθαι.
And whoever received him, he gave to them the right to become children of God. (John 1:12)

9. Clauses

A clause is a unit of thought that forms part of a larger sentence. Clauses normally have their own (stated or implied) verb, infinitive, or participle. A compound sentence consists of two more coordinate clauses, and a complex sentence has at least one clause that is subordinate to another. Dependent or subordinate clauses may add meaning to the main clause of a sentence in a variety of ways, indicating such elements as time, purpose, result, cause, condition, manner, or means. See the Overview of Syntactical Structure under Participles, Circumstantial, for a more complete list of ways in which clauses can modify main clauses.

A. Concessive clause. A clause that expresses an action or a state of affairs that occurs or exists despite what the main verb or clause asserts. This is often best expressed in English with "although."

B. Conditional clause of expectation. A protasis ("if" clause) of a general conditional sentence that expresses the expectation that the condition will be fulfilled and conveys less doubt than other protases in general conditions.

C. Dependent clause. A dependent clause is a clause in a complex sentence that adds meaning to a main clause and cannot stand on its own as a complete sentence. Such clauses can function as nouns, adjectives, or adverbs with respect to the main clause.

D. Final clause. A clause that expresses the purpose or result of the action of the main verb. In cases where it is difficult to distinguish between purpose and result, the clause is often identified as a final clause.

E. Genitive Absolute. See section on Genitive Absolute above under Participles.

F. Impersonal clause. A clause in which the verb's implied subject is impersonal.

καυχᾶσθαι <u>δεῖ</u>.

<u>It is necessary</u> to boast. (2 Cor 12:1)

G. ἵνα clause (of purpose, of result). A clause that begins with ἵνα (usually followed by a subjunctive verb), expressing the purpose or result of the action of the main verb.

H. Purpose Clause. A clause that expresses the purpose for which the action of the main verb takes place. Two common types of purpose clauses are participial (see above under Participles, Circumstantial, Purpose) and ἵνα clauses (see previous entry).

I. Relative clause. A clause introduced by a relative pronoun or relative adverb that relates the clause to an antecedent in the main clause of the sentence.

Glossary of Other Terms
and Constructions

Adverbial phrase A phrase that functions as an adverb.

Adverbial phrase of manner An adverbial phrase that describes the manner in which the action of the controlling verb was accomplished or conducted:

> προσδέχεσθε οὖν αὐτὸν ἐν κυρίῳ <u>μετὰ πάσης χαρᾶς</u>.
>
> *Therefore, receive him in the Lord very joyfully* [literally, <u>*with all joy*</u>]. (Phil 2:29)

Adversative Indicating a contrast or opposition between elements in a sentence, paragraph, or section. An adversative conjunction or particle expresses opposition or contrast between sentences or elements within a sentence (e.g., δὲ, ἀλλά).

Anacoluthon A break in the flow of thought in a sentence, such that the writer does not finish a thought or grammatical construction.

Anaphora/Anaphoric Repeating the same word or phrase in successive clauses.

Anarthrous A substantive that lacks a preceding article.

Antecedent An earlier substantive word, phrase, or clause to which a pronoun refers.

Apodosis The "then" part of a conditional sentence that sets out the consequences of the fulfillment of the condition set out in the protasis (the "if" part).

Apposition/Appositive A construction in which a noun or substantive is used adjacent to and often in the same case as another substantive to further describe, identify, or define it. The modifying noun may stand between the main noun and its article or it may have its own article. An appositive is a noun that stands in apposition to another noun or substantive.

> Ἐπαφρόδιτον <u>τὸν ἀδελφὸν</u>
>
> *Epaphroditus, <u>the brother</u>* (Phil 2:25)

Arthrous/Articular Occurring with the article. An articular infinitive is an infinitive used with the article and having the force of a substantive.

Ascensive Having an intensifying or heightening force, sometimes translated, "even," or "indeed."

Asyndeton The literary device in which words or phrases are put together without the conjunctions normally used to connect them.

Attributive position See Syntax Overview under The Article, With modifiers.

Causal (Instrumental) A word or phrase that indicates the means or instrument by which an action is accomplished; often translated with: "through," "by means of," "because of."

Chiasmus A crosswise or "a-b/b-a" arrangement of parallels lines of text in which the order of the words or ideas of the first half are reversed in the second half.

πολλοί εἰσιν θεοὶ
καὶ κύριοι πολλοί
there are many Gods
and lords many (1 Cor 8:5, 𝔓46)

Cognate A word that has the same root or origin as another word.

Collective Noun A singular noun that stands for a group; e.g., when "Israel" refers to all those who are Jews.

Comparative A word that expresses comparison or contrast with another element in the sentence. The comparative degree of the adjective, along with the genitive case or the comparative particle ἤ, both normally translated "than," are commonly used to form comparisons. Adverbs such as μᾶλλον ("more," "rather") can also be used to signal comparisons.

ἰσχυρότερός μού ἐστιν
he is mightier than I (Matt 3:11)

Compound direct object A construction in which two or more substantives serve as direct objects of a verb.

Compound object A construction in which two or more substantives serve as objects of a verb or preposition.

Compound subject A construction in which two or more substantives function as subjects of a single verb.

Concessive Expressing an action or state of affairs despite what the controlling verb asserts. This is often best expressed in English with "although."

Conditional conjunction A conjunction that introduces the protasis or apodosis of a conditional sentence.

Conditional imperative The use of the imperative in the apodosis of a conditional sentence that issues a command that depends on the fulfillment of the conditions of the protasis. See Wallace, 489-91.

Conjunction A word that expresses a relationship between parts of a phrase, clause, sentence, or paragraph. Common examples in English include "and," "but," and "or."

Conjunctive particle A word that signals a joining of two or more elements in a sentence.

Consecutive A word or phrase that expresses a result.

Contrastive particle A word that signals a contrast or distinction between two or more elements in a sentence. Categorizing a usage in this way indicates a weaker contrast than identifying it as an adversative.

Coordinating conjunction A conjunction that relates elements of discourse (words, phrases, clauses, sentences, paragraphs) on an equal plane. The most common coordinating conjunctions in Greek are καί and δέ, both meaning "and" when used this way.

Copula A verb, most often a form of εἰμί, that simply couples a subject and predicate.

Copulative A word that connects words, sentences, or clauses, or a sentence containing a copula.

Correlative conjunction A conjunction paired with one or more other conjunctions to express a variety of relationships such as: either … or; both … and, etc.

> μεμύημαι, <u>καὶ</u> χορτάζεσθαι <u>καὶ</u> πεινᾶν
> *I have learned <u>both</u> how to be full <u>and</u> how to go hungry.* (Phil 4:12)

Crasis The combination of two Greek words into one by dropping a vowel at the end of the first word.

Deponent verb A verb that occurs only in the middle and/or passive forms, yet often has an active meaning (e.g., ἔρχομαι, "I come, I go").

Disjunctive particle A word that relates two or more words as alternatives (e.g., ἤ as "or" or as "to" as in the phrase "three to four days").

Distributive singular The use, particularly with abstract nouns, of a singular to refer to members of a group.

Divine passive When God is the cause of an action (i.e., would be the subject of an active verb), writers sometimes avoid speaking of God directly and so express the idea by using a passive verb without indicating who performed the action (Phil 1:29).

Elision/Elided The dropping of a short final vowel from the end of a word when the following word begins with a vowel.

Ellipsis The deliberate dropping of words necessary to the sense of the statement for rhetorical effect.

Enclitic A word that attaches itself to the preceding word, often losing its accent in the process. The words are to be pronounced together rapidly.

Epexegetical A word or phrase that serves to explain another word or phrase.

Gnomic The use of a verb tense or other construction to express a general or timeless truth.

ἱλαρὸν γὰρ δότην ἀγαπᾷ ὁ θεός

For God loves a cheerful giver. (2 Cor 9:7)

Hapax legomenon A word that appears only once in a given body of literature.

Hendiadys A figure of speech, used for emphasis, in which two words, joined by "and," are used to express a single idea.

κατὰ <u>τὴν ἀποκαραδοκίαν καὶ ἐλπίδα</u> μου

in keeping with my <u>hopeful expectation</u> (lit. *my expectation and hope*) Phil 1:20

Homeoteleuton An error in copying texts in which a scribe's eye jumps from one portion or line of the copied text to another with a similar ending, causing the scribe to skip over and omit material in the new copy.

Improper preposition A word, usually a noun or an adverb, that, over time, begins to be used as a preposition. E.g., παραπλήσιος, *near* (Phil 2:27).

Indefinite pronoun See Syntax Overview under pronouns.

Indirect discourse The use of the direct object clause to express reported thought or speech. The discourse clause usually follows a verb of perception and is often introduced by the particle ὅτι. Unlike direct discourse, which involves a direct quotation, indirect discourse recasts the thought or statement into an indirect form.

Instrumental See Causal.

Intensive pronoun See Syntax Overview under pronouns.

Interrogative A word that indicates that a question is being asked. Interrogatives may be particles or pronouns.

Intransitive The use of a verb without a direct object. English verbs such as *sleep* and *talk* are intransitive.

Negative coordinating conjunction A word that connects two constituent parts of a sentence and negates what follows it. E.g., μηδὲ, *and not* (Phil 2:3).

Negative particle A particle that expresses negation or opposition. E.g., οὐ, μή.

Optative of wish See Syntax Overview under Verbs, Mood.

Parataxis A literary device involving the juxtaposition of a series of coordinate clauses, with or with out the use of connective conjunctions. Parataxis should be distinguished from hypotaxis, the frequent use of subordinate clauses. See Phil 4:4–7.

Paronomasia A rhetorical devise whereby similar words or phrases are deliberately confused for humorous or dramatic effect.

Particle The catch-all term for a number of (usually small) uninflected words for which there is no clear grammatical classification (e.g., ἄν, γέ, μέν, οὐ, μή, etc.). Conjunctions and adverbs are sometimes referred to as particles as well.

Periphrastic construction The use of more words than are commonly used to express an idea.

> τὴν δέησιν ποιούμενος
> *making (the) prayer* [i.e., *praying*] (Phil 1:4)

Periphrastic participle The use of a participle and a verb of being (e.g., εἰμί) to express an idea normally expressed by a single finite verb. See Syntax Overview under Participles, Periphrastic.

Pleonasm/Pleonastic The use of more words than are necessary to convey an idea, redundancy. It may be used to give greater emphasis or clarity.

Polysyndeton The repetition of a series of conjunctions, particularly when not all of them are necessary or expected.

Postpositive A conjunction or particle placed after the initial word(s) of the sentence. Often postpositives, such as γάρ or δέ, should be translated first even though they do not occur first in the sentence.

Predicate nominative The use of the nominative case to form the predicate of a verb of being, knowing, or thinking.

Predicate position See Syntax Overview under The Article, With modifiers.

Preposition A word that defines a relationship between its complement phrase and another element in the sentence. Such relationships include temporal (e.g., *before, after*), spatial (e.g., *over, under, in, out*, etc.), or abstract (e.g., *for, from*).

Prepositional phrase A preposition and its complement phrase, including its object and all terms that modify that object. Prepositional phrases are normally adverbial (that is, modifying the verb), but can also function adjectivally.

Protasis The "if" part of a conditional sentence that sets out the condition on which the state of affairs in the apodosis (the "then" part) depends.

Relative adverb An adverb that introduces a relative clause. Among the common NT relative adverbs are: ὅπου (*where*), ὅπως (*how*), and ὅτε (*when*).

Relative pronoun See Syntax Overview under Pronouns, Relative pronouns.

Solecism A form or element of syntax that differs somewhat from the more proper grammatical form.

Substantive/Substantivize A noun or a word used in place of a noun (e.g., adjective, pronoun, participle). A substantivized word or phrase functions grammatically as a noun.

Superlative The form of an adjective or adverb that expresses the greatest degree of a feature or quality in comparison to three or more things. E.g., μάλιστα, *most, especially* (Phil 4:22). It is to be distinguished from the comparative degree, which expresses the greater of two compared objects (e.g., *more*).

Temporal conjunction The use of a conjunction to express something about the time when an action occurs in the clause or phrase it introduces; e.g., ἄχρι, *until* (Phil 1:5).

Transitional particle A particle that signals a change of subject or movement in the flow of thought or argument of a text. E.g., τὸ λοιπόν, *finally* (Phil 3:1).

Transitive verb A verb that takes a direct object.

Resources for Further Study

—∞∞∞—

Grammars

Blass, F. *A Greek Grammar of the New Testament and Other Early Christian Literature*. Edited by A. Debrunner. Edited and translated by R. Funk. Chicago: University of Chicago Press, 1961.

> This book (often referred to as *BDF*) is based on the 1896 grammar by Blass that was supplemented by Debrunner and then again edited and translated into English by Funk. While its intention is to describe the grammar of the New Testament and other early Christian literature, this work draws on a yet wider body of material to describe the uses of particular grammatical constructions. The writers are always careful to note the distinctions between Classical and Hellenistic usage and to note what uses appear primarily within Christian literature. This book is a standard resource whenever the details of New Testament grammar are being discussed.

Dana, H. E. and J. R. Mantey. *A Manual Grammar of the Greek New Testament*. New York: Macmillan, 1969.

> This intermediate grammar addresses the student who is ready to expand his or her knowledge of Greek beyond that of first-year studies. It covers the range of topics that one expects in advanced grammars, but it does so in a way that helps those who are not yet Greek scholars. This book helpfully places in an appendix all the full paradigms of all the parts of speech that one needs to know in order to read New Testament Greek.

Moule, C. F. D. *An Idiom Book of New Testament Greek*. 2d ed. Cambridge: Cambridge University Press, 1959.

> This intermediate grammar focuses on the syntax of the New Testament. Besides including a basic treatment of how the various parts of speech and constructions are used in the New Testament, Moule offers insightful observations about unusual New Testament constructions and usages. As in the other grammars in the present list, the indexes of Greek words, subjects, and passages in Moule's book enhance its usefulness.

Paine, Stephen W. *Beginning Greek: A Functional Approach.* New York: Oxford University Press, 1968.

> This beginning grammar uses an inductive approach to learning Greek. The Greek readings in the first half of the text are from the Gospel of John, while the second half has readings from Xenophon's Anabasis. There are also grammatical and syntactical helps and summaries that remain helpful to intermediate students.

Smyth, H. W. *Greek Grammar.* Revised by G. M. Messing. Cambridge: Harvard University Press, 1956.

> This standard reference grammar of ancient Greek encompasses a wider range of usage than what is found in early Christian literature. It deals with the development of the language and explains uses of various forms through different periods of ancient Greece. It is helpful for the New Testament student to see the many uses that grammatical constructions can perform, even when a particular usage is not found in the New Testament. Noticing such diverse uses can help readers of the New Testament to see the ranges of nuances that a construction may have. Care must be taken to notice, however, that some meanings of particular constructions are limited to time frames or regions, perhaps even specific authors.

Wallace, D. B. *Greek Grammar Beyond the Basics: An Exegetical Syntax of the New Testament.* Grand Rapids: Zondervan, 1996.

> Wallace's book contains a detailed description of the New Testament use of each part of speech. He provides not only definitions, but also extensive examples of various elements of the usage with New Testament examples. He also discusses disputable instances of a particular usage, giving the reasons why he thinks that it falls into the category in which he places it. Discussions here are often more extensive than those in BDF, but these discussions deal with the evidence of the New Testament rather than also treating the nonbiblical evidence as BDF does. Wallace's book is user friendly and very helpful.

Lexicons and Dictionaries

Bauer, W. *A Greek-English Lexicon of the New Testament and Other Early Christian Literature.* Revised and edited by F. W. Danker, W. F. Arndt, and F. W. Gingrich. 3rd ed. Chicago: University of Chicago Press, 2000.

> This standard lexicon (known as BDAG) of early Christian Greek is a substantial revision of the previous standard Greek-English lexicon (BAGD) that was based on Bauer's Greek-German lexicon. Danker's extensive revisions have made this tool easier to use. It contains detailed definitions of all the words

in the New Testament and many others that appear in other early Christian literature. The meanings given function for the words' uses in early Christian literature and usually do not reflect meanings that words have in other literature, unless that meaning is relevant for its early Christian usage. Entries for words include examples of the various meanings from early Christian writings and other sources and sometimes references to recent scholarship on particular words. Serious students of New Testament Greek need this tool.

Kittel, G. *Theological Dictionary of the New Testament.* Edited and translated by G. W. Bromiley. 10 vols. Grand Rapids: Eerdmans, 1964.

This set of books (known as TDNT) is among the most influential and helpful word study tools for New Testament students. This set contains an entry on most New Testament words and extensive discussion of their meanings from Classical times through Hellenistic times, including their use in the Septuagint and other Second Temple Jewish literature. The authors of the entries were many of the leading German New Testament scholars of the first third of the twentieth century. No word study is complete without noting how a word is treated in TDNT. This invaluable tool does, however, have its limitations. Often its presentation of Judaism, particularly Second Temple Judaism, denigrates that tradition, especially if it makes comparisons with Christianity. In this it participates in the biases of its time.

Liddell, H. G. and R. Scott. *A Greek-English Lexicon.* Revised and augmented by H. S. Jones. 9th ed. New York: Oxford University Press, 1996.

This work (known as LSJ) is the standard Greek-English lexicon of ancient Greek. It is broader than BDAG in its scope. It has numerous examples of the various meanings that words possessed over the course of the centuries. A look at the broader use of a word sometimes helps New Testament readers think about the nuances that the word may have in the New Testament. Readers who do not have access to this reference work may think about using the abridged version, which has many fewer examples of the various meanings of words but still is helpful.

Spicq, C. *Theological Lexicon of the New Testament.* Translated and edited by J. D. Ernest. 3 vols. Peabody, Mass.: Hendrickson, 1994.

This set of books (known as TLNT) contains word studies of most New Testament words, all from Spicq, a highly respected New Testament scholar. This set sometimes gives the reader a nuance on a word different from what one finds in TDNT. The entries in TLNT are usually more brief than those in TDNT, but they can take advantage of advances in understandings of some words made since the original publication of TDNT in the 1930s. So this is a good supplement to one's reading in TDNT.

Concordances

Aland, K., H. Riesenfeld, H.-U. Rosenbaum, and C. Hannick, eds. *Vollständige Konkordanz zum griechischen Neuen Testament: Unter Zugrundelegung aller modernen kritischen Textausgaben und des Textus receptus.* New York: de Gruyter, 1978.

This thorough concordance has the advantage of being based on more than a single edition of the Greek New Testament. This broader base means that some readings that UBS⁴ considers textual variants are listed among the occurrences of a word in the New Testament. This can be helpful in coming to understand the meaning of words.

Moulton, W. F., A. S. Geden, and I. H. Marshall, eds. *A Concordance to the Greek New Testament.* Revised by I. H. Marshall. 6th edition. New York: Continuum, 2004.

This work has been the standard concordance for the Greek text for one hundred years. It is a very good, useable tool. It had the original weakness of being based on the Westcott and Hort 1881 edition of the Greek text, but the more recent editions are based on the latest critical text. Further, Moulton and Geden included a significant number of textual variants in this work.

Wigram, George. *The Englishman's Greek Concordance of the New Testament.* London: Samuel Bagster & Sons. Repr., Peabody, Mass.: Hendrickson, 1996.

This classic work, originally published in 1903, gives those without a knowledge of Greek many of the advantages of a Greek concordance. By looking up a particular Greek work (or by using the Strong's numbering system to find the word), the user can find every location in which the word is used in the New Testament. Excerpts from each verse are in English (KJV), with the word or words that correspond to the Greek entry in italics. An English to Greek index also provides a ready reference to the Greek word or words from which each English word is derived.

Young, R. *Analytical Concordance to the Bible.* Revised by W. B. Stevenson. 22d ed. Grand Rapids: Eerdmans, 1955. Repr., Peabody, Mass.: Hendrickson, 1980.

This classic work was first published in the nineteenth century and has gone through many editions. It is valuable for the Greek student who does not have access to a concordance of the Greek text. Although based on the language of the KJV, it provides good information about word usage in the Bible. The words are alphabetized in English, but under each word its appearance is listed by what Hebrew or Greek word the English comes from. Of course, a Greek word may have been rendered with several different English words, so readers should not assume that the passages that appear under a Greek term represent an exhaustive accounting of the use of that word in the New Testament.

Still, this work can get the reader started in trying to understand the use of a word in the New Testament.

Critical Commentaries on the Greek Text of Philippians

Fee, Gordon D. *Paul's Letter to the Philippians.* New International Commentary on the New Testament. Grand Rapids: Eerdmans, 1995.

This commentary provides a careful and artful reading of Philippians. It engages a very broad range of interpreters on many topics. Readers will find no more complete commentary on Philippians. Fee treats questions of reading the Greek text with depth and thoroughness. At the same time, he also addresses theological issues that the letter raises as he engages other interpreters on such issues.

Martin, Ralph, and Gerald F. Hawthorne. *Philippians,* Word Biblical Commentary. 2d ed. Waco, Tex.: Word, 2004.

While this commentary is not as focused on the Greek text as the others in this list, it does address issues of grammar and structure and takes up critical issues as well. In addition to presenting clear arguments for many exegetical and interpretive decisions, each section begins with a helpful bibliography.

O'Brien, Peter T. *The Epistle to the Philippians: A Commentary on the Greek Text,* New International Greek Testament Commentary. Grand Rapids: Eerdmans, 1991.

O'Brien offers a helpful commentary that discusses exegetical problems from the Greek text. He engages critical and interpretive issues in helpful ways. This commentary is more detailed than Hawthorne, particularly in its engagement of word studies. O'Brien is careful to look at the ranges of meanings various words possess in their first-century usage.

Vincent, Marvin R. *A Critical and Exegetical Commentary on the Epistles to the Philippians and to Philemon,* International Critical Commentary. New York: C. Scribner's Sons, 1897. Repr., London: Continuum, 2000.

While this commentary is rather old, it offers a good analysis of grammatical structure. More recent commentaries and other interpreters will often be in conversation with this series (which is now being rewritten by new interpreters).

Index of Subjects